Robert and Myrtle Unruh

A Legacy of Christian Service and Goodwill
in Paraguay, 1951-1983

by
Gerhard Ratzlaff
and Philip Roth

in collaboration with
Edwin Neufeld, Chaco, Paraguay

English translation by
Erwin Boschmann

Robert and Myrtle Unruh
A Legacy of Christian Service and Goodwill in Paraguay, 1951-1983

Library of Congress Number: 2009903678
International Standard Book Number: 978-1-60126-177-9

Printed 2009 by

Masthof Press
219 Mill Road
Morgantown, PA 19543-9516

Table of Contents

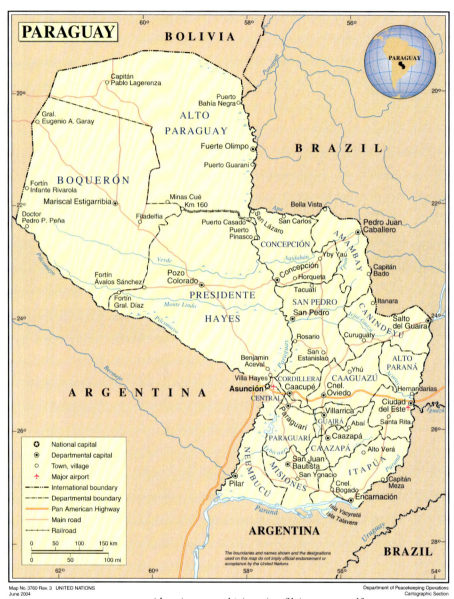

PARAGUAY

BOLIVIA

BRAZIL

Capitán
Pablo Lagerenza

Puerto
Bahía Negra

20°

Gral.
Eugenio A. Garay

**ALTO
PARAGUAY**

Fuerte Olimpo

Puerto Guarani

Fortín
Infante Rivarola

BOQUERÓN

Minas Cué
Km 160

Bella Vista

22°

Mariscal Estigarribia

Doctor
Pedro P. Peña

Filadelfia

Puerto Casado

San Lázaro

San Carlos

Pedro Juan
Caballero

Puerto
Pinasco

CONCEPCIÓN

Yby Yaú

Capitán
Bado

Concepción

Horqueta

Fortín
Ávalos Sánchez

Pozo
Colorado

PRESIDENTE

Verde

Tacuatí

SAN PEDRO

Itanara

Fortín
Gral. Díaz

Monte Lindo

HAYES

San Pedro

Salto
del Guaira

24°

Pilcomayo

Rosario

Curuguaty

Benjamin
Aceval

San
Estanislao

**ALTO
PARANÁ**

Villa Hayes

Yhú

Hernandarias

Bermejo

ARGENTINA

Asunción

CORDILLERA

Caacupé

CAAGUAZÚ

Cnel.
Oviedo

Ciudad
del Este

CENTRAL

Villarrica

Santa Rita

26°

Paraguarí

GUAIRÁ

Abaí

PARAGUARÍ

Caazapá

CAAZAPÁ

Alto Verá

San Juan
Bautista

ITAPÚA

Capitán
Meza

Pilar

MISIONES

San Ygnacio

Cnel.
Bogado

Encarnación

NEEMBUCÚ

Parana

Isla Yacyretá
Isla Talavera

Uruguay

28°

ARGENTINA

BRAZIL

The boundaries and names shown and the designations
used on this map do not imply official endorsement or
acceptance by the United Nations.

Legend

- ⊛ National capital
- ⊙ Departmental capital
- ○ Town, village
- ✈ Major airport
- ▪—▪—▪ International boundary
- —▪—▪— Departmental boundary
- — Pan American Highway
- — Main road
- +++ Railroad

| 0 | 50 | 100 | 150 km |
| 0 | 50 | 100 mi |

Map No. 3760 Rev. 3   UNITED NATIONS
June 2004

Department of Peacekeeping Operations
Cartographic Section

www.un.org/depts/cartographic/map/profile/paraguay.pdf

iv

Introduction

by Gerhard Ratzlaff

Visitors to the Chaco are constantly amazed at the high standard of living among the Mennonites who supply about 50% of the national demand for milk and its derivatives, and 90% of the market for peanuts. Thousands of well-fed cattle from prime stock graze on cultivated and well-managed pastures. It is with deserved pride that Mennonite ranchers report that the best and most nutritious beef is produced in the Chaco, particularly in the Mennonite settlements. The popularity of the beef on the world market has resulted in record sales.

It wasn't always so. In the 1950s the Mennonite colonies were very poor; crop production was weak and barely provided enough for survival. A cow produced no more than a quart of milk per day. In 2006, the average was 4 to 4.5 gallons per cow, and in some instances much more. In his 1984 memoirs, Unruh says that in the 1950s local cattle required five to six years to fatten to 900 or 1000 lbs; today it takes just two to two-and-a-half years. The cattle birth rate then was around 60%, today it is 80 or 90%, and in some cases it is 95%. In the 1950s all farming was done by hand or with horses; today it is totally mechanized, and horses are bred as a hobby by horse enthusiasts.

How does one explain such dramatic change in just a few decades? There are many contributing factors that will simply be mentioned here and not discussed further: The Trans-Chaco road to the colonies was completed in 1961; the million dollar loan with low interest and a 30-year pay-off period; the settler's industriousness and tenacity. This book describes the contribution of *Robert and Myrtle Unruh,* whose work was crucial to the economic boom for the Mennonite colonies. Agronomist Wilhelm Giesbrecht, Menno colony, who spent several years working with Robert Unruh at the experimental station, says: "Both in farming and in ranching he showed us the way into the future."

It is the book's intent to first and foremost recognize the extensive pioneering service and far reaching impact of Bob Unruh, as he was generally known, and that of his wife, Myrtle. It was said that they came to give, not to receive; to serve, not to be served. Edgar Stoesz, who knew Bob well, says what characterized Bob Unruh were his service and his constant readiness to serve. Jakob T. Fehr, for many years the manager of *Servicio Agropecuario* (SAP) in Loma Plata, also worked closely with Bob Unruh. He agrees with this sentiment when he says that Unruh literally served the colonies by "kneeling," and that his commitment must not be forgotten. Walter Thielmann recommends that the experimental station be named after Robert Unruh. Annie Thielmann, his wife, suggests that the school for home economics in Neu-Halbstadt be named for Myrtle Unruh. (See Introduction, p. 194)

The proposal for this book came from Philip Roth, who served with MCC in Paraguay under Vern Buller's supervision (along with four other PAX men) helping to build the first roadway to Km 145 (End Station) and inter-colony roads that connected the colonies, in 1955-56. Verney Unruh, Bob's younger brother, graciously supplied new data and information. Verney passed away on July 8, 2006, and some information about his brother will thus remain unanswered. Other major contributors from USA were Elizabeth (Unruh) Leite, the Unruh's only child.

The challenging idea to write about Bob Unruh was mentioned to Fernheim colony's *Oberschulze*, (governor) Dr. Rudolf Kaethler, who immediately endorsed it. With the *Oberschulzen* from Menno and Neuland colonies, financial support was offered to the project. Encouraged by *Oberschulze* Kaethler, Edwin Neufeld worked with great care and personal devotion to obtain background material from the *Mennoblatt*, the

Fernheim archives, and the *Servicio Agro-Pecuario* (SAP). He found appropriate photographs and conducted interviews with various persons in all three colonies. Edwin Neufeld deserves special recognition for a very thorough job! Carmen Epp, Asunción, translated the long quotes from English into German. Edgar Stoesz and Phil Roth, from the USA, Heinrich Ratzlaff and Andreas Sawatzky from Menno, Edwin Neufeld, Sieghart Dueck, and Hans Duerksen from Fernheim, and Jakob Warkentin from Neuland all read the drafts with critical eyes, and offered helpful suggestions for improvement. Grammatical corrections by Lily August. A great debt of gratitude goes to each one!

The book's purposes are:

1. To provide a general overview on the life and service of Robert Unruh, and his wife Myrtle.

2. To honor their self-sacrificial commitment, and to promote thoughtful reflection on their lives.

3. To sustain the memory of the Unruh's lasting service to encourage its imitation among others.

Foreword

by Philip Roth

Being responsible humans with the ability to reason and control our behavior, we need stories about people who make a difference such as Robert and Myrtle Unruh. These people—particularly those without privileges of birth or position, or without larger than life personalities—confirm to us that the potential to perform better than we have in the past is valid. Their stories should give us pause to rethink our values, to inspire or change us, or at the least to propel us forward. They give us something worthy to strive for. We do not need to make them heroes to appreciate their contribution. We only need to recognize that they did something beyond average expectations and understand how or why it happened after having grasped the background dynamics.

Moreover, good history it seems to me, tries to reflect how things were when the recorded event took place, warts and all, from as many varied perspectives as reasonable. Enamored or tongue-in-cheek or muted details in story telling would seem to be bad history. How better then, to understand and benefit from the past than hearing from the people who experienced the event? Following that, we empathize using our own experience and intuition, coming to some personal conclusion about the event's historical validity for us individually.

Having spent eighteen months in the Paraguayan Chaco from January 1955 to June 1956, concurrently with the Unruhs, the experience made an indelible impression on me. Was it the absorbing Russian Mennonite colonists—a few I remember fondly, or this end-of-the-earth place with its puzzling ambiance, or something ethereal and inexpressible, or all three? I know not which.

This six year (part time) effort has been a labor of love. I hope you are in some manner strengthened, stirred or find merit in Bob and Myrtle's life's work.

We might use emotional capital metaphorically to illustrate sound judgment and taut sensibility. Bob Unruh appears to have had a sizeable emotional bank account, likely because he rarely invested emotional capital on anything that didn't earn a double-digit return; pettiness was unthinkable. He had a Midas touch about emotional investment opportunities—to serve others was his central focus and his driving motivator. Only once that we can tell, did his emotional investment yield a negative return, the Indian Settlement Board malfunction. Like a good businessman, he shrewdly made an early attempt to cut his losses, realizing it was not humanly possible for a "subordinated outsider" to lead others, for their own reasons, where they adamantly refused to go.

Bob also had a tenacity of purpose difficult to comprehend. In 1955 a once-in-100-year weather event wiped out long-established Experimental Farm trials. We ask ourselves, "How does this man keep his shoulder to the wheel and remain so light-hearted facing such adversity?" A possible answer: Bob and Myrtle were two humble, principled and trusting persons with an abiding faith that whatever happened beyond their control was God's will and that they need not waste their emotional capital on self pity or blaming others. Better to stand up, dust themselves off and keep going.

However patient and resilient the Unruhs remained to trying events, however dramatic and intense the situational dynamics, they owe their measurable performance to the Russian Mennonites' instinctive ability, their tradition, their progressive circumspection and their hard work. The colonists' collective response and will to persevere was equal to the Unruhs, making the Unruh legacy possible.

Parts of the addendum might strike you as superfluous to the Unruh story, but provide interesting details on the time and place. The Unruhs embodied the essence of Mennonites in a helping profession and their legacy should be recorded before their contemporaries, who can tell us how it really was, pass from the scene.

Much has already been written about the Paraguayan Chaco Mennonite "experiment" and makeover. So why do we need yet another book on the subject? Given the human yearning for precise explanations and an authoritative point of origin, the Unruhs' self-effacing life style was at variance to the typical perception of how leadership works. For instance, they met their obligations or discharged their responsibilities in a prosaic manner, scrupulously methodical, patient, nonassertive, nonjudgemental. So the depth of their imprint in this complex evolutionary development was hidden by their restraint, gentleness and humble demeanor. Gerhard and I hope to discover, to examine, to interpret, to illuminate and to bring their contribution into focus through this writing. (See Preface and Prologue, p. 188)

1

Robert Unruh's
Childhood and Youth

Everyone's character is shaped by the events and experiences of childhood and youth, and so it was with Robert Unruh. His success in the Chaco was, in many respects, the direct result of early experiences during his growing up years in the USA. It is from this viewpoint that we consider his early years, which were a precursor to his selfless and impact-laden service for the Mennonites in the Chaco.

1.1 Difficult Economic Conditions During Early Childhood

Robert Gilmore Unruh was born the second child to Anthony and Anna Unruh on April 26, 1921, in the rough high country of Bloomfield, Montana. His parents were pioneers in the virgin prairie. His older brother Willard was born in 1919. After Robert came Verney (1923), Helen (1925), Leslie (1926), and a girl born in 1929, who died a week after birth.

The early years in Montana seemed to be promising economically, but then things changed drastically. Drought, failed crops, and the economic crisis after World War I ruined many farmers. Affected by these conditions, the Unruh family found itself in desperate straights. (See 1.1, p. 195)

In an attempt to better their condition they rented land in Freeman, South Dakota, where the family moved in 1924. South Dakota was Anthony's birth place and some of his relatives still lived there. They hoped for a better life! His half section (320 land acres) in Montana was entrusted to his brother Peter with whom he had homesteaded there in 1913 at age 20. He married Anna Albrecht in 1918.

Anthony's economic situation did not improve after four years in South Dakota. The land owner called in the rent contract to make the farm available for his recently married son. The family had little choice but to move back to Montana. The move took place in March 1929 with five little children and Anna Unruh in an advanced pregnancy. Bob was almost eight years old. His older brother Willard recorded the move and the new beginning in Montana:

. . . Uncle Pete, who owned the adjacent half section, had moved to Avon, S.D., so we would have a full section to farm [in Montana]. *That half also had a good house and other buildings. Early spring 1929 we had a farm sale in South Dakota and looked to better times in Montana. Little did we know! . . . We kept the best milk cows, the best team of horses* [matched dapple-grays, Mike & Beauty] *and Pat, the saddle pony. In Montana dad would get unbroken horses and train them to do field work.* [It took a team of 6 horses to pull a two bottom moldboard plow. Getting his field work done in that training year was the trade for the training, care and feed before the broken horses were returned to the owner in the fall.]

All our earthly possessions [were] *loaded into a boxcar for the trip. In those days the railroad had a special immigrant rate for people going west.* [One railroad car cost $80 and would transfer to two independent railroad companies and took a week from Freeman, S.D., to Terry, Montana.] *Dad went along in the car to take care of the animals. It was sort of a miniature Noah's ark. Temporary feed bunks had to be constructed. . . . Enough grain and hay was loaded for a week. When waiting at stations for switching to the next connecting train* [Dad] *hoped it wouldn't be too far out of town so carrying water . . . wouldn't be a problem. He had to have a place to sleep and carry his food too.*

Switching the car from one train to the next could cause bedlam.
To save time the engineer would give the car a good bump so it would roll
across the switch to the next track, rather than having to travel with the car
across the switch and then drive the train back. Inside the car the animals
might go down [be thrown off balance], *household goods fly about. If it*
was cold and a stove had been set up to keep warm, the fire had better be
out, lest the stove upset and set everything ablaze.

I was rather reluctant to leave Rose Valley School in South Dakota.
The teacher was reading Huckleberry Finn *to us by installments just after*
lunch each day, and there was talk that the school board might install a
Giant Stride, a much-to-be desired piece of playground equipment. I con-
soled myself [with the thought] *that maybe Huck Finn would be in the*
library in Montana and the school might even have a Giant Stride. (See
1.1.1, p. 196)

After Dad was gone with the freight car several days, Uncle Joe Gra-
ber, with whom we had been staying, took us to Marion [S.D.] *to board*
the passenger train. There was Mother and Uncle Emil who had come from
Montana to help her with us five children. I was nine years old.

We were only about 80 miles from our destination but it would take
all day to get there. In Terry an incident happened that I recall clearly. We
three older boys were out on the station platform playing. I took Bob's hand
and swung him around me and then let go. He would go scooting across
the platform. One time he fell and hit his head on a bench, cutting quite
a gash. What to do now? I guess it took some time, but the station agent
produced a strip of white cloth to wind around Bob's head. He was quite
a sight.

We got on the Northern Pacific main line to Glendive, and then took
another train to Sidney, then a spur line of the Great Northern to Lam-
bert. Dusk was falling as we got off the train to see Grandpa Albrecht with
a team and bobsled to take us the last 18 miles at nighttime. It was still
winter in Montana [March]. [After four train changes and 38 hours] *We*
were out where the coyotes howled at night in a place where men were men
. . . and smelled like horses.

After arriving in Montana, a daughter was born on March 15. To the family's distress, the newborn died a week later.

1.2 A Widower With Five Children

On April 4, 1932, a seventh child was born, however, two weeks later, on April 18, Anna died, and four days after that the infant died. Anthony was now alone with his five children whom he had to educate and care for.

The oldest child was thirteen, Robert eleven, and the youngest, Leslie, just five years old. Friends and relatives offered to take care of the children, or even adopt them. Anthony Unruh politely rejected the well-meaning offers. He just could not separate himself from the children he loved: "With God's help, we will find a way to stay together." Father Anthony had strong faith. His three surviving children remember that before eating breakfast he would read a section from the Bible and offer a prayer. "We doubt dad missed a single morning devotion his entire life," say all three. Surely this deep and abiding faith must have affected Bob and contributed to shaping his character.

Leslie remembered life without a mother:

My mother died in the spring of 1932 when I was only five years old. Dad must have been down for a short period but I remember him as generally upbeat, a pretty positive person. Dad kept us all together . . . My Grandmother Albrecht baked bread for us every week. We took our dirty clothes to church where my Dad's sister (Susie Schmidt), *would take them and exchange the clothes she washed the previous week. We always planted a garden where there was enough moisture to raise potatoes and other garden things. We always had hogs. Our diet was mostly potatoes, meat and then some bought canned vegetables and dried beans. We usually went to Glendive* (40 miles South) *pretty much our trading town. Sometimes to Richey* (NW 21 miles in 1930). *We had a Model T Ford but in the winter we used horses. My sister and I stayed with our aunt* (who did the laundry) *most of the summers. Willard, Bob and Verney were older and*

The Anthony Unruh homestead Bloomfield, Montana, 1920 or 1921. The barn is front center and the house to the right.

The Unruh house on the eastern Montana prairie, 1929.

helped Dad on the Farm. One summer one of our bachelor uncles came to cook and keep house. For school we were always at home. School was only one mile from the house, a one room school, one teacher, for 8 grades. We walked except in the coldest weather then dad would take us to school with a team and sled.

1.3 A New Homemaker and Stepmother

The 1930s were economically very difficult years. For the Unruhs without a homemaker and mother it was doubly difficult. The children hoped fervently that father would bring a new mother into the home, but it seemed their waiting was to no avail. Friends suspected that when Anthony visited some relatives in Kansas, he had secondary reasons—but again the waiting seemed to be in vain. It now had been some four years since their mother died, and the children's wish faded. But in June 1936 they experienced an exciting and happy moment, which Willard, the oldest then at 17, did not forget. He recalled that in their family there were no secrets, and this included the mail. When the mail came, the children were always free to open it without asking father's permission. Willard wrote:

> *. . . It was always the custom that when we children got the mail, we would open it. . . . One beautiful, sunshiny day in June, 1936 we got the mail which contained a rather strange postmark and return address, Pretty Prairie, KS. We didn't think we knew anyone there, but we opened the letter anyway. To our amazement it read, 'Dearest darling'. What in the world is going on? After that, the letter with that postmark was left unopened!*
>
> *1936 was another year of drought. Cattle were on the verge of starving for want of grass so the government set up a program of paying $4.00 for a poor cow and $6.00 for a good cow. Harvesting what little shriveled wheat there was, hardly paid for the fuel to run the threshing machine.*
>
> *Where Dad got the money to go to Kansas for a wedding I don't know, but it was against that backdrop of hard times that our new Mom*

The Anthony Unruh family in 1937. L to R: Verney, Robert, Willard, Helen, stepmother Frieda, Anthony, Leslie.

was willing to come to Montana, a thousand miles away from her family, to take over another family of five children.

The children were happy. Leslie says: "We had a mother again and a cook. Yes, things got better."

From this new union emerged yet another five children: Evelyn, James, Betty, Phyllis and Gerald. Despite the big difference in age between the first five and the second five, all nurtured and sustained strong family ties. (See 1.3, p. 196)

1.4 Robert and School

Ties among relatives were important to Bob. It was for this reason that he decided, after completing grade school in 1935/36, to go on a family trip to visit relatives in South Dakota and Kansas. Only Willard remained in Montana to stay in school. As a result, he attended high school two years later, but now was in the same grade with his brother Verney, who was two years his junior, and who, due to his academic aptitude, had earlier skipped a grade.

In 1937 the entire wheat crop was destroyed by grasshoppers. How would they now be able to continue with school? Bob's older and younger brothers, Willard and Verney, wanted to continue their schooling. In this difficult situation Robert showed a characteristic that became a trademark of his life; to defer his own interest in favor of oth-

Anthony with team 'Mike' & 'Betty'.

L to R: Leslie, Verney, Robert with Helen, Willard. A six-horse team was required for a two-bottom moldboard plow.

Bob riding 'Babe' with half-brother Jim in 1947.

ers. Bob offered to stay and help on the farm so that his brothers could go to school.

Bob loved Paraguay, its people, and the responsibilities. In return he earned respect. He always deferred personal interest in favor of others. Bob was patient; he faced difficult situations without complaining, he did not allow his temper to flare up. Despite resistance now and then, he always kept a calm demeanor.

Bob worked on the farm helping his dad through a critical situation and was able to save a bit of money in preparation for the upcoming 1938/39 school year by hiring himself out to neighboring farmers during the busy spring planting and summer harvest season. It was likely a contributing experience in preparation for his extraordinary service in Paraguay.

It became clear that Bob was a good farmer. His quiet manner was a special gift, even in the way he handled farm animals, especially horses. Younger brother Les said: "Bob liked horses. He had a beautiful mare that was difficult to ride. She was a one-man horse; he was the only person who could ride her. She threw him one time though. He had a scar on his forehead forever after."

Bob's grades were average. He excelled in sports, especially in football playing guard. In his junior year he helped Glendive High bring home the Class A Montana State Football Championship. He graduated from high school at age twenty.

This was the time of the Second World War. When Bob registered he was classified as 4-C, for "work of national importance" (farming and food production one statutory provision) thereby exempting him from military service.

Bob in his 1940 football uniform.

1.5 Bob as Farmer: an Eventful Road

After finishing high school, Bob decided to become a farmer. In 1943 a half section next to Anthony came up for sale. Bob bought the 320 acres for $8,750. While the price was high, he justified it since the land bordered his father's farm. He borrowed $6,000 from a non-Mennonite retired neighbor friend at 4% interest.

A defining moment occurred in May 1945 that upset his equilibrium and affected his deepest inner feelings. World War II had ended. Soldiers returned from Europe's bloody battlefields, and among them was his girlfriend's former boyfriend. Almost immediately she ended her relationship with Bob, and simultaneously announced her engagement to the returned soldier. Bob realized he had been manipulated— held in reserve in case her first choice didn't return from war. This great disappointment and hurtful experience in the end deepened his spiritual life, and he decided to attend Bible school. At first he thought to attend *Grace Bible Institute*, however, at brother Verney's urging, he chose *Bethel College*, North Newton, Kansas, a progressive Mennonite General Conference college. After the harvest in 1947 he decided to begin his studies that September. His father and his younger brother Les took over his farm.

1.6 Bethel College

Bob enrolled at age 25. Universities place great value on academic training but life does not revolve around theoretical knowledge alone. It is for this reason that Bethel College placed equal emphasis on practical student internships, in the college and in nearby churches to prepare them for service to churches and the mission field. Bethel prepared many missionaries and MCC workers for foreign service. (See 1.6, p. 196)

Bob participated on several levels in this work. For him, the practical aspect might have taken precedence over the theoretical. He sang in the college choir, played football (a football accident later ended his sports activities), participated in many activities, and on weekends he visited churches, assisted in services at jails and hospitals.

The freshmen in 1946 were demographically different: 190 students, a record for the college. Also this class had 130 students who had done alternate service or served in the military. Thus they were older students with varied experiences. Only 60 were "traditional" students.

Living in the dorm his freshman year he shared a room with John Gaeddert, who wrote in 2004:

Bob laughed frequently in conversation and was somewhat light hearted in spirit. He had a deep commitment to the church and to justice concerns. . . . he belonged to the ministerial group of students interested in entering pastoral work and mission interests. . . . He was very gentle and soft spoken, not the boisterous kind. He had his direction set as to his major and interest beyond college. He was focused on what he wanted to accomplish. I remember we both played football. . . . Football and his disposition of kindness and gentleness seem a bit out of character, but I think he loved the game having played in high school in Montana. We also both sang bass in the college choir.

In his sophomore year the roommate was Peter Voran, who one day challenged Bob to double date with his girlfriend's roommate, Myrtle Goering. Peter says, "We went out together several times. Bob and Myrtle hit it off and eventually got married."

They were engaged on April 3, 1949, and planned the wedding for June of that year. Everyone has since agreed that they became a nearly ideal couple. (See 1.6.1, p. 196)

1.7 Pathway to the Mission Field

Bob's early intention was to study medicine, however, the rush into that field by the veterans returning from the war was so intense, that Bob could not meet the competition. His average grades might have been a contributing factor. On March 20, 1949, he wrote to his brother Verney and sister-in-law Belva, who had been commissioned by the Mennonite General Conference to be among the first missionaries to Japan:

I haven't decided yet whether I'm going to apply for med school again next year but it's doubtful. I wouldn't be too surprised if we went out on the mission field somewhere as industrial missionaries if an opportunity should present itself (as did older brother Willard). *I've often wondered whether God instilled in me a love for hard work, open air, farming, etc. because he had a definite place to put me. Perhaps this is his way of teaching me not to rely so much on my own plans. . . . I'm still waiting and looking for his leading.*

This letter preordained Bob and Myrtle's future. Verney in response to Bob's letter wrote to William T. Snyder, MCC Assistant Executive Secretary in Akron, Pennsylvania, relating his brother's interest in overseas service and recommending an agricultural position. Snyder knew Willard and Verney, and respected their recommendation. He wrote to Robert and Myrtle and had in mind a service position in Africa. (See 1.7, p. 197)

Bob graduated from Bethel College in April 1950 with a B. S. in Natural Science. Soon afterward Bob and Myrtle contacted the Mennonite General Conference mission office. But, again, agriculture was not the conference mission's domain. Still, Bob and Myrtle firmly held to their goal; to serve in an overseas mission. That summer Bob worked as equipment operator with a follow-the-harvest combine crew in Lind, Washington. Myrtle cooked for the entire crew. Bob enrolled by fall at Cornell University, Ithaca, N.Y. The course was in preparation for agriculture mission work in third world countries. At the same time Bob accepted an associate pastorate with a calling to unify four small Methodist churches.

In the middle of this activity they received a letter from W. T. Snyder dated December 12, 1950 that informed them about a possible agricultural assignment in South America. The letter included an application form:

Brother Orie Miller has been informed of your interest in agricultural work and is at the moment in Paraguay. The present Fernheim experimental farm director's term expires in April next year and Brother Miller will look into the situation there.

Cautiously eager, the Unruhs responded to Snyder on December 16:

In answer to your letter of December 12, we hardly know what to say as our primary interest thus far has been toward missionary work. We would have no serious objection to serving under MCC but we would like to have a few more details about the work. With whom would we work? What would the work be like, that is, what would we be expected to do? I grew up on a farm in southeastern Montana and farmed myself for a number of years before going to college. . . . I didn't leave the farm because I didn't like the work but rather because I felt God had a greater work for me. When I started I had interest in medical missionary work but not being able to get into medical school I felt that my next best op-

The MCC Executive Committee, 1951. L to R: back row, H. A. Fast, C. F. Klassen, H. S. Bender, C. N. Hostetter, Chairman. Front row: O. O. Miller, P. C. Hiebert, J. J. Thiessen.

portunity for service lay in the field of agriculture. . . . Myrtle grew up on a farm near Moundridge, Kansas, but I fear our German has become quite rusty through disuse. . . . We feel we should have a little more information about the work and more time to think this over before turning in our applications. (See 1.7.1, p. 197)

It was on January 21, 1951, that Unruhs decided to fill out and send in the application forms and prepare for the work in the Paraguayan Chaco. The application said that after completion of their course on July 1, 1951 they would be prepared for their assignment. At the university they now concentrated their studies entirely on this goal and with high expectations they looked forward to the new venture. They decided to accept the agricultural mission service for a term of five years. Bill Snyder thought that Paraguay was ideal, mentioning the service among distant Mennonite relatives from Russia.

1.8 The Unruh—Paraguay Chemistry

Bob and Myrtle were the right people, at the right time, in the right place the judgment of several settlers in the Mennonite colonies who personally knew and loved the Unruhs. What experiences and circumstances shaped them for their service in Paraguay?

Bob grew up in a region and in a time that in many ways mirrored the difficult situation the Mennonites found themselves in the Chaco during the 1950s. Though climatically and economically different, the difficult settlement years in Montana helped Bob to better understand and help the Mennonites in the Chaco. It will be instructive to list other factors that shaped and prepared Bob for his work.

First, as mentioned, there were the environmental conditions during Bob's growing up years. The conditions in the U.S. in the 1920s and 1930s in many ways paralleled the 1950s in Paraguay: difficult settlement years, virgin soil, unreliable weather, a fight for survival, poverty, and pioneer work with occasionally untrained animals. Land in Montana and in South Dakota was open with little rain, and often resulted in crop failure. The virgin soil was tilled with horses. Pioneers in this region fought a battle for survival under the most primitive conditions. Low grade livestock resulted in a constant search for a better breeds. Horses and buggies were the usual transportation. It was not until the 1920s that the automobiles, tractors, radios and electricity found their way into Montana. As Bob experienced the transition into mechanized farming as a youth—a process he relived in the Chaco—he had a strong advantage in providing leadership in Paraguay.

Second, his home was spiritually and practically well grounded. His father's example, who in extreme situations remained firm in his faith, loved his children, was a friend to them, all this certainly shaped Bob's life.

Third, the church where Bob grew up had been founded in 1910 by pioneers under demanding and primitive conditions. The first meetings were in a barn with a straw floor. It was the similarity of this condition with Jesus's birth place that led the founders to aptly name their church Bethlehem. The church was blessed with talented and mission-minded pastors who devoted their lives to the church and sacrificed for it. Such great leadership examples shaped its members

During the first 75 years, this church commissioned 25 missionaries and MCC workers who went into the four corners of the world. Two Bethlehem member families crucially impacted Paraguay: Bob and Myrtle Unruh and Vern and Violet Buller. Vern for example, gave the decisive impetus to construct the Trans Chaco Roadway with the first roadway construction of a road from the railroad station at Km 145 to the Chaco colonies.

The Bethlehem congregation leaned toward practical service work, seasoned with a drive for missions. At thirteen, Robert was baptized on November 4, 1934, by the Rev. Jacob F. Sawatsky. He remained a member until 1986 when, after thirty-two years serving in Paraguay, he joined Myrtle's home congregation, the Eden Mennonite Church, in Moundridge, Kansas.

Fourth, his extracurricular activities at Bethel College where the-

The Bethlehem Mennonite Church, Bloomfield, Montana, 1936.

ory was balanced with hands-on activities. The work at the Cornell University was also applied science. Since they knew about their Paraguay assignment before their study ended, they were able to plan and study soundly. They prepared themselves for Paraguay by gathering as much information as possible about the Chaco and its Mennonites.

Fifth, his character. Bob was not a charismatic person. He was quiet, thoughtful, and inclined to do what is realistic and useful. People said that his temperament was patient, pious, and gentle—with a clear goal in mind. He loved the church, gladly sang in the choir, and participated in hands-on activities. He manifested a deep sense of justice and was always willing to serve. He carried himself according to the principle: *pretend less, be more.* He was always willing to forgo personal interests, favoring others. Disappointments and frustrations strengthened his spiritual life and steeled his character. (See 1.8, p. 198)

Sixth, Myrtle's influence. Studies have shown that marriages where the wife is the older, are generally stable. Be that as it may, Myrtle was the right wife for the right husband in the right place. For their work in Paraguay they were the right team, and no one who knew them had doubts about their compatibility.

All these factors contributed to defining the Unruhs as the right people for the right place at the right time. Bob was well prepared when he came to Paraguay. He made a difference in Paraguay the second time around not simply as a passive participant as in his youth, but by helping to direct the Chaco Mennonite farming and ranching transitional development. (See 1.8.1, p. 199)

2

The Mennonite Struggle for Survival in the Chaco, 1927-1945

To appreciate Robert Unruh's contributions in agriculture and ranching, we need to consider the difficult situation the Mennonites faced in Paraguay's Chaco. And to describe the efforts Mennonites had already undertaken before the Unruhs arrived in 1951.

2.1 Mennonite Settlements in the Chaco

The first Canadian settlers arrived in Asuncion aboard the Argentinean riverboat *Apipé* on December 29, 1926. President Eligio Ayala and his entourage boarded the ship and greeted the settlers, speaking in German, "Paraguay is not big and mighty." But he added, that it was his heartfelt wish that they would experience "fortune and prosperity" (Friesen, 1977, pp. 5-6) as they settled in the central Chaco, a region that he—even as President—did not know. On Friday, December 31, 1926 an unusually hot day, the group arrived at Puerto Casado. They met with extreme disappointments and unpleasant conditions, described elsewhere (Friesen, 1977 and 1987) that will not be detailed here. Taken aback but not discouraged, they were the first white people to settle in this undeveloped and wild region. It was a costly undertaking that claimed 196 lives in the first two years (A total of 1,763 persons in 279 families in seven assemblies). (Stoesz & Stackley, *Garden in the Wilderness*, CMBC Publications, Winnipeg, Manitoba, 1999, p. 28)

Still, the Menno colonists experimented in agriculture by testing various seeds in the native soil. They learned quickly that various Kaffir (sorghum) varieties grew nicely and provided needed income and feed for animals during the difficult pioneering years. Martin Friesen wrote about these tests:

Starting in 1927 small experimental plots were established along the road (Pozo Azul, Hoffnungsfeld, Palo Blanco, Loma Plata and Km 218) *to the settlement hoping to learn what would grow in the Chaco. Settlers were particularly interested in testing Canadian wheat varieties. Paraguayan grains were tested in a plot in Pozo Azul. Americans* (New York banker Samuel McRoberts and associates) *organized Corporacion Paraguaya (CP) in Paraguay to help Menno's settlement and expedite financial transactions. CP had the authority to purchase land from the Casado landholders and to resell to the Canadian Mennonites. Also CP was to do the land surveys, assist the settlers wherever possible in finding appropriate*

Menno temporary camp, 1927—Mennonite Church USA Historical Committee Archives, Goshen, Ind.

clearings for the villages, finding and digging water wells, and building the first temporary shelters for the settlers.

CP planned the experiments and local settlers carried them out. The Americans sent a Swedish immigrant agronomist, Erik Lindgren, to work at Pozo Azul. He was most helpful with grain tests in the tropics. He had lived the past 20 years in East Paraguay.

It was decided to plant crops such as cotton, peanuts, mandioca, bananas, beans, potatoes, corn and watermelon. Lindgren also visited the other testing plots. The settlers were not always willing to listen to his advice. After all, they were accomplished farmers and could decide for themselves best management practices. After the first year with villages established and the fields ready to plant, the 200 families looked at the results from the Pozo Azul experiments and decided to plant native crops. The insights gained from Pozo Azul had been helpful. (Friesen, 1992, p. 5; and Friesen, 1987, pp. 227-229)

In contrast to the Menno Colony, 2000 Russian Mennonites arrived penniless from 1930 through 1932 founding Fernheim Colony. It was the considered opinion among Fernheimers to learn from Menno's pioneering know-how and experience. But still, the beginning was very, very difficult.

In 1947-48, World War II refugee Russian Mennonites arrived in the Chaco, organizing Neuland Colony. Their situation was doubly difficult because more than half the families were widows and widows with young children. Like Fernheimers, they also came with little more than a suitcase.

2.2 Early Difficulties

Menno Colony

The Canadian Mennonites came to the Chaco in 1927 with high expectations and great hopes. While they came voluntarily and expected to make sacrifices, the beginning was more difficult than anticipated. They were accustomed to bitter cold and found the temperatures in the Chaco soaring over 100°F, they foresaw southern fruits but found none, and they discovered the native grasses were unsuitable forage for the cattle. Early in 1928 Abram Giesbrecht wrote from Puerto Casado to his relatives in Canada: "I have told people repeatedly that the pastures in the Chaco are not good, feeding perhaps a cow and a pair of oxen. There seems to be much pasture grass, true, but they are all inedible, often called Bitter Grass. It is going to be difficult if not impossible." (Friesen, p. 26) Giesbrecht decided to go back to Canada. His first assertion that, "it is going to be difficult" was correct. In fact, the entire venture could have collapsed. Another settler wrote: "Here we have less than nothing and life is extremely difficult." (Friesen, 1977, p. 19) Completely devastated, Mrs. Ginter wrote, "Sadness and suffering are everywhere." (Friesen, 1977, p. 25)

Fernheim Colony

It was in April 1930 that the first Russian Mennonite settlers arrived in Asuncion on the *Apipé*, (the same river boat that three years earlier transported the Menno settlers). President Dr. Jose P. Guggiari, and other high ranking persons gave them a warm welcome and encouraged them on what would be a difficult venture. There were many questions after his welcome, all economic in character: "What grows here? What stock can be bred? What fruits are common?" These and other questions were asked and answered satisfactorily, according to the April 26, 1930, issue of the Buenos Aires *La Plata Post*. As it turned out, the questions were really not "answered satisfactorily," a task that would take decades.

A commemorative writing was issued on Fernheim's 25ᵗʰ anniversary in July 1955: "This writing is to inform our descendants of the difficulties and suffering during the early years, of God's help during our need and is dedicated to the pioneers of the difficult early years in

Fernheim's 25ʰ anniversary monument unveiling, 1955. Heinrich Duerksen and Fern-heim officials on left with Zentralschule chorus. Photo credit: Phil Roth.

the Chaco." When the first settlers came into this "untouched wil-derness," this writing says, "The arid clearings did not have much to encourage us. Should we be surprised that many women knelt in the Bitter Grass and wept?" (Wiens/Klassen, 1955, p. 9)

Heinrich Duerksen, for many years Fernheim's *Oberschulze* (chief administrator), wrote in retrospect: "The early settlement years were marked by reversals and disappointments . . . man and na-ture were openly hostile to one another." (Duerksen, 1990, p. 99) He cites the chief enemies in the beginning being drought and heat. But then there were other hardships, the lack of potable water, the many grasshoppers who in a matter of hours could destroy the harvest, the great distance to the market, and the absence of roads. (Duerksen, 1990, pp. 99-103) (See 2.2, p. 204)

Questions such as: "What do you need?" or "How might you best be helped?" were answered by Peter Rahn in May 1931 as follows: "We need everything." He concludes stoically by being practical, "If I cannot do as I want, then I have to do as I can." (*Mennoblatt,* May 1931; compare H. Wiens in *Fuenfzig Jahre*, 1980, p. 76) To accept this wise and realistic attitude was easier said than done. The tribulations the settlers had to deal with were enormous; among them some were mentioned repeatedly during the pioneer years: potable water, the weather (heat and the northwind sandstorms) many periods of drought, lack of roads and means of transportation. Ants, caterpillars, aphids to name a few pests, were troublesome creating a great challenge for the farmers in the Chaco. Locust came unannounced by the millions and attacked the fields creating devastation in a matter of hours, along with any hope the pioneers might have had. Devastating threats to Kaffir fields were masses of birds such as pigeons and parakeets. As harvest drew near, the fields had to be guarded for weeks on end. Also, for decades the colony development was hindered by the unsolved questions about transportation and marketing.

Adding to this apparently forlorn situation, the Chaco War (boundary dispute with Bolivia fought in and around the two colonies) erupted in 1932 continuing until 1935. And in 1937 Fernheim lost nearly a third of its citizens in an exodus to east Paraguay, organizing Friesland Colony.

2.3 Farming Efforts in the Chaco

During the first few decades, economic survival for the Mennonite settlers depended entirely on farming. For the first thirty years however, Mennonites in the Chaco labored under a cloud of continuous doubt about their economic future. Fernheimers made a valiant effort from the earliest beginning at agricultural experimentation.

For example on June 19, 1930, a meeting took place at Trébol just a few weeks after the Mennonite settlers from Russia arrived, then known as "*Corporationsplatz.*" Twenty-nine leaders and their assistants; ordained pastors and the village leaders (Schulze) from the first eight villages met together. The meeting was chaired by Johann J. Funk, the first group's leader (Fernheimer's arrived in seven separate ocean trips over six month's time). An early organizational task was creating a "cultural/scientific committee," later simply known as "Agricultural Committee," charged to promote agriculture, the foundation for the settlers' existence. The *Mennoblatt* carried articles on observations and recommendations for farming. On October 15, 1930, Johann J. Funk wrote optimistically:

> *Nature presents us with various opportunities for field and garden crops. Naturally, the Russian farmer will have to dismiss the idea of raising wheat. But there are many other possibilities. Beans, peanuts, Kaffir, corn, sugar cane, and other crops thrive in this environment. In the gardens we can raise turnips, cucumbers, and radishes. The tasty watermelons thrive very well. Looking around, one can see that gardens are being planted, and in the near future we will cultivate our proud gardens, trees, shrubs of Russia. Bananas, lemons, oranges, peaches, grapes and others do well here. Mulberries do well here also, which promise a bright future for silk worm farming. But as can be seen from the previous list, our people will miss the familiar bread crops. While we have corn and kafir, which can be made into good bread, these are unfamiliar. Currently flour is being imported from Argentina, which of course is expensive. And products which we draw from our neighboring colony* (Menno) *while we are waiting for our own to mature, this also takes funding.*

Please note the quotation's reference to the Russian homeland. The raising of fruit trees and garden crops had not yet been tested—a work that still had to be done. For the time being, Fernheim settlers copied from their neighbors in Menno Colony. Immediately after arrival, R. S. (full name not recorded) wrote with hope: "As soon as we have enough wells dug, we will receive two oxen and a cow per family. The livestock, however, are quite wild and need tamed. In September/ October the rains come and with it spring, so that we can plant, and with God's help, we will eat our first watermelons and vegetables from our own gardens." (*Dein Reich komme*, [German monthly] December 1930, p. 324; compare Wiens/Klassen, 1955, p. 9)

No one knew if fresh fruit and vegetables would be on the table at Christmas. But in difficult situations it is a good thing to be optimistic.

In March 1931 the Agricultural Committee organized a fact-finding ox cart trip through several villages in the Menno Colony. Writing for the Committee, Heinrich Pauls concluded: "Life in the Chaco will likely always be difficult; however, we could improve our existence if we had better marketing and the means for processing our products." Pauls perceptively addressed two basic problems; farm product processing or preservation and marketing. It would take decades to solve these problems.

Pauls wrote a detailed report about the visit to seven villages in the Menno Colony. He gave recommendations for the Russian Mennonites and here is an example from his lengthy report:

We saw 40-day old corn, and it is not much . . . What we saw is no comparison to the decent corn harvest we are used to from the Ukraine. Sudan grass is tall, sowed by hand and harvested by harrowing. The kafir is bound in sheaves, placed in small heaps, and later transferred to the barn for cattle feed. Prior to the frost, the mandioka is cut down and buried two feet and covered with hay for protection. If this is not done the plant roots freeze. After the first rain in the spring the plant is cut into 8 inch pieces, placing two pieces across from each other, and planted about three inches in the ground. . . . (Mennoblatt, April 1931, p. 40)

Everything was so different from Russia, and everything had to be learned anew. The group saw makeshift, improvised mills to process Kaffir into flour and peanuts to peanut butter; they saw mills to clean and thresh; they saw bean planters and sugar cane presses. A detailed description was given on the harvest and cotton baling. (*Mennoblatt*, April 1931, pp. 3-4) Cotton was the only exportable crop bringing cash into the colony. Menno's experience and progress was taken seriously. Menno people were also quizzed about disease and insect control for vegetables. Pauls writes:

Vegetables are protected against disease by Paris Green (copper (II)-acetoarsenite), *and a weak solution of nicotine* (neurological toxin) *is sprayed to control caterpillars* (larvae). *The soil in Menno villages is sandier than ours; so many plant Bermuda grass in their yards. This is to prevent dust from kicking up* (soil erosion), *for better appearance, to control weeds, and to improve the soil. We recommend this! (Mennoblatt,* May 1931, p. 3)

Besides listing observations and giving recommendations, the committee also collected vegetable seeds, ordered piglets, saw the manufacturing of useful tools, learned about Chaco lumber and brick making and firing. Attempting to reverse the commerce flow and reduce Fernheim's cash drain, the committee succeeds in selling only three *Mennoblatt* subscriptions. The report sarcastically laments, ". . . we regret the Menno people have no time for reading."

All these are basic and simple practices, ". . . but still quite remarkable," according to Pauls. "Our task is to write about the good and the best." (*Mennoblatt,* May 1931, p. 3) This was easier said than done. The longing for the wheat fields in Russia remained. Peter Rahn, writes in 1931, "[Compared to schools] the farmer's situation is even worse. They have to be re-trained totally; from Russian wheat farmers to South American planters, and we hope they will do this. It is as difficult to accomplish this as if a teacher who does not speak Spanish were to attempt teaching in Spanish." But Rahn comes to this realization: "Those of us in Fernheim will be forced to imitate our neighbors in the beginning." (*Mennoblatt,* May 1931, p. 3)

Mennonites in the Chaco were compelled to fall in line with local economic conditions and forget the glorious wheat fields of Russia and Canada. It soon became clear that this would not be easy because it demanded enormous courage and patience from the settlers. Tradition and culture accumulated over centuries cannot be forgotten easily. When despair overwhelms, settlers recalled the wonderful freedoms enjoyed in the Chaco: "God be praised for our freedom!" (*Mennoblatt,* February 1931, p. 4) This freedom outweighed all difficulties even though they had to experiment, test and relearn anew.

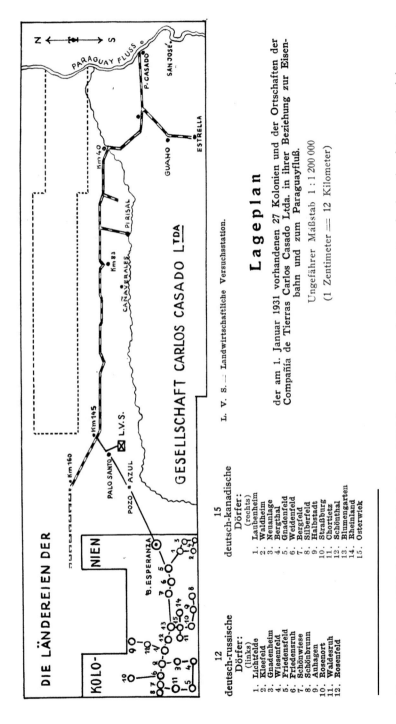

Map from January 1931 showing 12 Fernheim and 15 Menno villages in relation to Puerto Casado, the railroad, Km 145 and three experimental farm locations. L.V.S. is Palo Santo. Esperanza is Hoffnungsfeld.

2.4 Agricultural Experiments

When the Unruhs arrived in the Chaco in 1951 they were quick to acknowledge that the Mennonites had already experimented much with agriculture—some successfully and some not. Bob was able to build on these foundations and encourage the settlers despite the great difficulties they faced. He encouraged them to continue their good efforts in spite of many hardships.

Recall that Fernheim's Agricultural Committee counseled adaptation to local conditions and to benefit from the agricultural achievements in Menno Colony by applying Menno's practices until improved practices were developed. What remained for Fernheim was to evaluate the agricultural experiments supported by *Corporación Paraguaya.* (On behalf of Fernheimers, MCC contracted with CP to help Fernheimers in their settlement.)

Personnel employed by CP in 1931 were found at Trebol, but they did not fulfill their duties. Worse yet, the new settlers were cheated at every turn, as recorded by the *Mennoblatt's* first editions and by Walter Quiring (1936, pp. 125-140). All commodities and services were excessively inflated (at times with a five-fold price increase) to the impoverished settlers who were fighting for their subsistence (Quiring, *Deutsche erschliessen den Chaco,* 1936, pp. 131-134) The Fernheimer's became so outraged that by the late 1930 they decided in concert with MCC (G. G. Hiebert and Orie Miller) to take fate into their own hands and demanded resignations from CP personnel. Some said that the Menno settlers with their practical examples had more to offer than the CP agents with their experimental station. The last CP agent left the Chaco by May 31, 1931. Walter Quiring writes:

At Hoffnungsfeld travelers always meet the CP agents headed by Alexander Langer. But the immigrants just shake their heads at this curious operation; they had hoped to get answers to many of their questions about tropical crops, but instead see nothing but puny experiments. Even later

this station, which cost CP some $25,000 was of no value to either colony.
(Quiring, 1939, p. 143)

The editor of the *Mennoblatt* refers to these "CP people without a conscience . . . whose goal it is to ruin the colony," saying that they have hurt the "young colony" far more than nature's parasites. He quotes Schiller, the great German poet:

> It is dangerous to wake a lion,
> And awful is the tiger's tooth
> But the most terrible of horrors
> Are human beings in their deception.

MCC's G. G. Hiebert worked on the settler's behalf during these difficult and dangerous times, and he did so in a selfless and heroic manner. At one point he was physically assaulted by CP officials. In recognition for his service, Fernheim named village No. 13, Hiebertsheim. (*Mennoblatt*, June 1931, p. 4, and November 1932, pp. 2-3) (See 2.4, p. 205)

2.5 Experimental Station *Palo Santo*

At considerable expense the Casado Corporation set up around 1930 or 1931 an agricultural experimental station at *Palo Santo*, located some 8 miles south from Km. 145 rail station, and some 63 miles from Filadelfia. This created great hope among the Fernheim settlers since the plan called for young men from both colonies to spend six months, with free lodging and food, at the station learning about Chaco agriculture, and then apply this knowledge in the colonies. (*Mennoblatt*, 1931, pp. 3-4; June 1932, p. 2; March 1933, p. 4; and August 1934, pp. 1-2)

In the June 1932 *Mennoblatt* issue (page 2), Nikolai Siemens writes that over 20 young men, 3 young women, and a young married couple work at the station. "If this station is managed properly it will be a blessing to the colonies." In August 1934 Siemens journeys to the station now managed by Ernst Oehring, an experienced German agronomist. "It is unbelievable," writes Siemens, "what is happening at the station:"

> *Hope comes from the many southern fruit trees like oranges, tanger-*
> *ines, lemons, guava, figs, mangos, Paradise trees in many rows, Australian*
> *eucalyptus (growing to 36 feet in four years) and several fiber oil bearing*
> *plants like tung, sisal, sesam and olive trees. Even young apple and pear*
> *trees appear healthy. Ten grape acres show promise with about half ready to*
> *produce their first fruits. (Mennoblatt,* August 1934, pp. 1-2)

According to Siemens, of the 212 cultivated acres, 62 are cleared bush, proving that properly prepared bush land can also be productive. Siemens concludes optimistically: "If it was possible to bring about these results, then those in the colony will be equally successful. But by early 1935 the Casado Corporation dismissed Mr. Oehring. (*Mennoblatt,* February 1935, p. 6) Soon the promising experimental station went quiet and the Mennonites are once again, on their own. (Quiring, 1936, p. 182) Why this promising experimental station went under was a mystery to the Mennonites, *Mennoblatt* editor Siemens' effort to promote it notwithstanding.

It was a fact that the economic situation in the Chaco became increasingly difficult and at times the settlers did not have enough food. The Chaco war brought some relief, since the military bought perishable farm production that was not otherwise marketable due to the long distances. The financial situation worsened after the Paraguay-Bolivia peace treaty was signed. (*Mennoblatt,* May 1933, p. 3) For years cotton remained the only exportable cash crop. Official records from February 1, 1935 show the colony had 1,580 acres in cotton.

The year's 1935 and 1936 were exceptionally dry, encouraging rapid emigration. In September 1937, 740 persons departed Fernheim Colony to organize Friesland Colony in East Paraguay. 1937 is some-times referred to as a "crisis year." However, 1937/38 was an unusually good year with farmers expanding their crop acreage that in turn boosted income beyond expectations. This elevated people's spirits. F. Wiens wrote optimistically, "All in all one can say that Fernheim has conquered its financial crisis and is looking into the future with great hope." (*Mennoblatt*, February 1938, p. 5) (See 2.5, p. 205)

2.6 Peter Esau

Peter Esau, a young man from *Schönbrunn* village, known as the "best vegetable and fruit gardener," was sent to eastern Paraguay by the colony administration to "gain further knowledge in gardening in the Chaco." (*Mennoblatt*, January 1939, p. 6)

Esau proposed a concrete plan: concentrate on guava, all citrus fruits, and especially grapefruit that were "mostly unknown" in the Chaco. To survive the dry winter months, Esau suggested cultivating the ground around the trees right after the summer rains, and then covering it with straw to prevent evaporation. He also suggested to prune out extra foliage and unnecessary water sprouts" (to promote fruiting). (*Mennoblatt*, March 1939, p. 5) MCC recognized Esau's work and supported it financially, saying that it was money well spent.

To great dismay, this promising young man from *Schönbrunn* died from appendicitis at age 26 on August 30, 1940. (Balzer/Dueck, 2005, pp. 233-236) (See 2.6, p. 206)

2.7 1941 to 1945

In the meantime, the Western Hemisphere was drawn into World War II, with grim consequences for the social, religious and economic life in Fernheim. Many in Fernheim looked forward to a victorious Germany, thinking this event would ease their return to Russia or Germany. Many put their economic interests on the back burner during the war years. (Duerksen, 1990, pp. 115-128) Menno Colony however, was not affected by this sentiment having no link to Germany except language. In Fernheim tensions developed between opposing ideologies. During this time there was little agricultural detail recorded in the Chaco. With Germany's defeat May 1945, the longed-for return to Europe and Russia evaporated. Fernheimer's were required to undertake a new beginning. (See 2.7 p. 206)

3

Fernheim's Experimental Farm— 1946 to 1951

3.1 Historical Perspective

Germany's unconditional surrender and massive destruction from World War II, crushed all hope for returning to Russia among Fernheimers. The war's end brought to Fernheim a sense of vulnerability, helplessness, utter despair. The bond with Germany was broken, expecting assistance from the 'fatherland' now a memory and senseless wish. For many Fernheimer's "tears welled up," the mood among many was akin to the pioneer women in 1930 that knelt to cry in the bitter grass. The often debated issue, German allegiance, caused a tense and quarrelsome mood in the colony and in the churches.

Before and during the war, difficult colony issues were sometimes brought to German Professor Benjamin H. Unruh—"Uncle Benjamin"—for his advice and counsel, much valued (Unruh assisted in shepherding Fernheimers through Germany in 1929. A major street near Filadelfia's center is named B. H. Unruh in his honor). After the war such dependency on Uncle Benjamin was out of the question, and Germany—who had so graciously welcomed them when fleeing Russia—could not help them politically, financially or emotionally. Remembering the heated arguments about German allegiance, some were reluctant to renew close ties with their Mennonite North American brothers, even if they were Mennonites and brothers in Christ. (See 3.1, p. 207)

Despite all this, "Big brother in the north" came to the aid of "Little brother in the south," an expression prevailing for many years. From 1930 US and Canadian Mennonites chiefly through MCC supported Fernheim spiritually, socially, and economically. One successful example is the agricultural experimental farm in Fernheim. The experimental farm's founding is documented in English and German reports and in minutes from Fernheim archives. In the beginning agriculture was the sole economic engine for Mennonites in the Chaco. Later ranching followed; clearly the future depended on farming and ranching (See 3.1.1, p. 207).

3.2 A New Approach

Although cotton and peanut production had increased from the early years, the standard of living was at a stand still, going nowhere. Chaco Mennonites remained poor and deeply discouraged. MCC decided to set up a 'country office' in Asuncion in 1943. As the war ended, it was known several thousand more Mennonite refugees from the Soviet Union would require resettlement, the Paraguayan Chaco a likely refuge. Negotiations for this third immigration were already in full swing by war's end. Rather than re-immigrate to Europe, as some Fernheimers had planned to do during the war, it appeared they would be joined by several thousand more refugees from the Soviet Union. It was clear to all, north and south, the Chaco colonies faced a crisis. (See 3.2, p. 207)

A desperate situation, MCC gave increased attention to the Chaco. Imperative was a productive and stable agriculture for the Chaco if the colonies were to survive and support an increasing population. The new settlers would also be dependent on agriculture; another reason agricultural know-how must be a priority. With this in mind, Fernheim's administration and MCC collaborated, agreeing in 1945 that MCC recruit a North American to guide the Chaco's agricultural development. In 1946 a young, energetic and capable Canadian agronomist, Menno Klassen, arrived in Paraguay having agreed to serve for three years. His mandate specifically, "to act as intermediary between the colonies in the Chaco and STICA (*Servicio Técnico Interamericano de Cooperación*

Agricola) at *Caacupé* in East Paraguay and second to provide counsel for colony farmers." STICA was important to the Mennonite colonies agricultural development.

Assistance from the US government to Paraguay began in 1942, during the Second World War, and concentrated in three areas: health, education and agriculture (STICA). In conjunction with the Paraguayan government, STICA was founded in December 1942 near Caacupé, East Paraguay to promote agriculture and ranching. In the early years STICA was administered by Americans with assistance from Paraguayans and MCC voluntary service young men who then took skills learned to East Paraguay Mennonite colonies and for brief terms in later years, to the Chaco working at the experimental farm. Several young men from Fernheim got their first agricultural training with STICA in Caacupé then returned to Fernheim to work at the experimental farm. Menno Klassen, founder of the experimental farm in Fernheim, worked closely with STICA as did Robert Unruh, experimental farm administrator beginning in late 1951.

Between the years 1942 and 1944, STICA conducted the first agricultural census in Paraguay. According to this investigation, Paraguay had 94,500 agricultural operations, with 48% less than 12 acres. 25,600 operations had fewer than 2.5 acres, but included 153,600 persons. 74% of all farmers had no title to the land they worked, and 74% of all farmers had no metal plow, 55% did not own a plow or wagon, and the few tools they had were an ax, a spade and a machete. Usually an ox provided the pulling power.

Ten years later in 1954 the census showed that 1.7% of Paraguay's total land area was tilled or1,730,000 acres tilled. In 1966 tilled acreage increased to 2,223,000 acres, then 2.2% of Paraguay's total land area. (See 3.2.1, p. 209)

3.3 Menno Klassen

After spending some months with STICA in East Paraguay Menno realizes that Chaco climate conditions are greatly dissimilar and that it is not possible to directly apply STICA's recommendations to the Chaco. Also the plant varieties STICA proposes for East Paraguay were more or less useless in the Chaco's dryer climate. Menno concludes the situation is not simple; something basic must change. Menno writes, ". . . and so my task had changed considerably. We needed to find other ways and means to solve the problems the farmers face. . . . The conditions are much different here and I have no direct experience to make recommendations. We need to discover what works and what does not work in the Chaco and to find the best method to teach the colony farmers how to solve their problems. To do that efficiently and in the quickest manner the colonies need to set up their own experimental farm."

Fernheim's committee minutes from June 7, 1946, state, "Menno Klassen, who was sent by MCC to help us, laid out his plan." Curiously, the details of this plan are not mentioned. "His plan" was not questioned, instead the discussion centered on another structural detail; whether such a station should be organized and administered by the colony as a whole, or by a farmer's association. The committee decides this is a task for the entire colony. They authorized Menno Klassen and Jakob Isaak, Jr., also a several months 'graduate' from STICA, "to find a suitable place for this undertaking." Also discussed, would MCC be willing to fund Menno's Plan?

Following the June 7, 1946, committee meeting, Menno Klassen, Jakob Isaak, Jr. and Amos Yoder, another MCC volunteer, took Jakob's wagon and his magnificent horses and began searching for a suitable place for the new experimental station. They chose a site where the experimental farm stands today, four miles northeast from Filadelfia, with roughly 125 acres in open savannah. (See 3.3, p. 209)

3.4 The Experimental Farm's Beginning

On July 5, 1946, the committee proposes "Menno's plan" to the colony, where point 6 reads:

Establishing an Experimental Station by Menno Klassen:

The colony convocation finds the station proposal acceptable and votes to accept responsibility for it, rather than creating a separate farmer union. Brother Orie Miller has proposed that the colony organize the station, and that MCC will purchase the required machines and finance the experiments as well. This proposal is accepted gratefully by those present (See 3.4, p. 209).

The minutes from July 20, 1946, read, in part:

Menno Klassen gives a report and details a plan for the upcoming work for this and the following years. This plan is accepted. Jakob Isaak is hired with a salary of G80.00 (likely Guaraníes per month, G3.09 = $1.00 in 1946 or $25.89/month). *The colony is to supply the lumber. A construction foreman is to be found, and workers are to be hired so that the project can progress quickly.*

Menno proposes to establish a nursery garden to provide vegetable seedlings the colonists might transplant in their own household gardens, an experimental vegetable garden, do various seed trials and find grasses suitable for pastures, determine how best to protect against destructive insects, learn about fertilizers, chicken breeds, better cattle breeding, seed cleaning and inspection, find suitable horse drawn implements to improve productivity and much more.

Construction got under way immediately with rapid progress. Menno set up a tent and lived on site to lend a hand and to oversee construction.

At the beginning we lived in a tent. It was cold but we did not expect snow. The two horses were tied to the wagon and were fed from the wagon. We found suitable trees, cut these down and brought them to the saw mill (in Filadelfia) *and the lumber was used for the well* (casing; the well hand dug about 4-5 feet diameter) *and the barn. The living quarters were built later.* (Spoken by Menno Klassen on radio ZP-30, June 12, 1979)

Menno recognizes the importance for clear communications in promoting colony wide support for the farm. He is concerned about farmers clearly understanding what "a real experimental station" might do for them. To better inform farmers he traveled to villages and, "We spoke freely at special meetings like farmers do across the fence." He prepared a formal progress report December 1946: "250 acres have been surveyed, a well was dug, bush cleared, plowed, many palo santo posts have been set, a barn was built, and a house erected to the roof, and a cistern built to collect (and store) rain water." (*Mennoblatt*, December 1946, p. 3)

Menno wrote about his broad and far sighted vision for the experimental farm. In an English report he hoped for farmer gatherings, competitions to advance agricultural accomplishments and he anticipated agricultural shows at the farm. This all seems a bit premature and too ambitious but his vision is prophetic; all these things came to

Fernheim youth group evening meeting at Experimental Farm, November 1955. Photo credit: Phil Roth.

be. Moreover, Menno did not forget that, "Man does not live by bread alone." The experimental station is to be a place for conferences, excursions, Bible meetings, and more. "I pray that colony wide agriculture will result in a deeper spiritual life that extends to missions among the Indians and to leprosy patients." (*Paraguay Notes*, October, 1946, p. 7) Indeed, Menno set forth a grand plan and vision for the experimental farm and the Chaco Mennonites.

With characteristic enthusiasm Menno begins implementing his plan.

Preparing palo santo logs for the experimental farm shop. It demanded a great investment in hard work with ax and saw.

As far as known, most Fernheimer's supported the effort. This heightened activity was not without set-backs however. Menno mentions a nine-month drought and "locusts and ants that gave no one peace." And the threat from hostile Moro Indians, dormant for twenty years, suddenly surfaced. The much feared Moros (today known as

Ayoreos) were one day seen at a clearing's edge by the peaceful Lengua Indians working at the new Experimental Farm. Whereupon all the Indian workers immediately ran off into the bush toward Filadelfia in a panic. Doing manual labor for the Mennonites in exchange for food and clothing, these friendly Indians had been telling frightening stories to the colonists about Moro ferocity for many years.

This reaction was not totally unfounded. Not but one year later on the remote Stahl homestead about 3 miles farther north from the experimental farm, Paul Stahl and three of his five children were massacred by Moros on November 28, 1947 (from Edwin Neufeld). Justifiably alarmed by the peaceful Lengua workers having fled to Filadelfia, the colony workers also reacted by moving off the experimental farm to the nearest village *Auhagen* (#9), about 4 miles east. Commuting by horse and wagon to the farm for work each day and without Indian laborers, slowed progress to the point Menno was not able to meet his planned objectives during his three year term. (See 3.4.1, p. 210)

Even so, to his credit, he provided decisive direction for the experimental farm and started several crucial projects to "solve many agricultural problems:" first silo tests for winter feeding, growing fruit trees and vegetable plants for colony citizens, experiments with pasture grasses not native to the Chaco and others. Menno planned and supervised, with Fernheim's administration, the first Mennonite agricultural exposition successfully carried out on July 8, 1949, in Filadelfia. ("First agricultural exposition of the Chaco Mennonites in Paraguay" *Mennoblatt*, July 1949)

His MCC service nearing an end, Menno wrote a brief report for North American readers, *Guide for Better Agriculture in Subtropical Paraguay*, published in Fernheim. Menno writes that much still needs to be done: control for diseases and insects, pastures and winter feed for cattle, fruit and vegetable growing, soil improvement and conservation, cattle raising and milk production. And Menno acknowledges: "Really, we just made a small start in our adventure for discovering the secrets that lie hidden in the Chaco soil." (*Southern Notes*, January 1949, p. 4)

Persistently with enthusiasm and with determined colonists, Menno made a good beginning. We will later see how Robert Unruh built on Menno's excellent foundation to advance and expand the Chaco farming and cattle ranching. Unruh's work had lasting and far reaching benefits beyond Mennonite colony borders.

This young man from Canada had a love for nature and for his Chaco Mennonite brethren. His encompassing vision for an experimental farm is proof. But wait, there is more to tell.

The third immigration wave to the Chaco mentioned earlier in this chapter, happened in 1947. Menno fell in love with one expatriate, Aganethe Enns, then working in Fernheim. They were married on January 13, 1948. Thirty years after leaving the Chaco, Menno returned with Aganethe January 1979. With Robert Unruh they toured the experimental farm and progressive colony farms and watched sleek cattle grazing on lush Buffelgrass pastures where earlier there had been thorny bush and bitter grass. They admired the social and economic progress, which Menno said, works in "harmony with Christian faith."

He commented with overwhelming pleasure that "the 'green hell' is emerging as a paradise." Did Menno fully comprehend that this astonishing transformation grew from his legacy? That his idealism from long before was the basis for this conversion?

Between Menno Klassen's departure and the Unruhs arrival, Abe Peters from Oklahoma supervised the Experimental Farm for two years. And for five months

Experimental Farm staff early 1951. L to R: Peter Klassen, Mrs. Klassen, Peter Schellenberg and his three children, Ernst Oehring, Abe Peters and Mrs. Schellenberg, far right. Photo credit: Robert Snyder.

after Abe's departure, two MCC voluntary service workers, Robert Snyder and Darrell Albright also from the U.S., temporarily came from East Paraguay to hold the farm together and keep the experiments growing until the Unruhs arrive, October 1951.

4

Getting to Paraguay

After much preparation, perhaps difficult to understand in today's rapid and easy travel, the Unruhs were ready to set sail. They departed New York on the *S.S. Brazil* on August 23, 1951, bound for Buenos Aires. Bob was 30, Myrtle 34. With them were John and Clara Schmidt and their five children (the youngest 5 months). The Schmidts had served with MCC in Paraguay July 1941 to late 1942 for John alone and 1943-1946 with Clara. Their mission was to start the leprosy station at Km 81. On the trip the couples surely must have talked about Paraguay and the Chaco. Clara Schmidt wrote that after 20 days at sea they reached Buenos Aires and were greeted by Martin Duerksen who worked there, ministering to the scattered Mennonites who in 1947 refused to go on to Paraguay. In 1947 others did go on to Paraguay but organized Volendam in East Paraguay, never reaching the Chaco.

From Buenos Aires the two families traveled separately; the Schmidts stayed for a few days in Buenos Aires, and the Unruhs traveled to Uruguay and to Brazil. Traveling by boat to Montevideo, Uruguay, they visited a new Mennonite settlement where people lived under appalling conditions. Then they went to the newly formed settlement at Bage, Rio Grande do Sul in Brazil before returning to Buenos Aires. From there, upriver to Asunción, Paraguay. (See Chapter 4, p. 212)

Bob and Myrtle spent ten days in and around Asunción. Of special interest was the leprosy station being built. Johann Teichgraef, a Chaco Mennonite, was busy repairing some dilapidated houses and restoring these into living quarters for the first workers soon to arrive. They must have had interesting impressions seeing the primitive living conditions, first in Uruguay and Brazil, and now at Km 81.

On October 6, 1951, the Unruhs left Asunción going upriver to Puerto Casado where they arrived at midnight after a one days delay on the river. They stayed in Hotel Casado, and early the next morning they had their first "typical Paraguayan breakfast of half raw meat and hot *Yerba Mate* tea," Myrtle wrote later in their first activity report to MCC. They then took the *Auto Via* (narrow gauge rail truck) to Km 145 where they ate a hasty lunch, climbed onto a heavily loaded truck to travel the

Auto-Via. Photo credit: *Garden in the Wilderness Collection,* Mennonite Heritage Centre Archives (Winnipeg).

last 60 miles to Filadelfia. Myrtle writes that "the tree branches whipping across the truck made sure that we were not bored. The constant tumbling and lurching of the truck trying to avoid mud holes saw to it that we did not have a single dull moment." After this first trip into the Chaco one thing became clear to Myrtle: a high priority for the Chaco was roads! Well, she thought, before they settled here they should have built roads. From today's perspective it seems irresponsible to have been settled in the Chaco without roads. (See Chapter 4.1, p. 212)

By October, Darrell Albright had returned to North America. Bob Snyder remained to greet the Unruhs on their arrival in Filadelfia. He said in a 2003 recorded interview:

I tried to get the little house in Filadelfia ready for them and be there to greet them. I remember very well when they arrived. It was late evening very dark, a new moon. I remember the truck loaded high with freight, stopping in a cloud of dust in the street by the house. When the truck's engine and lights cut off, it was quiet for a few seconds and in the cool night air the first sound I heard coming from the top of the load was a woman's dead serious, commanding voice,

"Thank Goodness, only 1,765 days until we can go home!"

Their trip from New York to Filadelfia took 49 days. Myrtle's folks donated a wood burning kitchen stove no longer needed in Kansas. Shipped from Newton, Kansas, it did not arrive in time to load on the *S.S. Brazil.* There were personal items packed in a steel drum that also didn't ship on the *S.S. Brazil.* Arriving five months after the Unruhs, the stove and drum opened in Paraguayan customs was minus Bob's .22 caliber rifle and ammunition.

5

First Term:
October 1951 to August 1956

5.1 Introduction

Robert and Myrtle Unruh were active in the Chaco from October 1951 to December 1983 with furloughs lasting from a few months to two years. According to Ingrid Epp, their service periods were as follows:

1. October 1951 to August 1956
2. April 1958 to April 1961
3. August 1961 to August 1964
4. October 1966 to October 1969
5. April 1970 to April 1973
6. April 1974 to May 1977
7. October 1977 to September 1980
8. December 1980 to November 1983

Little doubt the Unruhs considered the Chaco Mennonite's living conditions primitive. The Russian immigrants coming in 1947 (Neuland Colony) occasionally referred to Fernheimers as "White Indians." However, the Chaco Mennonites saw "respectable progress." One's viewpoint reflected a varying starting point. When longer term settlers compared their life in 1951 with conditions twenty years earlier, they could easily distinguish "respectable progress." For instance, agricultural expansion especially in cotton and peanuts, increases in cattle, an industrial complex with a saw mill and electricity (in Filadelfia only), a creamery, a cotton gin and telephone service were all evident. (See 5.1, p. 216)

The Unruhs, however, came from the most progressive country in the world where the economy and technical advances flourished. From their perspective the Chaco Mennonites lived in appalling poverty. The younger generation in the Chaco was accustomed to this living standard and did not find it as oppressive as the 1947 newcomers. When today's Chaco Mennonites look at pictures from those early years, they are astonished at the living conditions. (See for example the films taken in the 1930s by Hans Krieg, or Phil Roth's amateur 8mm movies from the mid 1950s)

Street scene on Filadelfia's main street near the Cooperative, 1955. Photo credit: Phil Roth.

The Unruhs acknowledged but never spoke judgmentally about the deficiencies. Indeed, they shared in the paucity and contributed to its elimination. They always recognized the Mennonites for their good will and commitment, even if at times they might have felt taken for granted. Their own experiences growing to adulthood gave them empathy toward the *chaqueños* (people living in the Chaco). What follows in this chapter comes almost entirely from MCC activity reports, archived reports in Fernheim, and personal correspondence.

5.2 Work at the Experimental Station

In an agreement with Fernheim citizens, MCC sent Robert and Myrtle to supervise the Experimental Farm, working in agriculture and ranching, and thereby hoping to better the living standards. Bob began with small and elemental things. He always tackled the initial need at hand and later the bigger problems. While helping Myrtle set up their household, he immediately plunged into Experimental Farm details. First was the fight against ants. Unruh writes "We poisoned a great number of Ants" and dismissed the issue without elaboration, as was his nature. The facts were that ant control was a difficult agricultural problem that had to be addressed on an emergency basis and did not find a satisfactory long term solution for several years. (See 5.2, p. 218)

Early Fernheim Experimental Farm, date undetermined.

At the same time he pursued his longer term vision for the station and test-seeded small plots. Unfortunately, the rains did not come, the summer heat was scorching, and sand storms raged so that it became impossible to do much work outside. Bob provided Jeep transportation and accompanied Dr. Schmidt to Neuland to discuss the leprosy station and seek voluntary service personnel when they were caught in unexpected heavy rain. Bob immediately rented a wagon and horse to get back to Filadelfia leaving the Jeep with Dr. Schmidt in Neuland. The 22-mile trip took seven hours at night, needing to immediately plant experimental trials at the farm the next day. (Bob wrote in a family letter, ". . . the horse wasn't anything to brag about.") Bob later reported that germination was excellent, but no less the weeds, "The weeds removed all thoughts about unemployment," wrote Unruh.

Experimental Farm, 1962. Photo credit: Maurice Kaufmann.

Heinrich A. Wiens had recently been married and worked with Bob Unruh at the station. In 2006 he described Unruh as energetic and knowledgeable. But at first it was difficult for him to adjust to how things worked in the Chaco. Wiens writes:

As an employee of Mr. Unruh, an expert, one is careful with advice, but I have to mention one incident. Mr. Unruh came from a land of machines and cars, of course. If repairs had to be made, parts were available, but here the situation was different. In the Chaco a farmer or a wagon master had to have two things with him at all times to fix just about anything: wire and a pair of pliers. Mr. Unruh had to learn that even the Jeep could be repaired with such handy tools.

Bob read in the *Mennonite Weekly Review* that a bulldozer and pull grader for building and maintaining inter-colony roads in Paraguay were to be a shipped to Paraguay. He immediately wrote to Bill Snyder asking if the shipment might also bring a used grain combine for the experimental station. He specified that it should not be a large machine, a pull type most practical and concluded ". . . it will be put to good use."

(Myrtle's brother-in-law Philip Waltner, a Kansas dairyman, donated a used Allis Chalmers Gleaner combine. Edwin Neufeld reported that this combine was then rented and later purchased by Hohenau village.)

Next, Bob addressed the need for a balanced diet among the Chaco Mennonites. Fruits and vegetables were unavailable for long periods. But at times, in season, there were surpluses that spoiled. He proposed that extra beans, cucumbers and so on, should be canned, but there were no canning containers. So he urged Bill Snyder to solicit North American Mennonite constituencies to donate canning jars for Paraguay. "We know people in the states who would donate canning jars if MCC undertakes such a project." Bob writes. "As ocean shipping rates are figured on volume rather than weight, these jars could be filled with raisins, dried fruit, brown sugar, and vegetable seeds. All these things are desperately needed here." (See 5.2.0, p. 218

In January 1952, Bob came down with hepatitis, misdiagnosed at first as malaria until his complexion turned yellow. Stricken with a high fever he was unable to work for three weeks. During this time

A large tomato harvest at the experimental station. Vegetable growing was an early priority for the Unruhs. L to R, Bob with Heinrich Duerksen, Fernheim Oberschulze.

Bob with vegetable display. Experimental Farm house in background.

cotton fields became infested with ". . . small, grey moths that strip the leaves," Bob wrote in his activity report. "To date no control has been found although sprays from the States might work. But then, they have no machinery for spraying so every farmer must walk his fields spraying with hand methods."

The January 1952 activity report also mentioned digging a sweet water well at the farm, ". . . wells good enough for drinking water are indeed rare for the Chaco. The well is about 100 yards from the buildings but we hope to some day pipe the water to the yard."

In February 1952, he reported worms in the cotton fields. Farmers attempted to spray with Paris Green (copper(II)-acetoarsenite) but without success. Another insecticide Gammezane, (chlorinated hydrocarbon compound similar to DDT) was used with great success not only for cotton but other plants as well. But spraying applications became a major burden because it was dusting, all done by hand, a tedious and unhealthy procedure. A better solution must to be found.

Fernheim's Cotton Gin, 1955. Growers bringing cotton in horse wagons (pictures right). Processed cotton loaded on trucks headed for End Station on the left. The cotton seed was used for cattle feed. Photo credit: Phil Roth.

In the meantime, Myrtle attempted teaching Mrs. Wiens, who was also employed at the station, how to can beans. Canning was unfamiliar to her and she didn't seem particularly enthusiastic. Not to be discouraged, Myrtle hoped in time food preservation would become an accepted practice. Patience. During the winter months, (July and August) when more vegetables were available, Myrtle planned to do a series of demonstrations with her pressure cooker, another new idea for the Chaco. The farm bought a tin can canner from Ernst Harder with about 100 usable cans and lids. Although people did show an interest in this process, the absence of glassware and cans was a problem. (See 5.2.0.1, p. 219)

5.2.1 Cattle Genetics, Better Cattle Feed and Care

Cattle in the Chaco were substandard by any measure; often sick, especially with TB and brucellosis. In March 1952, STICA experts

Early silo production, cutting kafir with a machete. In front is Robert Unruh.

Fernheim bought a used Hammermill from STICA in 1954. Man far left is packing a masonry (brick) pit silo. Two MCC VS men working with STICA in East Paraguay, Marvin Miller from Virginia and Harry Neufeld from Kansas came to the Chaco to set it up and are shown here feeding the Hammermill.

examined 150 cows in Fernheim and Menno colonies. Healthy cows that cleared the screening, were bred to pure bred bulls on loan from STICA. Not everything ran smoothly, but Bob was convinced that "it is a start in the right direction." (See 5.2.1, p. 219)

A "small experiment" the Unruhs conducted on their cornor house lot in Filadelfia caused quite a sensation in Fernheim. Bob built a small trench silo for winter feed for their cow. The "hole" for storing cattle feed was a curiousity. The hand-driven chopper was an old English model dating from the 1800s. Bob removed the crank and replaced it with a pulley, and drove the cutter (hammermill) with Fernheim's Farmall M farm tractor. When he started the rig up, the cutter made such a loud and unfamiliar racket that people gathered to see the "demonstration." He wrote, "Several onlookers said that if this works they too will try it next year. Maybe there is some good that can come from this." (See 5.2.1.1, p. 220)

Delivering the morning's milk, 1954. Photo credit: Nancy Flowers, Mennonite Church USA Historical Committee, Goshen, Ind.

Bob's MCC activity report (April 1952) noted two happenings: a Moro attack with *Lengua* Indians killed and their teaching duties.

They conclude their report with the note that their work has increased considerably, and they ask for prayers that they might do the tasks correctly. They add humbly that they can do only a small part of this work. (See 5.2.1.2, p. 221)

Encouraged by the silo experiment's success in Filadelfia, in May 1952, Bob continued experimenting with silage at the experimental station. Indians chopped the Kafir on the field, and brought it by wagon to the trench silo near the buildings. The process was similar to that used in Filadelfia with the exception that instead of using a tractor, his Jeep was used. It was set on blocks, put in four-wheel drive, a belt was placed over the front tire, (the other front wheel anchored from turning) and he wrote that "this sounds crazy, but it worked."

Harvesting 'Honey Drip' Sorgum, 1952. Photo credit: MCC, Mennonite Church USA Historical Committee, Goshen, Ind.

Another sign of progress at the experimental station was harvesting peanuts with a combine. He did not describe this further, but wrote with obvious pleasure "People were very much surprised at the time saved and were enthusiastic about the harvestors."

Peanut harvester in operation.

With favorable weather, the Farm's vegetable garden produced abundantly. In one week the station sold some 18,000 vegetable seedlings to the citizens. An additional 3,500 seedlings were set out at the station to later sell the resulting produce to the hospital where vegetables were always in demand.

Rain was, of course, needed for production. But the roads—little more than trails through the bush—became impassable. Traveling every day between Filadelfia and the Farm, Bob understood the need to improve the roadway. In his June 1952 report, ". . . would hardly pass for a good road in the States but it is no doubt the best road in the Chaco now." (See 5.2.1.3, p. 221)

In August 1952 Bob began the second step in his cattle improvement program fencing 80 acres at the Experimental Farm. He planned a breeding program to demonstrate improved milk production. In those days, half a gallon per cow per day was top production. This low productivity was unacceptable. His plan was

"Improved" road to the experimental station. Looking southwest from the farm toward Filadelfia.

to show that proper care and feeding when combined with breeding would bring about increased productivity and profitability.

5.2.2 Farm Extension Education

Bob throughout his tenure stressed the importance for "extension"; adult education about research results to practioners. To this end, he often traveled to the villages to inform and give counsel. And

During the early 1950s the experimental station was new and interesting and served as a field trip for schools and youth groups.

he also invited the farmers to visit the experimental station, to personally see the experiments.

In September 1952 Bob drove to Menno Colony to transport Menno's *Oberschulze* and other colony leaders for a visit to the Experimental Farm. The Unruhs reported that previously Menno had viewed the farm with a dismissive I-can-take-it-or-leave-it attitude. After this visit Bob perceived a change of heart to showing some interest in the Farm's activities.

Bob also encouraged visits by the high school students and the teacher's training school. For instance, a "September 1953 Highlight," Myrtle men-

High school juniors in Filadelfia, 1955. Second row middle Robert and Myrtle Unruh. Robert taught agronomy. Myrtle taught home economics. Peter P. Klassen, school principal, seated front row center.

tioned 40 high school students visiting the station. It was the "Ag" class' practical aspect.

Pulled by a Jeep and driven by Bob, all students rode a trailer four miles to spend the day at the station. Though the day was hot, the students nevertheless enjoyed it. They learned about the various projects and the Experimental Farm's significance for colony agriculture. For most students this was no doubt their first visit to the farm.

Bob's German was not the best and that reality sometimes caused confusion and at other times laughter in the classroom. Although the students joked about Bob's inauspicious command of German, he was reported to be a good sport and not defensive about his limitation. All things considered, former students said it kept his classes interesting, lively and instructional quality apparently little impaired. (See 5.2.2, p. 221)

Of "key importance" during the months August/September 1952, was the raisin distribution from churches in California. Unruhs reported that this "distribution was a joy." According to Reverend Walter Thielmann, even today people still remember this event with affection.

A 1958 lattice shade constructed for tree nursery. Peter Klassen, specialist in tree propagation shown.

In October 1952 Bob reported on progress with a cattle breeding project. Some good cows, a few heifers, and a Holstein bull were bought from STICA and kept at the Experimental Farm for breeding purposes to upgrade herd quality.

In the meantime, Myrtle started a unique vegetable canning project for the personnel at the hospital. All glassware, including borrowed jars, were filled. The Unruhs hoped that this would become a regular practice.

5.2.3 Experimental Farm's North American Public Relations

In a letter dated November 28, 1952, and addressed to Marion W. Kliewer in Akron, Pa., Bob gave a detailed description of station personnel: Ernst Oehring, originally from Germany had experience in Africa, Argentina, and with Casado at *Palo Santo* Experimental Station. Ernst worked mainly with fruit trees and vegetables, and his assistant,

Experimental Farm pond, known as "Tajamar" used to water vegetables and experimental tree plots.

Hans Unruh, was then visiting STICA for a few months for training. Peter Klassen—known as forest Klassen—was a recent immigrant (Neuland) with experience as a Russian forest ranger. Edwin Neufeld says that Klassen experimented with reforestation using *paraiso* and eucalyptus trees. Bob also mentioned Heinrich Wiens, an excellent yard manager, and his wife, a cook at the station.

The letter contains a detailed description of buildings and living quarters, pointing out they were meager and inadequate. Peter Klassen and his wife lived in the same house where poisons and seeds were kept, something that had to change. Except for the combine (peanuts), all other work was done either by hand or with horses. He added an explanatory note saying that at the station there is no "research" only "experiments" with a variety of plants and seeds coming from overseas. "We are experimenting with many grass varieties and one type looks particularly promising." It was Buffelgrass, originally from southwest Africa, which seemed to thrive in the Chaco. "Perhaps this is exactly what we need in place of the native bitter grass," he casually added.

Kliewer was interested in colony farmer acceptance to the Experimental Farm's program and Bob answered this question thus:

Reaction to the farm varies a great deal. Those for it are definitely in the minority. Many think the farm is unnecessary because of the money it takes to run it. So far the recently introduced Landwirtschaftliche Schaufenster (translation: Agricultural Window. A periodic extension newsletter from Bob, 4-5 times a year) *has been well received. . . . Regrettably only Fernheim has a financial interest and so the other colonies are not as interested as they should be. Menno Colony always claimed they were agriculturally ahead but since my taking a few colony leaders to see the farm, they don't talk like that so much anymore.*

The greatest vulnerability was locusts and leaf cutting ants, wrote Bob. It is too bad that the government (Paraguayan) does not provide any assistance for insecticides or seeds. Other factors suppressing development are the low prices for produce, and the transportation difficulty to the market. Again Unruh emphasized that mechanization was needed, since virtually all work was done with horses, which limits personal productivity.

Concluding his report to Kliewer, Bob listed his priorities; the need to improve cattle through a breeding program, pasture improvement, developing a quality feeding program and better animal care.. He expressed the hope to someday import breeding stock directly from the U.S. if financing can be arranged. Following that are Experimental Farm building improvements, better weed control for all crops, improving crop rotations, variety trials, *Schaufenster* and teaching high school agriculture classes. (See 5.2.3, p. 221)

5.2.4 Activity Reports

The tenor of the Activity Reports continues much the same month after month; a continuing struggle with recurring problems. For example; heat, drought, periodic crop failures, locusts, ants, aphids, and various diseases. But Bob would not give up the battle to overcome these major setbacks. He continued experimenting with cattle and various crops. Trial progress was slow and appeared of little consequence, requiring much time to mature from a seedling to harvest. Trials needed repeating for several years to be certain of results in the long run. He conducted hundreds of experiments with grasses, fiber plants, vegetables and more, most are forgotten today, and only a few brought the expected result. Getting to these satisfactory results took monumental patience.

In March 1953, Bob reported harvesting kafir with combines that generated enormous excitement. Everybody concerned regarded the combine as a big step toward mechanization. He also mentions that 1953 Kaffir and peanut yields were better than average. (See 5.2.4, p. 222)

However, the report's optimism was dampened by continued Moro sightings and just as important, "emigration fever." Many didn't see a future in the Chaco and decided to leave, causing land prices to drop dramatically.

All in the colonies were shocked over the death of 15 year-old Kornelius Peters who, along with 20 year-old Hans Schmidt, were lost in the Chaco bush looking for their wayward mules. When they were found, Kornelius had died of thirst but Hans was saved. These incidents were mentioned in Bob's activity reports. (See 5.2.4.1, p. 223)

The April 1953 report cited "most important news," the acquisition of two Zebu cows for breeding purposes. The plan was to mate with STICA's Holstein bulls. The hope was this cross breed would tolerate the heat better than pure Holsteins and produce more milk than purebreds. The price, Gs.5,000 each (roughly $500 in 1953) was high however, they came with a money back guarantee for six months (can return if not satisfied). At the same time Neuland Colony purchased 20 Zebu bulls from a ranch 160 miles south from Neuland. (See 5.2.4.2, p. 223)

5.2.5 Mechanization

While the work at the station continued to progress, after twenty months on the job, Bob thought it was time to press MCC to consider serious mechanization. Farmers in the Chaco wanted to see results and not empty promises of a better future. That the Experimental Farm should lead the way by example going beyond small hand plot demonstrations that might or might not have practical applications for commercial farmers, were two points in a letter written to William T. Snyder, on May 2, 1953.

Bob was convinced that the Farm must be ahead of the farmers by several years and he saw the need for a tractor at the Farm as urgent. In this letter Bob says the logic that Chaco farmers worked with horses and that the Experimental Farm should also work with horses—was an invalid argument. It was the purpose of an experimental farm to lead the way into the future. With a tractor it was possible to work faster and efficiently. Moreover, Fernheim was already on the path to mechanization. Machines increased yield as seen by the example of Fernheim having bought three peanut threshers. He writes that, "I am of the opinion that in the next ten to fifteen years the methods of agriculture will be changed completely." He also argued for a tractor saying he had been in touch with Neuland and Menno Colonies who had agreed to each plant 2.5 acres of dwarf Kafir. He would then go to the colonies with the combine to harvest the Kafir, as a demon-

Robert Unruh with FARMALL-M.

stration for each colony. He was so convinced of the need for a tractor that he was willing to appeal to friends in the USA and pay off the debt doing custom work in the colonies.

It was an uncharacteristically persuasive letter to Bill Snyder and his forthrightness carried some risk he might be censored by MCC as

"Pre-mechanization at the Experimental Farm.

Shipment of surplus horse-drawn implements loaded on railroad car at Puerto Casada, 1953. Photo credit: Mennonite Church USA Historical Committee, Goshen, Ind.

overstepping his authority. How this tractor came to be is not documented in Paraguay but a new tractor did arrive in Asuncion a few months later. (See 5.2.5, p. 223)

In July/August 1953, harnesses, a wind mill, and a grass cutting machine arrived as a gift from Kansas and Montana Mennonite Churches. The horse drawn mower was to convince people of its usefulness in hay production, and in addition within financial reach of the colony farmers. Though a hard frost brought some crop damage, vegetables such as cabbage, lettuce, carrots, onions, and others escaped injury.

The young bulls auctioned at the station early 1954 was a special event; the first cross bred offspring from Zebu cows and STICA Holstein bulls. Although there were only three young bulls, the interest and participation by the farmers was good. Bob wrote because most farmers did not see breeding as their obligation, he hoped to have an annual auction to improve milk production in the Chaco.

In his first 1954 activity report Bob noted the North American visitors streaming into the Chaco. "Our one complaint being MCC representatives is that we spend too much time showing people around and as a result our work at the Farm suffers. January was taken up with one set of visitors after another." In their three year service, there were about two dozen MCC workers in east Paraguay and all wanted to visit the Chaco. That there being no other provision for sightseeing than Bob's Jeep, to travel with them throughout the three colonies was becoming a burden.

Despite progress, some perceived a dim future for life in the Chaco. In February 1954 an emigration from Fernheim to Bolivia took place with five fully loaded wagons. (See 5.2.5.1, p. 225)

In August that year Bob reported major sand storms and drought. In some villages' cattle died for lack of pasture and water. In contrast was a successful wheat harvest by combine from a 27-acre Experimental Farm plot. He wrote that it is hard to imagine the surprised faces of the children when they saw their first combine, and even more surprising were the faces of the older persons who remembered their beloved wheat fields in Russia. The big conversational topic in the colony was "Wheat in the Chaco as we used to have it in Russia." The yield varied between 7.4 to 10.5 bushels/acre, not great, but the event was a big morale booster for the farmers if not everybody.

The last two reports by the Unruhs came in March and July 1955, mentioning a dry January. From February 11 to March 11 with Vern and Violet Buller, the Unruhs took their first vacation, visiting Argentina and Uruguay.

July 1955 was Fernheim's 25th anniversary that brought a renewed wave of MCC visitors for the Unruhs. (See 5.2.5.2, p. 227)

Looking at the last 25 years, according to the Unruhs, there were many developments to report that gave courage to all. But Bob also reported a "natural catastrophe" for the Chaco. After several warm days, a cold wave swept the area with two night's temperatures falling to 19°F, and the succeeding nights to 21°F and 26°F. Bananas, papayas, potatoes, *mandioca*, many small fruit trees, and most vegetables were completely destroyed. Bob estimates the loss at around $300, which is high compared with an annual budget for the entire Farm around $1,000 that year.

5.2.6 "A Day off in the Chaco," by Myrtle Unruh, May 1952

For two months it seemed there was no time to relax. Sundays were crowded with activities like every other week day. Although activities on Sunday were religious activities, we felt we should take Sundays to relax. Finally, one Friday it seemed that the coming Saturday might be made into such a day. At 5:00 a.m. we would say goodbye to Peter Epps who were leaving for Asuncion via End Station and down river. Then we would go out to meet the plane and say good-bye to the Sherrills, bring in the (MCC) mail and distribute it, come home and then relax as we read the week's accumulation of mail.

When the alarm clock sounded we hurried out of bed to finish packing the lunch for Epps to take on their way to End Station. A few minutes later a knock at the door, someone came to say good-bye to the Epps. Shortly the truck pulled away and we came back to the house to finish organizing the mail going out on the plane. At 6:00 a.m. we decided it was breakfast time. In the next hour there were five more callers, each getting something, bringing something, or asking something.

Then Oberschulze Duerksen brought MCC's Jeep back. He had borrowed it the night before because his had a broken fuel pump. So Bob pushed his jeep to the repaid shop and lent him our Jeep. After that there were four more callers before the plane came at 9:00 a.m.; one brought mail, one borrowed tools, one wanted to know how slide projectors worked, and one asked if we would take him to the Farm in the afternoon? Goodbye siesta!

We hoped for a siesta after lunch. But we are always happy to show the Farm and appreciate this interest. As it turned out we learned something from this Menno Colony farmer. (See 3.2.6, p. 227)

When we heard the airplanes, Dr. and Mrs. Dollinger jumped into the Jeep with us and we drove to the airport. In half an hour we were back, sorted out the mail and started dinner for our guest from Menno. Before dinner was ready we had five more callers, delivered the mail, and answered seven phone calls. There were two more phone calls during dinner.

After dinner Bob and the guest drove to the farm while I started to put the house in order again and to replenish the pantry because we had to change our plans for spending Sunday in Neuland.

When Bob got back from the farm he went to get a barrel of water from a nearby well. While he was gone an urgent phone call sent me rushing down the street to bring a neighbor to the phone. (See 5.2.6.1, p. 227)

At 7:00 we set down to relax—supper over and the dishes done, baths taken, hair washed—to read our mail of 24 magazines, newspapers and several letters to enjoy. Our broken radio came back from Asuncion so we should see if it works. In a few minuets another visitor at the door; a man had died at the hospital. Because there is no telephone service at night, would we drive 12 miles to tell the family? While Bob was away I answered the door three more times. By the time he got back the current was off for the night (10:00 p.m.) so we went to bed. The mail has since been read and the radio works. It would have been such a nice day to relax, but we just couldn't find the time to do it.

5.3 Paraguay's Affairs of State, 1950-1956

To better understand the situation in the Chaco we should consider Paraguay's demographic and political environment during the Unruhs' service term.

Until 1954, Paraguay was marked politically with unrests, insecurities, and revolutions. For example, during the two years 1948 and 1949, Paraguay had six presidents, a situation hampering economic development throughout Paraguay. Except for Asunción and its surroundings, there were no roads worth mentioning and all transportation was river traffic or by railroad between Asunción and Encarnación. Most 1,425,000 inhabitants were living along the rivers. Those living in the hinder lands relied on the ox and donkey for transportation and all goods for Asunción markets were brought on the backs of donkeys or ox carts. In this sense the Mennonites were far more advanced than the native population.

The first elevated and solid roads in Paraguay's backcountry were built by Mennonites. It was Harry Harder in 1953, using one bulldozer and grader, who built access roads to the ports for Friesland and Volendam. Later these machines were sent to the Chaco to improve that road system. Vern Buller came in mid-1954 with additional road-building equipment. The Bullers were also from Bob Unruh's home church congregation. The task: to build the road to the train station at Km 145. He finished this work in 1955, and then improved the roads between villages, built water holes (*tajamares*), and cleared bush where Bob could plant Buffelgrass. These happenings were the start for rapid development in the colonies in the next few years. (See 5.3, p. 229)

5.4 Unruh's First Service Term: Summary Conclusions

Looking superficially at Activity Reports, the Unruhs wrote during their first term, one gets the impression of mediocrity; the reports are not very impressive. Fortunately, there are many letters to family and correspondence with MCC that expands our view.

First, the Unruhs did not draw attention to themselves; they were not inclined to exaggerate. They considered themselves brother and sister among brothers and sisters. They showed no disdain for the Mennonites in the colonies, their poverty, or their backwardness. On the contrary, the Unruhs were humble people who found a way to integrate themselves into the social environment. They did not complain, but when something was needed to work efficiently; a refrigerator or washing machine or kitchen equipment for the Farm, then MCC or their home churches were informed quickly.

They knew that their standard of living was above that of the general population. They might have lived as the average population did but because the goal was to elevate the standard of living for everybody it became necessary to be a step or two ahead both at the Farm and at home. Their life style served this purpose well, to their credit. The Unruhs led in tiny steps whenever it was in the realm of possibility for the colonists; to can fruits, to build a silo for winter feeding, a small pasture of Buffelgrass for the home cow, a horse-drawn cutter bar mower. These were inexpensive and practical yet convincing examples people could adopt.

Life in the Chaco compared to that in their homeland certainly was one of deprivation. Sometimes they privately noted these deprivations: a home without running water, without a refrigerator, food shortages and limited variety and insects on the rampage. There is no documentation that shows they complained about bugs in their beans, or rationed flour that was distributed according to the "number of souls" in the household (jokingly referred to as "soul flour"). This "soul flour" needed to be warmed to kill the worm eggs and then sifted to separate out the worms which were then thrown out the kitchen window for the chickens. Vern Buller wrote that it was frustrating to discover the flour was both rationed and wormy. That at first it was hard to eat the bread but when he looked around, ". . . and it dawned on me that everybody else was using the same flour and looked healthy, so I decided to eat it and not think about it anymore." The Unruhs must certainly have had similar thoughts.

In another example, Myrtle wrote in family letters about the vacation trip they took with the Bullers in 1955 visiting Argentina and Uruguay. Myrtle enjoyed shopping in department stores and seeing dresses that could be purchased, ready to wear. She compared this to Filadelfia, where every dress was hand-sewn from bulk cloth purchased from the Cooperative Store. In the Chaco the selection was meager and many women appeared in their Sunday best wearing the same cloth.

On an intellectual level, Bob writes on one occasion that he spent several days at STICA and it was stimulating and refreshing to be able to exchange ideas and talk with like-minded experts. But in the next sentence he wrote that he was happy to be "at home in the Chaco."

In a few years the colonists captured the Unruhs into their hearts. People stopped briefly to say hello, to thank them for some service or act of kindness, or to invite them into their home for fellowship or a meal.

Available documentation suggests that Bob never officially proposed grand or tentative ideas. But it is clear he had firm goals in mind. He considered the need, whether it was controlling destructive plant insects and diseases or whether a restricted diet needed to be improved with fruits and vegetables. He conducted many experiments with different crops and exhausted all reasonable possibilities to share the results with farmers in a productive manner. For example, ventures to breed cattle, improve milk production, provide winter silage and urge better animal care.

Unruhs were MCC employees at the Experimental Farm. But their actions showed that their horizon extended beyond Fernheim's boundaries. Bob's approach reflected MCC's philosophy for mutual aid and regional development. Again and again Bob traveled to Neuland, visited and counseled on agricultural problems inviting farmers and cattlemen to visit the Experimental Farm. He was especially eager to engage Menno citizens, exercising patience and sensitivity leading to eventual and lasting success for Menno Colony.

In January 1956, Bob announced that the *Mennoblatt* would carry a regular column from the Experimental Farm, which would attempt to answer questions from farmers: ". . . a column for agricultural questions!"

5.5 First Term Recognition for Service

Abram J. Loewen was asked to write an appreciation in the *Mennoblatt* recognizing the services of Bob and Myrtle Unruh. Here are some excerpts:

Their departure has created a void. Five years ago they came under the sponsorship of MCC and having completed their term, will now return to their homeland.

All these years they lived in the little white house at the corner of Bender and Central streets. They did not hurt anyone, and in their humble spirit there was no self aggrandizement and no air of self importance. And yet these dear people radiated a blessing to the entire colony that left no one untouched. Through tireless devotion they have touched our lives, and, in part, even changed our lives.

Through the leadership of this prudent and experienced man the experimental station stimulated and led all agriculture of Fernheim.

Mr. Unruh fought with difficulties just like all farmers in the Chaco do: ants, aphids, worms, heat, and drought. It was not always possible to master these difficulties, and it was during the hard fight with nature's forces that Mr. Unruh's patience, tirelessness, and perseverance defied all difficulties. His tireless activity was crowned with successes, which were evident at the experimental station and on virtually every farmstead in Fernheim.

Mr. Unruh did not limit his activity to practical affairs only, but taught agricultural classes in the high school to encourage the next generation of farmers.

Mrs. Unruh also had an assignment in the high school where she taught cooking and baking to our young girls. This knowledge was then applied in the homes of these girls, and thus Mrs. Unruh's superb recipes found wide acceptance in all homes. She was also active in the Fernheim women's circles where she was appreciated and loved by all.

During their farewell, the question came up repeatedly whether they might consider an eventual return. Mr. Unruh did not deny such a possibility. Perhaps in a couple of years they might return, but that has not been determined.

This is the hope we cling to. We wish these dear people a safe journey and a well-deserved vacation. And with hope in our hearts we call out to them, "Aufwiedersehen." (*Mennoblatt*, September 1956, pp. 5-6)

5.6 A Little Daughter Elizabeth

When the Unruhs came to the Chaco they were a family of two. When they departed they were a family of three, with an adopted daughter, Betty. In their Activity Report May 1954, they write that they have adopted a "sweet, little girl." Friesland's *Oberschulze* made it known a little girl in his colony, from a shattered, single mother family situation, needed adoption. The Unruhs thought and prayed about this and considered all angles, then went to Friesland to investigate. Bob wrote that when they saw the "sweet, little girl, the pathetic situation she was in, and how small her chances in life if she stayed there, we did not know how we should some day answer for it if we said no." They adopted her officially and wrote they could not then imagine life without her. "She is a source of much joy and we would not want

The Robert Unruh family, 1956.

to be without her anymore. We are thankful that we were led to her . . . and hope the Lord will bless us in this undertaking."

Betty wrote in 2006:

> *Coming home from school one day (about age 7) I told my parents that the other children kept telling me that they were not my 'real' parents. My parents told me I was 'adopted'. I never, ever had the feeling that I was adopted. To me, they were my real parents. They always told me, that I was a gift from God and that every gift from God was always right and real. As a child you do not understand many things completely, but I always understood and knew that I was truly loved without any reservations, unconditionally.*
>
> *I know that I was the source of much heartache and worry for my parents, but with God's help and the help of my parents we were able to overcome all the pain and worry.*

My whole life I never heard my parents argue or say unkind words to each other.

They would often see that people did unkind, bad or even evil things. But my father told me that there is hope for everyone. He would tell me that these people needed someone to help them discover the good in themselves and to help them grow and become people with hope and a fulfilled life. He said that we need to be willing to help others find the right path. In the end that is what will count, "Have you been helpful and made a positive difference in their life?" (See 5.6, p. 229)

5.7 Social Integration

Their Activity Reports often contained information on social and church activities in the colony. This seemed to be their nature. They attended church regularly, they reported on celebrations such as Christmas, Easter, Pentecost, Thanksgiving, and the special celebration on Fernheim's 25th anniversary. Of special interest to the Unruhs were the Indian missions and the occasional baptisms. In one letter Bob mentioned that he agreed with his predecessor Menno Klassen, who thought the Experimental Farm's work must be supportive of Indian missions.

Bob also wrote about evangelistic meetings deepening the faith for the colonists. Occasionally he noted gifts sent by people in the "north," especially his and Myrtle's home congregations. And he thankfully mentioned the simple gift of raisins, shared with others, a generous offering to equip the hospital kitchen, and clothing for those living in Neuland.

Edwin Neufeld remembers Unruh's activities among junior and high school boys, when he says:

It was his (Bob's) opinion that there was a need to educate the youth and he started such work. Gathering 12 to 15 year-old boys, they did voluntary work, had discussions, and made field trips. It was very important to him that young people be motivated through these activities to give their lives to Christ.

Robert Unruh with youth group, November 1954.

Edwin also writes that Myrtle addressed a vital social need.

> *Mrs. Unruh soon recognized a need among young mothers with small children. Often they were unable to participate in social activities, so she organized a circle for young women where their young children were included. The fellowship, the meaningful presentations for young mothers and book club activities afforded a blessing and uplifting change from the everyday routine.*

Bob showed a special love for music. He participated in choir practice and wrote about choir workshops and choir conventions in his letters. It was "music to his ears" when Hans Rempel, Neuland, came to Filadelfia with his choir and brass orchestra. That was entirely new for the Chaco. Bob compared the program quality with that in the U.S., and considered it a happy and blessed Chaco highlight.

Bob considered these events noteworthy in his activity reports to MCC. (It should be mentioned that many Neulanders had studied music in Russia [Soviet Union] and brought a few instruments to Paraguay [1947]. They used these instruments in their new villages during the difficult pioneer years, formed choirs, and even an orchestra with guitars, mandolins, balalaikas, harmonicas, violins, and in some cases, brass instruments.)

All things considered, the Unruhs' interest and influence extended beyond farming and animal husbandry. From the beginning they integrated themselves into the very fabric of life in the Chaco Mennonite Colonies.

Fernheim's Community Choir. Director, Walter Thielmann. Bob in the bass section, back row third from the left.

6

The Buffelgrass Story

Edgar Stoesz, MCC Secretary for Latin America (1967 to 1975) defined Robert Unruh's major gifts to Chaco Mennonites as having introduced Buffelgrass and his contributions to cattle husbandry. (Stoesz & Stackley, *Garden in the Wilderness*, CMBC Publications, Winnipeg, Manitoba,1999, pp. 94-97) Following its introduction, the facts became merged with myth. So in 1984 Edgar asks Bob for details about Buffelgrass. It is a story about incredibly good timing and coincidence. Translated into German and abridged in *Agrarian Technology* August 1995, a bulletin of *Servicio Agropecuario* (SAP) and again in the *Mennoblatt*, September 16, 1995, under the column "Pioneers Tell" the history is informative and legendary. This accounting richly conveys 1952-55 conditions and gives us insight into Bob's methodical thought process.

The year was 1951 and the time late October. Myrtle and I arrived in the Chaco a few weeks earlier, trying to adjust to new circumstances, climate and environment. My first indelible impression was the poor condition of the cattle due to lack of pasture. People told me this was normal and nothing could be done about it. I did not agree although the situation did look nearly hopeless. 90% of colony land was bush. The open land was mostly taken up for farming but what open land wasn't (cultivated) was covered over with native grasses; slow growing and unproductive. The unpalatable bitter grass (Espartillo) is dominant and crowds out better grasses. Colony farming was on a subsistence level and so no funds were available for fencing and clearing land for pasture. To top it off the market was limited to whatever might be consumed in the colony. The fact remained, better livestock nutrition was needed.

. . . while we waited for the first mail from USA we read and reread English magazines left behind by former MCC workers. There was an Oklahoma Farmer-Stockman *that contained a short article about a newly introduced grass proving itself adapted to Texas sandy soils.*[1] *I wrote for information and in time received literature and a full page color ad about "Buffelgrass" (Pennisetum Ciliare) It came from southwest Africa and was Introduced by USDA to Texas where it proved to be well adapted . . . Another grass, K-R Bluestem, introduced to Texas from India, was also recommended. After some deliberation, John Hostetler, MCC purchasing director at Akron, purchased and shipped 10 lbs of Buffelgrass seed and 5 lbs of K-R Bluestem. It took almost a year between reading the article until receiving the seed. On arrival we were surprised to find not one small bag but two large bags* (about the size of 50 lb flour bags) *for 10 lbs of Buffelgrass. The unhulled seed was hairy and fluffy. The second surprise was the price. No price was quoted so we expected around two dollars a pound, like other grass seed. It was* **twelve** *dollars a pound!* (delivered to Filadelfia) *This seed alone would take about ¼ the experimental farm's budget! Fortunately MCC came to the rescue with extra funds donated for special projects.*

The first plantings of Buffelgrass and K-R Bluestem were made at the experimental farm in late 1952, small plots roughly 20 x 30 feet. Both (varieties) *germinated and grew well but soon it was apparent that Buffel was much faster growing. A few months later larger plots were planted with good results. After the first year we could see Buffel was growing well and produced seed but had no idea how it might stand up to pasturing.*

At that time colony farmers only pastured oxen and horses on small plots of a half acre to one acre. Cattle were fenced **out**, *not* **in** *to pasture. The horse pasture grass was Guinea grass planted 40 inches apart in rows and cultivated*

---

[1] *Likely a subscription to Abe Peters, an Oklahoman, Bob's Experimental Farm director predecessor.*

to keep the weeds under control. We planted one horse pasture to Buffel at the farm to see how it might do. Small quantities of seed were given to a few farmers to try. One farmer discovered the fluffy seed could be planted using the seed plate for fuzzy cottonseed. This solved the uneven distribution—a problem with hand seeding—as well as a poor coverage problem.

During the first two years, comments and questions varied widely. How often would it need replanting? Would it be as nutritious as Guinea grass? There was concern Buffel grass might turn out to be a weed like Sand Bur that when planted for pasture mistakenly proved instead to be their worst weed when it invaded the cropland. A few were enthusiastic about it. All the early trials were on open sandy (campo) land because there was no cleared land available. Early 1954 I decided to try my own experiment. We had our own cow in Filadelfia that supplied us with milk. She was turned out every morning to scavenge for feed, along with every other cow in Filadelfia. There was a vacant lot across the street from us, land once covered by bush. I rented this lot, cleared the bush re-growth and then planted Buffelgrass. In a few months there was a lush stand of grass, up to the cow's belly. Soon she was fat and sleek. People in buggies driving by would stop and stare, not believing what they were seeing. Soon everybody in Filadelfia who possibly could was clearing and fencing a pasture lot for their milk cow. People in Fernheim villages began doing the same. Suddenly people realized the bush land was good for something after all! [2]

Large scale land clearing and Buffelgrass pastures got under way in the late 50s and early 60s when the $1,000,000 Smather's Loan, through the effort of C. L. Graber, interim SA director and Bill Snyder, enabled the colonies to purchase heavy land clearing equipment and fencing wire. The Trans Chaco Road was important for it made possible the marketing of cattle in Asuncion, something formerly impossible.

---

[2] In a 2003 interview John Peters, serving in the Chaco from 1964 to 1969 said, "Cleared bush land had such a hard base (high clay content) nothing would grow . . . it was useless. So they had all this bush land, harvesting trees from it, selling extract or using for lumber, firewood and fence posts. With the introduction of Buffelgrass . . . this cleared land started being used for pastures and beef cattle."

Land clearing and planting Buffelgrass continued not only in the colonies but on neighboring ranches and neighboring countries. Seed has been exported to Argentina and Bolivia for low rainfall areas. Buffel is doing well in Argentina's northern Chaco region.

New Buffel strains have developed recently. Last year I sent 106 Buffel varieties provided by Dr. E. C. Bashaw of Texas A&M to the Experimental Farm for testing. The variety first introduced in the Chaco was T-4464, now known as Common Buffelgrass, is still the most planted Buffel variety in Paraguay.

At one point we had about 50 grass species on test. A few looked promising but none were equal in drought resistance, rapid growth and nutritional value to Buffel. I've often wondered how long it might have taken before Buffelgrass found its way into the Chaco had we not seen the article in the Oklahoma Farmer-Stockman.

Robert G. Unruh, 1984

From June 1956 and years later, Bob received orders for buffelgrass beyond the experimental farm's ability to fill, a tribute to the value and buffelgrass's efficacy beyond the colonies. The Buffelgrass introduction along with livestock genetic improvements, energized the dairy and cattle industry among Chaco Mennonites. Buffelgrass' success eventually had far reaching consequences for Paraguayan ranchers and for southern Bolivia cattle producers. It is unlikely that Bob or any person anticipated in the 1950s that Buffelgrass would have such far reaching benefits. Introducing managed pastures brought attention to the advantages from better feeding and livestock care, leading to fencing cattle in rather than out.

One Buffelgrass myth:

Bob received the first seeds in a letter from his former professor with a note that this could be the solution for the Chaco. Bob puts these seeds into the ground and a few plants grew surprisingly fast and thus increased his interest. He harvested each new seed with a tweezers and replants these as well. After a short time beautiful grass appeared. Mr. Unruh is pleased and sees great potential and so places his first order for seeds from USA.

Having Bob's first hand account, we know the reality was a bit different than the myth. But such a dramatic myth underscores the importance of the grass for the Chaco and Bob's role in the region's agricultural development. (See Chapter 6, p. 230)

7

Second Term: April 1958 to April 1961

7.1 Re-socialization

Returning from furlough the Unruhs expressed pleasure having returned to Paraguay. In an open letter "Again in Paraguay" published in the *Mennoblatt*, May 1, 1958: (See 7.1, p. 232)

We are glad to be back in the Chaco and send greetings to everyone here. We traveled much and are refreshed. We visited and became reacquainted with many old friends and relatives whom we had not seen for years. We are grateful the Lord protected us from harm and accidents, and confident He will guide us and bless our work here.

But many colonists had had enough deprivation and families with connections or gifts from friends making possible immigration, particularly from Neuland and some from Fernheim, were moving to Germany or Canada. The mood was not good as the economic conditions in the Chaco were not improving and seemed hopeless. Robert Unruh began his second term knowing this migration flow must slow or stop for the colonies to survive. The *Mennoblatt* letter continues:

Farmers everywhere are facing problems. In United States beginning in 1952 up to the present, large areas are suffering with drought, so that many in the past five years have had little to harvest. Just last year at harvest time floods came making it impossible to harvest and crops rotted in the field. In addition, farmers there have the same problem as here; prices for supplies are rising while the prices for farm products are the same or going lower. Wheat and corn sell at the same price as fifteen years ago yet the price for tractors has increased three fold. Many US farmers are selling out and working off the farm. Statistics say only 12% of the US population are farmers and that number is calculated to go lower to perhaps 6%. Small farms are merging into bigger farms. Mechanization and borrowed money make this possible.

Bob concludes this open letter:

One thing is certain; immigrating to Canada or USA to make a living as a farmer is almost impossible. Immigration has as many or more problems than changing Chaco conditions. Think on Psalm 37.3. 'Trust in the LORD, and do good; so shalt thou dwell in the land, and verily thou shalt be fed.'

These comments show identification with the Chaco and the strength of his resolve to improve agricultural productivity. In an early second term letter he optimistically previews and again recommends growing vegetables for good nutrition as he had done years earlier:

It looks like a good year ahead for growing vegetables. It is important to cultivate your garden after each rain in order to conserve all possible moisture for the dry winter months. We have fungicides for tomato disease, and we hope to soon have Bayer pesticides for all vegetables and fruit trees. Please let me know if you have particular agricultural problems, and I will try to help as best as I can." (*Mennoblatt*, May 1, 1958, p. 7)

The late 1950s was a period of heightened activity and support from North America, change was in the wind. Only one short Activity Report for the second term was found and it describes the work from July to December 1958. Written by Myrtle, she reports how grateful they are to be warmly welcomed by so many people, ". . . we feel completely at home." She notes the improved living standard compared to 1951. There is a greater variety of goods available in Asuncion stores for instance. But arriving in the Chaco they discover the Cooperative has no flour that first week. Weeks later they can buy flour but no sugar or salt, "In the Chaco one must plan ahead about a month in advance," Myrtle writes. Myrtle also notes the continuing discontentment among Fernheimers.

7.2 Getting Back Into Harness

The experimental farm however was a different matter. After a nineteen-month absence, Bob discovers the farm had gone to rack and ruin. MCC sent an interim experimental farm director who as it turned out wasn't up to the task. With trials not cared for the projects are in disarray and overgrown. The silo program stubbed its toe and farmers were losing interest. The Farm's machinery was badly neglected; the Farmall M was inoperable with a damaged transmission, for example. Correspondence shows *Oberschulze* Duerksen had no confidence in the interim director and that the director had little rapport with colonists. Even worse the farm's employees were unhappy not having had inspired leadership and guidance during Bob's absence.

Early in this second term, Bob vents his frustration in personal letters wondering why his work is not finding more support among the three colony administrations and colony farmers. But his disappointment never rises to a level of resignation or public demands for greater farm participation. He understands the potential for good if the work is successful; his faith and conviction keep him on course and driven forward. The setbacks are mentioned and then suppressed, no more talked about. There is just enough success to provide "moral uplift" says Bob. Disappointments were carried quietly.

1958 was also the year that the Moros created much tension throughout Fernheim. Missionaries Kornelius Isaak and David Heins had for some months tried communicating with the Moros. On the morning of September 11, 1958, Issak died from a Moro spear wound the day before. The colonists and churches were called to reflection on the meaning of this event.

7.3 Second Term Highlights; Dairy

In chronological order and relying mostly on *Mennoblatt* articles for information, it was none the less a progressive three years.

Contributing to a successful push for dairying were buffelgrass and silage for winter feeding, Bob's first term standout successes. An article entitled: *Silo—Indispensable for Milk Production*, was printed in the *Mennoblatt*, June 16, 1958, p. 7:

I have noticed lately that interest in silo feeds has diminished, and I would like to make some observations. Some farmers are disappointed because they thought silo feed was a miracle feed to replace all other. Actually, it is a feed which replaces grass, and perhaps only part of the grain.

Others think silage is unnecessary because they can pasture year around. That is not completely true because when the dry winter months come the grass

Digging a trench silo at the experimental farm, Bob driving the Farmall M.

does not provide enough nourishment to keep animals healthy. Also frost and insect larva will destroy weakened pasture. To develop dairy farming we can not rely completely on pasture. From experiments and observations it is known that a good milk cow eats for eight hours and rests for eight hours if it has good pasture. If more time is required for finding food, less time is available to digest the food and milk production drops. Also it is known that a cow in good health needs half the food she eats for body maintenance. Not getting enough food means the same amount is used for maintenance leaving less for milk production. In other words, the cow provides first for body maintenance and produces milk from whatever is left over. It is no wonder that cows on bush pasture produce so little milk. It should be clear, to dairy farm in the Chaco or anywhere, silage is required. Silage has other advantages. First of all silage has 2 ½ times more food value than dry roughage in the same volume. Secondly there is less waste, the coarse stalk is eaten too. One must mention there is a down side to silage; it is low in protein content. We can adjust for this by feeding peanut or cotton seed meal. The cow's best feed is from 16 to 18 percent protein. Silage has only 1%, cotton meal 19.4% and peanut meal 39.6%. If one feeds only silage or only cotton seed or only peanut meal the cow gets unbalanced nourishment for body support and milk production.

There is much to learn about the best care for cows. In the USA for example at the research station for Iowa State College, healthy crossbred cows reached 5511 lbs of milk per year. Thus we should not overfeed nor neglect our cattle. If you have questions about feeding I will try to answer them as best I can. (*Mennoblatt*, June 16, 1958, p. 7)

This practical commentary was easily understood by all. At another time the high producers—without pedigrees—are listed to show that good care results in higher production when genetics are taken out of the equation:

The Dutch crossbreed Shokie Golden Joy cow in Delaware, USA after its second calf, produced 27,126 lbs. milk and 1,100 lbs. butter in 305 days. (*Mennoblatt*, August, 1958, p. 7) (See 7.3, p. 233)

7.4 Eggs

The improved road to End station at Km 145 enhanced the possibilities for marketing eggs, cheese, and butter in Asuncion. Before this road was built, shipping eggs to Asuncion was not possible. With proper packaging and careful handling, shipping eggs becomes an important possibility. The Chaco Mennonites were first to produce eggs on a large scale. Bob lists crucial data important to proper storage:

Proper Treatment for Shipping and Storing Eggs
>   1. *At 60 degrees and higher eggs begin incubation, immediately losing food value*
>   2. *At 80 degrees all food value is lost in 8 days*
>   3. *At 35 degrees eggs will store for over 10 weeks*
>   4. *At 33.8 degrees eggs will store for 6 months or longer, staying fresh*
>   5. *In the summertime eggs at room temperature are inedible over 1 week*
>   6. *Eggs should be packed with the round, thicker end up and refrigerated within 24 hours. Each day not refrigerated, eggs lose at least 10% of their weight and quality*
>   7. *Eggs packed with pointed end up tears the diaphragm. The yolks shifts upward and the egg loses freshness three times faster*
>   8. *Eggs laid on their sides lose 67% quality in 48 hours.*
>   (*Mennoblatt* August 1958, p. 7)

Given the strong demand for eggs in Asunción and rapid transport possible from the trans-Chaco road soon to be finished, Bob searched for ways to improve the poultry business. He thought to import chicks from the U.S. Clearly delighted, he writes: *"Chicks by jet"*

A year ago we tried to import pure bred chicks from outside Paraguay but without success. First we tried from Argentina but no supplier would assume responsibility for shipment. Brazil was willing to ship but the right breeds were not found. Finally chicks were found in USA but the airlines would not assume shipping responsibility. A few months ago we turned to the "Heiffer Project" an organization shipping cattle to many different countries. This is a relief organization organized by conscientious objectors after WW II to send breeding stock to war torn countries to replenish lost animals.

We were losing hope it could be done, but two weeks ago I got news that Pan American Airways would transport the chicks on Monday, May 16th. The jetliner departed New York at 10:00 a.m. At 10:00 p.m. that same day they arrived in Asuncion and Tuesday morning at 11:15 they arrived in Filadelfia (25:15 hours in transit).

We hurried to open the crates and found all 309 alive and lively. In a few days a few died but the prospects are good the majority will do well. The New Hampshire Red Breed is suitable for both egg and meat production." (*Mennoblatt*, June 1, 1960 pp. 6-7)

7.5 Mechanization

The *Ruta Transchaco* (Trans Chaco Roadway) opening was approaching, becoming a clearer reality. This direct, almost straight line connecting the Chaco Colonies with Asuncion was widely anticipated by most people in the colonies. The pros and cons were discussed and considered. Funds from the $1,000,000 Smathers loan were anticipated soon. Bob believed it was time to consider mechanization in the Chaco on a bigger scale. There were a few tractors but farming largely a matter of horse power, oxen by then gone from the scene. He again tries to lead the way:

One hears repeatedly about the coming mechanization in agriculture. Some farmers think machines will not pay their way, others are willing to try. At the experimental farm this year we looked at the economics of peanut mechanization. We worked 8 acres totally with machines except for hoeing young plants and knocking the dirt off after plowing up. Our records show:

	Man Hours	**Fuel consumption** - *liters*	
Winter field work	5.0	9	
Plowing	11.5	44	
Planting	7.3	20	
Cultivation, 5 times	20.5	49	
Spraying	4.3	10	
Digging	4.2	10	
Threshing	<u>35.6</u>	<u>26</u>	
Total	**88.4**	**168**	(44.38 galls)

Expenses

Diesel fuel @ gs14.5	gs 2,436	
Hoeing	1,460	
Cleaning dirt	180	
Chemical	<u>1,850</u>	
Total	**5,926**	

Total yield 3,000 kilo	10 gs/kilo	gs 30,000
less direct expenses	5,926	
less Depreciation and interest	<u>10,000</u>	
Total Expense		<u>15,926</u>
Net Income (Before grower labor)		**gs 14,074**

Based on these calculations we believe that the mechanization of peanuts is profitable, especially if the process is scaled up." (*Mennoblatt*, June 1960, p. 6)

In the same way, interest in egg production is ramping up as completion of the Trans Chaco Highway nears. Bob offers further elaboration in a *Mennoblatt* article dated September 17, 1960, pp. 6-7:

Because there is likely more growth to come from raising chickens in the colonies, following are good practices for the best results. First is to make

Combining peanuts in the 1990s.

Bob transporting harvest workers to the farm in 1958.

roomy housing so the chickens are not stressed by crowding. 40 sqcm per chicken for Leghorns and 60 sqcm for the heavier breeds is sufficient. Put in roosting bars, 15-20 cm per Leghorns and 25-30 cm for other breeds. The feeder trough should be 4-5 meters per 100 chickens and deep enough to hold feed for 2 days. The following table gives approximate rates according to production.

Eggs/week	kg feed/week
0	80
70	82.25
140	84.5
210	86.75
280	89
350	91.25
420	93.5
490	95.75
560	98
630	100.25

Water is no less important than feed. The egg is 70 to 75% water. Clearly a hen without adequate water is unable to produce eggs. 100 hens need about 25 to 30 liters of water per day, in hot weather much more. That means 9,000 to 10,000 liters per year perhaps more in the Chaco. The water containers must be cleaned and refilled with fresh water each day.

It is best to construct a "community" nest for 50 to 60 hens, 60 cm by 135 cm long. The floor is about 10 cm wider than the nest and diagonally from the rear forward so the eggs roll outside the nest as soon as they are laid. This way the egg cools, important for quality. Straw or bedding material is not needed. The nest is mounted on the housing wall around 75 to 100 cm high. Hang a rag in the opening so the nest is darkened. Make the cover diagonal so the chickens will not roost on the cover. Mount the nest where it can be easily cleaned. (See 7.5, p. 234)

7.6 Agricultural Fundamentals

From the beginning in 1951, Bob gave cattle genetics and milk production priority as the Chaco's agricultural future. With the Trans Chaco Highway and the $1,000,000 Smathers loan, a brighter future for the Chaco emerges. He makes a historical observation in a *Mennoblatt* article, "Opportunities for Milk Production" by telling what happened in North America, suggesting there were similar implications for Paraguay and the Chaco. Here are quotations in a carefully researched report:

If dairy farming is compared with industrial businesses, for example the steel industry, dairy farming is larger than the steel industry. Concerning money invested, the dairy industry has seven times more invested than the automobile industry and farmers hold 95 percent of these investments. Dairy farmers have about $27,000 invested per worker compared to $15,000 per worker for other industries averaged. Dairy Farmers have twice as much invested in machinery as the steel industry and five times more that the automobile industry. Moreover the dairy farmer is a customer for industrial products. Farmers make up the base that must exist before industry can happen.

*Why do I report this? Is it useless information about a foreign country? No, it shows that dairy farming is important for a stable economy in every country. There are many opportunities for dairy products in addition to butter and cheese already produced here. (*Mennoblatt*, December 1, 1960, p. 6)*

Bob comments on agricultural mechanization and technology. At the Experimental Farm three calves were conceived using artificial insemination (AI). This is a small beginning but a significant technical advancement. He writes about breeding cattle:

We think that there should be more emphasis on purebred cattle, since the earlier suspicion that they will not tolerate the climate, has been partially disproved. A particular breed's health is much more a question about care than climate. (Mennoblatt, June 1, 1961, p. 7)

Bob concludes his second term of service with an *Annual Report of the Experimental Station in Fernheim.* He notes experiments that failed and others that succeeded. The demand for citrus trees, roses, and other ornamental bushes was high:

1,786 citrus trees, 650 rose bushes, 454 ever greens, 306 grapes, 158 Kasuarinen, 586 cypress trees, 261 hedge bushes, and 262 other bushes were sold. Some 6,675 lbs of vegetables were sold, and many vegetable plants were also sold. (*Mennoblatt*, June 1, 1961, p. 7)

A grant from the Showalter Foundation ". . . brought new life into the Experimental Farm," writes Bob. The entire chicken project and other equipment acquisitions and building improvements were made possible. "Young students are also supported through this fund." he continues. Rudolf Kaethler studies veterinary medicine and Heinz Esau as an agronomist (both in Asuncion), and he writes "We hope in this way to gain specialists for the colonies." (*Mennoblatt*, June 1, 1960, p. 7) Bob points out that success in dairy farming and agriculture in the colonies will depend on Mennonite young people who train as experts and who then return to take on leadership responsibilities as soon as possible. (See 7.6, p. 234)

8

Third Term:
August 1961 to August 1964

During the third term, Bob served again as Experimental Farm director. Agriculture, cattle and poultry are again the focus (*Mennoblatt*, February 16, 1964, p. 6) and for mechanization. (*Mennoblatt*, August 1, 1964, pp. 6-7) A new experience for many was the agricultural exposition for the three Chaco colonies held on August 30, 1963 (the first exposition fourteen years earlier, was organized by Menno Klassen on July 8, 1949, see chapter 3). New ideas and production techniques introduced by the exposition stimulated questions. First, why an exposition? Bob answers the question straightforwardly. His direct but considerate approach to answering probing questions shows his humility, openness and wish to serve. He answers questions with fitting and practical examples, and he does so without a hint of manipulation or self service. The Mennonite community's welfare is paramount:

> *Most people know that this winter there will be an exposition. Many ask: "Why an exposition?" Some say that we want to show off. Others say it is done for the sole purpose of inviting government officials to impress them and influence them. It is good that these questions come up and I would like to attempt an answer.*
>
> *Why an exposition? It might be best to answer this question by quoting those who have much experience with expositions. A small pamphlet issued by STICA outlines goals for an exposition:*

1. *To promote the classification and evaluation of items at the exposition and to learn from the preparation of exibits. It is to promote an understanding of products people have made during preparations for the exposition. An exposition aids further advancements when understanding how things are classified and evaluated is made clearer.*

2. *To show how advancements in agriculture and ranching benefit every citizen.*

3. *To promote an interest in production improvements among farmers.*

4. *To offer an opportunity for farmers to participate and learn from other farmers.*

5. *To recognize and reward efforts to create better products.*

6. *To show to government officials the achievement potential of a region, and solicit their assistance in the continuing development of agriculture and ranching.*

7. *To promote the social and cultural life for the farming community, at the same time providing recreation and learning.*

8. *To promote better understanding among the urban population for farming and farmers.*

It is clear from these goals that an exposition is matter of the community and done for the community. Although we plan to invite persons from outside the Chaco, our concern is primarily what they can learn about the Chaco, not what they will think of us. This first year we are not going to emphasize top performers, because we are not ready for that. For me, of greater importance is that our young people recognize the characteristics of a good cow, a good horse, or good chickens. Then they will understand how to improve their own farm. With this in mind we are going to invite judges who will give us hints along these lines.

We hope that there will be an exchange of ideas among craftsmen and homemakers that might provide ideas both in time saving and entertainment. In other countries expositions are considered one of the best methods for the improvement of agriculture, and I am convinced this can be the case here as well. (Mennoblatt, July 16, 1963, pp. 6-7)

The exposition took place as scheduled on August 30, 1963. The event was considered "generally successful." Bob was asked to give an interview for the *Mennoblatt* to summarize the event for readers with more statistical data and to support enthusiasm for the future. Following are the questions and Bob's replies:

1. *What animals were at the exposition?*

    There were horses, cows, and other livestock such as pigs, sheep and chicken. Emphasis was placed on pure bred cattle.

2. *How many horses and what breed were they?*

    Twenty three horses were present. An English full blooded stallion and an Arabian stallion were the only pure bred horses. There were a few half-Percheron. Horses were generally classified as light weight, middle weight, and heavy weight.

3. *How many pigs and what breeds?*

    Eight Hampshire pigs and Spotted Poland China were exhibited. There should have been more pigs of each brand to do a fair evaluation. Apparently, there is not much interest in the pig business.

4. *How many cattle and what breeds?*

    43 head of cattle representing Holstein, Jersey, and Santa Gertrudis. There were several nice cows of a Holstein-Zebu crossing, and a few almost pure Holstein cows. Unfortunately, only theEexperimental Farm and Carlos Casado Co. had beef cattle.

5. *How many chickens and what were the breeds?*

    There were 53 Leghorn, White Rock, Rhode Island Red, New Hampshire, and Leghorn-White-Rock crossing chickens; most were Leghorns. The New Hampshire and Rhode Island Red had been brought from the USA or Brazil as chicks.

6. *How many craft items were brought to the exposition?*

    The quality of the items on exhibit was good. The tin items displayed by Jacob D. Neufeld, Loma Plata, were of excellent quality.

7. *How did women participate in the exposition? Needlework or foods?*

    Women participated with various crafts such as needlework, crochet, etc. as well as various foods. There were a total of 208 items: 60 food items and 148 crafts.

8. *Tell us something about the fruit and vegetables?*

    Participation was quite weak. This may have been because harvest was long ago and the frost we had destroyed some of the fruits, but another reason might be that it is not clear to many people what to bring to an exposition. Along this line, we should have done more preparatory work in the villages.

9. *What about vendor participation from the outside?*

    Firms such as Bosch, Cofarma, and Litoral participated by showing their products. Bosch presented electrical equipment, Cofarma showed insecticides, and Litoral brought various Allis-Chalmers pieces of agricultural equipment.

10. *How about a summary assessment of the exposition and ideas for the future?*

    Generally we can consider the exposition as successful. We met several goals such as recognition of accomplishments, the achievement potentials for the region, and the promotion of recreational life of farmers. In the future we would like to promote other goals which are equally important, for instance, much more time needs to be taken to judge cattle, to make farmers observe the process and learn the desirable characteristics of good cattle. I wonder if those who visited the exposition really recognize the importance of improving agriculture. Some may come to the conclusion that there is not much to improve! And for the women it would be of great help to provide a place to give demonstrations on the preparation of foods and provide other pointers for maintaining a home. Of utmost importance would be the inclusion of the youth by organizing clubs as learning opportunities, and then allowing them to present their projects publicly at the exposition. (*Mennoblatt*, November 1, 1963, pp. 6, 7)

Beginning in 1962 Bob also served as advisor for the Indian resettlement undertaking, considered in Chapter 12.

In August 1964 Unruhs completed their third service term in the Chaco. Despite "several disappointments," as he often called failed experiments, their service was noteworthy. Chaco Mennonites attest to this. Using the straightforward title "Robert Unruh leaves the Chaco," Peter P. Klassen, *Mennoblatt's* editor, wrote a fitting and meritorious appreciation for the Unruhs. Seen as perceptive and encompassing, it is reprinted here:

The great scientist Julius Liebig once said that "he who can make two blades grow where previously only one grew, has accomplished more then a general who has won a great battle." A man was given to us who has accomplished more than any general in the Chaco war. Mr. Robert Unruh, leader of the Experimental Station in Fernheim, accomplished the growth of blades, where no one believed that anything would grow at all.

Robert Unruh and his wife have worked in the Chaco for 13 years with brief interruptions, but now they return for three [sic] *years to be in their home in Montana in the USA. Farmers in the Chaco, especially in Fernheim, bid farewell to the Unruhs with a heavy heart. They know the debt of gratitude they owe for the Unruhs loyal, tireless, and wide-ranging activities.*

The wheat bread on our tables is the result of his steadfast belief that wheat ought to grow in the Chaco. Thanks to experiments at the Experimental Station we have large fields of planted pasture for cattle. The improvement of cattle, as well as good pig and chicken breeds are a direct result of Mr. Unruh's work at improving these. Chicks, bulls and pigs were imported directly by plane from the northern continent.

And this is due, in part, to the many experiments that Unruh and his coworkers performed over the last 13 years. Also to be mentioned are the roses that decorate our gardens, because man does not live by bread alone.

It always was a simple thing to call the Experimental Station for advice when something did not go right on the farm, i.e., when bugs invaded the fields, when chicken got sick, or when one needed trees.

Bob and Myrtle also worked in the schools. Each week Bob came to the high school to teach agriculture to the juniors, who, along with their fathers, were appreciative. In recent years he also traveled to teach in Loma Plata. All these years Mrs. Unruh led a cooking seminars in her home instructing senior girls in this noble art, and later success became apparent in the families.

We did not say good bye to the Unruhs. We hope that they will return. Mr. Unruh did not leave his place vacant since a young successor, Mr. John Peters with wife and child, from Manitoba, Canada, have been named to lead the station for three years. We hope he will adjust to the Chaco as quickly as did his predecessor.

"Two blades grow today where previously none grew." It is indeed the greatest accomplishment of the Experimental Station as we have learned that farming is not a matter of luck, but it is a science that needs to be fully supported. (Mennoblatt, September 1, 1964, p. 2)

Bob and Myrtle spent August 1964 to October 1966 in the USA for further studies. He graduated in July 1966, from Texas A&M, College Station, Tex., with a masters degree in agriculture. His thesis was entitled: "A Proposed Agricultural Education Program for the Mennonites in the Chaco."

During their absence the Experimental Farm was well and ably supervised by John and Edna Peters. The Peters remained another three years after the Unruhs' return in October 1966, when they shared responsibilites working together. The Peters returned to Canada in August 1969. (See Chapter 8, p. 235)

John and Edna Peters with Mark. Bob and Myrtle Unruh with Betty. 1964. Unruhs leaving for sabbatical and the Peters assuming Experimental Farm management. Photo credit: John Peters.

9

Longing for Wheat
as We Had It in Russia

This chapter shows that deeply engrained tradition might continue for many generations, creating tension between a hoped for possibility and the reality.

9.1 In the Beginning

When the Canadian delegation penetrated the Chaco in 1921 to explore possible settlement sites, the vision for growing wheat crops was uppermost in their mind. They brought wheat seed varieties along to plant at Puerto Casado. Returning after a several weeks long expedition, they found the wheat plants flourishing. But once settled they discovered growing wheat to maturity in the Chaco had some problems. Even so they did not immediately dismiss the idea and hoped that growing wheat in the Paraguayan Chaco might yet become a reality.

The Russian Mennonites (Fernheim) had an even stronger desire to grow wheat. And decades later the yearning for wheat lingered on, "as we had it in Russia." However uncertain and unprofitable wheat growing appeared as a commercial venture, the wish persisted. With few exceptions, all Mennonites in Russia (or more correctly the Soviet Union since 1922) were connected in some manner, to wheat farming. Mennonites had contributed substantially to Ukraine becoming Russia's bread basket. The stunning white bread made from wheat (Russian, *Bulka*; Low German, *Bultje*) and the *Zwieback* was their main staple in Russia. Grownups in Fernheim remembered these past good times that Communism had destroyed. They longed for these good old times and the passage of time only served to enhance the memory as heavenly.

In Paraguay, Fernheimers naturally enough, sought to duplicate the Russian model. That is, to build village settlements on their land, with a self-governing internal administration and a strong Biblical foundation. Again and again Fernheim's early minutes read "as in Russia" or something similar. And as in Russia they wanted to grow wheat in the Chaco. The younger generation having no Russian experience, found this attitude a bit puzzling and difficult to comprehend. Yet, given their elders situation living for generations in a culture where there were few opportunities except agriculture, this attitude was a natural inclination. Changing a longstanding tradition and doing so suddenly is not likely to happen.

Our fathers, grandfathers, and great-grandfathers who came into the Chaco and investigated agricultural possibilities (recall the Agricultural Committee in chapter two), reluctantly came to the conclusion that "the farmer who grew wheat in Russia must now learn to do without." One must adapt to growing local crops was the committee's conclusion after a Menno Colony fact finding tour. Despite this conclusion, farmers in Fernheim did not adjust to this conclusion and hoped the assessment would be proven wrong. And of course, it did not help when the *Mennoblatt,* in December 1931, reported in big bold letters that the Palo Santo" experimental station had **the first successful Experiments with Wheat in the Paraguayan Chaco**. The article stated that the experiments comprised 47 varieties of wheat and four seemed very promising. Young Mennonite men received six-month practical training at Palo Santo. Seven months later in August 1932, the *Mennoblatt* reports:

> *This month most villages have reaped the first wheat in the Chaco. To be sure, it was not a big harvest but we nevertheless have the satisfaction*

of seeing that wheat can indeed grow here, if the weather cooperates . . . Of course, one cannot expect the wheat to be as overseas (meaning Russia). *Everything is now done by hand . . . Harvesting does not happen with self binders* (as in Russia), *but the kernels are plucked off by hand. Some humorist suggested that doing it so, is the "real" self binder.*

9.2 The Reality

Despite more experiments through 1953, the hoped-for yields remained elusive, but not the expectation. Many opinions were tossed about, not only about the failed wheat crops, but also about the large amounts of wheat flour the Mennos and Fernheimers imported. An anonymous "farmer's son" writes:

I have some heretical views on the "Punkto" flour that I would not like to keep under wraps. In 1932 we imported 2,600 sacks of flour from Argentina and paid 594,000 Pesos; and in the two preceding years it was even more. The total spending for the three years was about 2,000,000 Pesos. For our settlement that is a whole lot of money, and I think we should become independent from this expensive foreign flour as soon as possible.

"Farmer's son" goes on to say the solution is not to grow wheat here but to grow more manioc, rice, and corn, and replace the white bread with dark sorghum bread. "Farmer's son" claims:

White bread is not nearly as healthful as dark bread, a fact we saw and heard of in Germany, where the whole population eats only dark bread. Besides in the Chaco, bread is not needed for the main meal. Eating so much bread is just a habit acquired through the abundance of wheat in Russia before the war. (Mennoblatt, May 1933)

Someone else said it would be good to eat more meat, because for one kilogram of expensive flour one can get almost three kilograms of meat. He too was of the opinion that, "We must change and adjust to local conditions

*and not eat that which grows in other countries." In the meantime he said,
"Growing wheat in the Chaco ought to be pursued more intensely." (Mennoblatt*, June 1933, p. 3)

A. Schroeder wrote, "It seems that the Argentinean flour will do us in. We must rethink and revise our policy . . ." (*Mennoblatt*, December 1936, p. 5)

9.3 Revived Energy and Expectations

The debate about wheat goes on, but gradually tapers off as time passes.

But thoughts about growing wheat were revived with the Experimental Farm's beginning in 1946 under the leadership first by Menno Klassen, continuing with Abe Peters, and five years later by Robert Unruh in 1951. Unruh reports in 1953 about successful experiments with wheat and hopes that soon the Mennonites won't have to import the expensive Argentinean wheat. A year later he reports to MCC that 25 acres were harvested with the donated combine, "You can hardly imagine the amazement on children's faces seeing a combine at work, nor the look from older people seeing wheat again being threshed, something not seen since leaving Russia. . . . The yields varied from 7 to 11 bushel per acre. . . . the quality this year was excellent." (Activity Report, August 1954) (See 9.3, p. 235)

Finally, "Wheat as in Russia." Mennonites would soon have their own flour and no longer depend on "soul flour" from Argentina. The Mennonite press in the U.S. and Canada reported this success in great detail. But growing wheat was unpredictable and to every person's disappointment never became a lasting practice. Four years later Bob wrote about the harvest for the year 1958:

The wheat harvest is long past but a short report. In Fernheim about 31 acres were planted in May and harvested in September, 9 acres in Friedensruh and 22 in Rosenort. The yield was between 11-14 bushels per acre. The quality was very good. We noticed a large difference in production when planted in different soil. Where the ground was heavier the grain was better formed and higher quality than when grown on sandier soil. So the heavier soil is best suited for wheat in the Chaco. Perhaps some might ask if it makes good sense to plant Chaco wheat? To grow wheat as a main income source is hardly practical. One should not count on a good harvest as this year for every year. But I believe that planting 5 to 7 acres for each family will provide flour for a year. Considering Fernheim spends G 300,000 each month for Argentina flour, growing our own wheat becomes important. (Mennoblatt, December 16, 1958, p. 7)

9.4 Analysis and a Fading Dream

In 1960 Bob wrote again on "Wheat in the Chaco:"

As reported in the last Mennoblatt *issue, generally the harvest this year was good in spite of an unusually dry winter. At the Experimental Farm we had 10.3 inches of rain between planting on April 20 and harvesting on September 6. We had many dark and cool days, but little rain.*

Farmer's say it is "simple with wheat." In comparison with other crops, wheat takes little work. It is planted on ground following peanut or bean harvest. Plowing and planting takes a few days, but then there is no work required until harvest. Harvesting with a combine takes about an hour per 2.5 acres. The yield depends on the ground. Darker soil seems to produce the best yield.

At the experimental farm this year we noticed yields were dependent on the number of seeds planted.

1. We sowed with 62 lbs/acre as STICA recommends.

2. The next field we sowed about ten days later and by mistake set the drill to 80 lbs/acre. At first we thought that this plot would not yield as much or give lower quality wheat. During harvest, however, we did not notice any difference in quality and the first field yielded 12 bushels/ acre and the second almost 18 bushels/acre. The ground in both fields was the same. Next year we are going to find out if it would not be better to use more seed. *Some people ask if wheat does not deplete soil moisture too much? I think just the opposite is true, since wheat needs moisture only during the first few months. Wheat also covers the field during the time that we get those north storms. It might be even more important that no weeds grow among the wheat where other fields are full of weeds that take up much moisture and soil nutrients. When wheat is harvested the straw and chaff go back to the soil to improve the topsoil by adding organic matter.*

There is a down side for wheat: First, to grow wheat on a big scale, more machines will be needed. We have ordered planters from the foundry in Friedensfeld *that we hope will be ready on time for sowing. One should not delay the sowing too much, because the land must be free for summer seeding by October, which also means that more combines must be available during September harvest. Combines must be imported. Finally, grinding mills must be available to process the wheat properly. Many ask if the risk with the added costs are worth it. Well, the three Chaco colonies pay about G20 million each year for flour. It would be an enormous help*

Robert Unruh worked many years to make Chaco wheat growing possible. He is shown consulting with a Neuland farmerette.

if farmers could offset this cost through work and use the money saved for other purposes. (Mennoblatt, October 16, 1960, pp. 6-7)

This report is less useful for describing progress, but more for insight into Bob's methodical approach. He was observant, precise, and detailed. And he thoughtfully looked forward; planned for the colonies best interest. Wheat production and processing into white bread for the Mennonites picked up momentum at this point. In 1964 and 1965 there were roughly 5000 wheat acres harvested and processed in the colonies. But suddenly production declined and soon stopped. Bob gave the reasons:

1. Severe frost damage
2. Low yields averaging 7.5 bushels/acre
3. Mechanization of peanut production yielded secure profits
4. Wheat flour was no longer as scarce as in the 1950s (see David Friesen, 1992, p. 40)

Nevertheless, Bob continued experimenting with wheat. He does not give up. By the end of 1972 he wrote, "Some Conclusions on Wheat in the Chaco":

1. Wheat can be produced successfully in the Chaco, but only under these conditions:
> *a. Dark open area ground or sandy bush soil must be used for planting.*
> *b. Summer fallow the land and cultivate it after each rain to store moisture.*
> *c. Planting between May 20 and 30 to avoid the danger of frost.*
2. As long as the prices for cattle, cotton and peanuts remain high, and there is sufficient wheat from Argentina, not much wheat will be grown in the Chaco. Still, it is not wise to ignore growing wheat completely since we can not know the future.

The last sentence was typically cautious Bob Unruh: ". . . since we cannot know the future." It should be added that wheat is grown successfully in eastern Paraguay which substitutes nicely for the expensive flour from Argentina.

9.5 Conclusions

Is there value to an accounting about the failed attempt to grow wheat in the Chaco?

1. First of all, on a short term basis attempts to grow wheat were not totally without success. For several years Mennonites produced their own wheat flour.

2. The account illustrates how goal-oriented and persistent Bob was throughout his career. We cannot help admiring his perseverance. He sought to serve.

3. All Mennonites in the Chaco, especially the Fernheimers, wholeheartedly supported the experimentation with wheat, which in turn cemented relations between the colonists and Bob.

4. The story also shows how a strong cultural and long standing tradition influence behavior, springing from 150 years of wheat production in Russia.

5. The example also moves us to reflect on how the past and present influence the future. Bob wrote about this at a later time. Are we in a culture of fattening cattle or producing milk and cheese? We don't know what the future holds for us, we can only build on past experience. (See 9.5, p. 235)

10

Agriculture and Theology;
The Unruh Perspective

Robert Unruh firmly held a faith clearly expressed in action, in reports, and spoken word. We might say a practical theology for farmers. In an article titled "My Field is God" written for young people, Bob comes to a biblical awareness about Mennonite farmers:

We Mennonites for centuries are known as farmers yet our responsibilities as Christian farmers are unspoken and often unclear. Here are three important responsibilities for the Christian farmer:

1. The farmer's responsibility to their families and their fellow man. *Providing for one's family is usually understood, but there is more:*

It goes beyond the family's material existence to mean responsibility to develop the gift from God in each family member. This responsibility extends to all Christian persons outside the family.

Unruh then asks:

What better witness that the love of Christ lives in us is there than the willingness to help those when misfortune strikes? For example, in my homeland when a farmer became ill at planting time the neighbors came with their tillage and planting equipment and planted the field in one day. There was joy on both sides for the helped and for the helpers.

The youngsters were then asked to consider opportunities for similar help and aid that might be found in their experience and colony environment. Doing good should be a joyful event.

2. The farmer's responsibility to help the less fortunate. *Bob pointed out that many millions go to bed hungry every day. For example:*

North American Mennonites try to fulfill this responsibility by sending aid to Russia, India, Germany and Korea. Often they give donations in kind, like farm products, cattle and hogs that are butchered and the meat canned. MCC has a mobile meat processor traveling to donating communities. Or often grain is donated, processed into flour and sent to the needy. Is it possible that might happen in Paraguay too? Some might say, 'We are still too poor.' But we should note that most donations do not come from the rich. Who could not spare an ox, a few chickens or other products for the poor in this or another country? There are many hungry in South America. It is not healthy to only think about providing for one's self. Some things have already been started such as the psychiatric hospital in Asuncion and the leprosy hospital at Km81. There is much more to be done.

3. The third responsibility is to be a good steward to the land. *Psalm 24 says:*

"The earth is the Lord's and everything in it; the world, and all who dwell therein."

The fields are gifts from God. The field is a loan to the farmer and he must treat it as carefully as he would if it was his own. The Christian farmer respects the field and takes precautions that the wind does not erode it away so that it becomes non productive. And when this happens we have sinned against God, having neglected his gift and also sinned against our descendants because they can not earn a living from this barren land that we did not care for. Farmers must answer for their failure to use their gift given from God in the same way preachers and teachers or other persons receive gifts from God. (Jugendblatt [youth supplement as an insert], Mennoblatt, April 16, 1959)

"My Field is God" was written in 1959 as the Trans Chaco Roadway construction was progressing toward the colonies. With the Mennonites still disadvantaged and isolated, Bob foresaw approaching social change and the need to prepare young people for this adjustment.

Bob consciously talked and wrote about "voluntary service" as a Mennonite ideal for young people. It has happened that many colony youth have participated in voluntary service.

Moving ahead eight years, on September 23, 1967, Bob was invited to speak to a young married couples retreat on the theme, "Looking to our Economic Future." Prosperity and social change were becoming evident to all. Some were beginning to ask, "We managed poverty but will we know how to handle wealth? Would this sudden new wealth be our undoing, a struggle of another kind?" It was interesting that a marriage retreat focused on broad, macro economic matters rather than marriage issues. Struggling farmers preoccupied and burdened with making ends meet, now reflected on social issues. Bob begins, "It is dangerous to talk about the future without first looking backwards to the past and to consider the present."

Bob pointed to the heavy burdens from the past; poverty, the hard work with crop failures and disappointments from many sources, no vocational opportunity except farming and that all citizens were uniformly poor, standing on the same platform struggling for survival. But today the picture was different.

For example, he mentioned the possibility for traveling easily to Asuncion, East Paraguay, and to other countries. That new ideas, opinions, life styles will find there way into Chaco Mennonite society. This will lead to changes and cautioned that change is not always progress or changes for the better. Then he continued in a positive manner saying that another substantial change will be increasing occupational possibilities. These opportunities will rise from mechanization, he says. Specialists in many disciplines will be needed. There will be opportunities for small independent business industries or shops. Further:

Thanks to increased production of agricultural products such as peanuts, milk, eggs, and chickens, the purchasing power and living standard increased as well. Bicycles and motorcycles, the increasing number of radios, record players and refrigerators are clear evidence of an increased stan-

dard of living. In spite of great progress, increases in farm acreage, and the introduction of machinery, interest in agriculture appears to be waning. One hears from all quarters that farms are for sale and plans are made to emigrate. Everywhere there is talk about leaving, why is it so? Most likely people think the future is brighter elsewhere than here. It is a paradox that finally after much success here, people still wish to leave. Has the older generation who endured the hardships, discouraged the younger people? How can we expect our youth to be interested in agriculture when they only hear about the difficulties and problems? The youth hear too little about the love for and wish for farming. …Or is it that we no longer believe farming is a blessed occupation? As the parents see things, the children will have similar desires. (*Mennoblatt*, November 1, 1967, p. 6)

At this point Bob expressed his personal philosophy about material wealth and religion:

Another question is whether the poverty and difficult years have influenced us too much for wanting physical comfort and accumulating wealth? That is not to say we should not live comfortably. The danger is that the more wealth we accumulate the less we think about God and our fellow men. We measure ourselves against other people rather than how well we have performed using our God given abilities to do good in the world. Driven for material wealth and physical comfort has gotten to the point we have forgotten some of our faith principles, or at least in danger of letting them fall. For example, we already consider it normal when trucks are loaded on Sunday and leave for Asuncion to be there on Monday. Another example, we miss church to do work on the farm. What is so important we can not take a few hours to worship? How do we reconcile this behavior with the firm discipline demanded of pre-baptismal candidates or with church doctrine we wish to implement?

Some will probably ask, "What has this to do with our future economic life?" I think a great deal. I believe it is important that our attitude about material possessions and social relationships will determine what we become in the future. It is extremely important to keep a balance between economic wealth and religious belief; they are inter-connected. The Chaco offers the opportunities to become relatively wealthy. But it is going to take our total efforts to keep pace with the building of our spiritual wealth.

Bob continued with concrete proposals for education:

1. Books and magazines that promote in a special way, "love and longing for agriculture."

2. A Christian agricultural school encompassing evening classes for adults:

A class for older youth and adult farmers teaching practical applications of faith to everyday living, perhaps titled "Christian ethics." For example, when are my responsibilities as a Christian farmer in conflict with responsibilities to the government and how should I deal with this conflict? What is the ethical use of money and power; when do I relinquish control over other people and how much property is enough? How do colony problems influence the church and my Christian response?

A three-colony cooperative agricultural school was established in Loma Plata in 1981, fourteen years later. To his satisfaction, Bob saw it happen before leaving the Chaco.

3. The Christian's use of money is important at this time:

Jesus says in Luke 12:31: "But rather, seek the kingdom of God and all these things shall be added unto you." Such men as R. G. LeTourneau, Colgate, manufacturer of soap and toothpaste, testify to the truth of this biblical covenant. Each of these men began small and remained faithful to their promise to serve God, to tithe and God has blessed them plentifully. So whether we are ministers, missionaries, farmers, craftsman or teachers we need to obey the prophet Malachi who years ago said in 3,10: "Bring the full tithes into the storehouse that there might be food in my house and thereby put me to the test, says the Lord of hosts, if I will not open the windows of heaven for you and pour down for you an overflowing blessing." This is every person's task, which so far as accomplished will solve the economic problems not only for today but into the future. (*Mennoblatt*, November 16, 1967, pp. 6-7)

For Robert Unruh his faith, his work and his actions were in harmony. Faith not applied to daily living was not real faith, it was dishonesty in Bob's view. He came to the Chaco intending to help the Mennonites into a position where they could help others. Receiving help obligates one to help others. In a letter to North American contributors Bob asks for prayer that Fernheim colonists recognize their responsibility to the indigenous Chaco people. We should note Bob walks the talk by participating in the Indian mission/settlement program. Bob is concerned that the colonists under stress from their difficulties are not able to deal with helping the Indians. He writes this as the Indian settlement program is under way but facing program uncertainties and disappointing progress. (see chapter 12)

What were the formative factors in Bob's approach?

1. Bob grew to adulthood under difficult economic circumstances.

2. His parents lived their religious convictions.

3. His church community and congregation from its organization in 1910 contributed to mission work. One later example, the Bethlehem congregation donated kitchen equipment for Filadelfia's hospital.

4. His training at Bethel College stressed humanitarian service and Christian responsibility. Bob from adolescence to maturity had exposure to the Mennonite ethos, service in the name of Christ.

5. Dr. John Schmidt came to Filadelfia in 1941 as a physician. The Unruhs and Schmidts traveled together for a month on board the SS Brazil to South America. Schmidt's leprosy hospital was the Mennonite thank you project to the Paraguayan people for opening the coun-

try to thousands of Russian refugees. Harry Harder came to Paraguay to build a road from Volendam and Friesland to the Paraguay River influenced in part by John Schmidt. Harder later supervised building the Trans Chaco Roadway. A year later Schmidt also challenged Vern Buller to come to Paraguay. Correctly, Dr. Schmidt never referred to the leprosy mission as an MCC project, instead referred to it as a Paraguayan Mennonite program for Christian service.

We do not know with certainty but it seems reasonable that the Schmidts and Unruhs exchanged ideas for encouraging voluntary service for Chaco young people to volunteer at the East Paraguay Leprosy Mission (Km 81). In any case, Bob's theological insight that he continued to share with Chaco citizens had a firm and established foundation in Mennonite culture; service to others.

11

Myrtle Unruh in Paraguay

Myrtle Hilda Goering was born on February 11, 1917, in McPherson County, Kansas. Her parents were Kansas dairy farmers, Benjamin and Anna Goering. Myrtle's ancestors on both sides came from Switzerland, migrated to Palatinate, then to Volhynia and in 1874 to Kansas. The Goering family held membership in the Eden Mennonite Church, formally organized in 1895. Peter Dyck, a major contributor to helping Russian refugees to Paraguay in 1947-48, was the pastor there between 1951 and 1957. Eden was a large and active Mennonite congregation in Kansas. Myrtle and Robert Unruh were married in 1949. Myrtle died on September 23, 1996 in North Newton, Kansas at age 79.

In 2003, Myrtle was remembered by her siblings as quiet and shy, introverted and not outstanding socially. She was also remembered as conscientious and reliable with administrative talent; a good organizer with an ability for getting things done.

A cousin, Jacob Goering, Ph.D., recalls:

I saw Myrtle growing up as the always quiet, reserved person. It was as if she was building up a reservoir of potential energy and competence which then blossomed in Paraguay. She was like a jewel, a diamond, gradually being polished until its true value was revealed.

After marriage and coming to Paraguay, the 'jewel' was indeed revealed; a husband and wife team at the right time in the right place.

Edgar Stoesz visiting the Chaco on MCC's behalf as Secretary for Latin America stayed with the Unruh's during those visits. "Myrtle was a person with boundless energy" he said. Peter P. Klassen said Myrtle "was supportive;" confirmed by many who knew the Unruhs. (Klassen, 2004, pp.173-193) We must honor Myrtle's work in the Paraguayan Chaco and join Klassen in appreciation with this chapter. Many colonists confirm that Myrtle was a partner with Bob in Paraguay, occasionally writing activity reports and typing other reports prepared by Bob. Fernheimer's had a soft spot for Bob and Myrtle, even in a time when some harbored post World War II anti-American feelings.

As the only MCC representatives in the Chaco and North Americans, the Unruhs receiving visitors meant added work for already busy Myrtle. Peter P. Klassen lists Myrtle's contributions as her instruction in Filadelfia's high school, encouraging and counseling young mothers, building a home economics curriculum and her work with indigenous women.

11.1 Finding Her Niche

In Paraguay, Myrtle's initiatives were no doubt in response to the urgency she felt for better nutrition. By 1970 her leadership and teaching abilities were acclaimed and validated when a fully equipped department in the high school was established (earlier *Zentralschule* and by

Sunday afternoon on the Filadelfia house steps, 1962. Photo credit: Maurice Kaufmann.

1970 *Colegio Filadelfia*). The separate building was financed 75% by "Bread for the World" and dedicated during Fernheim's fortieth anniversary celebration July 29, 1970. Myrtle gave the commemorative speech with students and their parents present. She emphasized the importance of housewives to the healthy development of a society and the people. She said:

The housewife has a crucial occupation. Can it be learned in the classroom? Years ago there was a magazine article, Wanted: 30 million young housewives who are ready, willing and able to dedicate themselves to their home and family. Conditions for each housewife:

1. *She must know about food groups and how they are prepared.*
2. *She must know about child care and children's education.*
3. *She must know something about relations in the family—between men and women, parents and children, brothers and sisters.*
4. *She must understand about clothes, laundry and sewing.*
5. *She must know something about appliances, home décor and household maintenance.*
6. *She should have high ethical standards and teach her children the same.*
7. *She should keep herself healthy, be pleasant and happy.*
8. *She must have an interest in the school and community.*
9. *Be prepared to nurse the sick and give early assistance.*
10. *She must manage the household finances.*
11. *Above all, she must spend time with the family.*

Her reward is the love and loyalty from her family. Sometimes the result is feeling exhaustion and aches. But the greatest reward is knowing she has contributed to the education of a future generation and perhaps community leaders. Besides this she will enjoy an intimate relationship with her husband and psychological satisfaction.

Much is required from homemakers. There are many interruptions in our work. Sometimes after doing our best, we are criticized by those outside the family. But what matters is the satisfaction in service for the love of our family. And it helps if sometimes the husband and children show their appreciation. (Mennoblatt, August 1, 1970, pp. 5-6)

Myrtle goes on to say that the Ministry of Education has pre-scribed "Education for the Home" as compulsory for girls and boys. She concludes:

Dear girls, if you at school and at home fulfill your role, you will be a blessing to all those around you and the community and bring honor to all women. (See 11.1, p. 236)

11.2. Instructional Examples

Myrtle's contributions cannot be overstated. Her instruction re-sulted in a healthier family life and beyond that a healthier society in Fernheim. Recall the stressful state at that time; food was limited in quantity and variety, fruit and vegetables from the garden available only in season, no home refrigeration until the mid 1960's and few in num-ber. In this meager resource situation, Myrtle said to her students, "It is important to make everything count in the Chaco." (Klassen, 2004, p. 179) It was a matter of adjusting to "What the Chaco gives." Recall from Chapter 5 the Unruh's appeal to MCC to ship canning supplies.

Filadelfia's hospital was the first benefactor of Myrtle's instruction in food preservation.

Myrtle always took a practical approach in homemaking matters, here are two examples:

1. A paper on "Cooking Date Fruit" and available to all those interested:

Robert Unruh showing an Experimental Farm date palm, before 1955. The Unruh's hope for dates becoming a productive and healthful crop in the Chaco was not fulfilled.

For Americans, dates are served on special occasions but I did not know how to preserve them. Some friends here showed me their preserving methods and each year we tried to find easier methods to simplify the work. We wrote to several friends in other countries to learn how to simplify the process. Last year I ran several tests and I would like to suggest one method.

After harvesting, sort the good dates from the immature dates. Place them in the direct sunlight for complete ripening. In the Chaco dates ripen nicely in Rex jars in sunlight. After the dates are fully ripe, wash and dry them. Remove the pits and put into sterilized jars. Seal the jars without water or sugar and cook in a water bath for 25 minutes. In a pressure cooker 15 minutes with 10 lbs pressure. (*Mennoblatt*, February 1, 1963, pp. 5-6)

2. Canning red beets:

Although not as tasty as other vegetables they are nutritious, high in Zinc, iron, vitamins A & C. When we vary the diet, our body is better nourished. Do not like beets? Then add carrots and beets together,

> *2 cups beet, already cooked and chopped*
> *¼ cup carrot soup*   *2 tablespoon butter*
> *1 tablespoon flour*   *2 tablespoon sugar*
> *1 teaspoon vinegar*   *½ cup sour cream*

Bring to boil until the broth is thick. Serve over the meat dish. "Mommy, more beets please, today they taste extra good" says little Hans. (*Mennoblatt*, October 1, 1967, p. 4)

Myrtle heard it often, "We have no money to buy these things." So she collected practical homemaking ideas and asked the young homemakers to test and evaluate her suggestions at home. The suggestions were about food, household care, and laundry:

Food:
   1. Use as much as you can from the garden when it is available and inexpensive
   2. Spend money carefully being certain you really need the item
   3. Buy in slightly bigger quantity when the item is less expensive than usual
       a. Preserve fresh fruit and vegetables
       b. Dry green beans, yellow carrots, kohlrabi, parsley, cucumbers, chives, guayaba, dates, sorrel.
       c. Gather all ripe beans and peas in the garden for later use
   4. Learn recipes for using leftovers. If you do not have an item or it is expensive, try the recipe without that item. (Mennoblatt, July 1, 1968, p. 5)

At another time Myrtle wrote, "Making things last longer is saving." For example she wrote, "Bed sheets worn in spots might be sewn for a baby crib sheet or made into a little night gown." (*Mennoblatt*, January 16, 1983, pp. 4-5)

Cooking Class in High School. Myrtle Unruh with recipe book. Mennonite Church USA Historical Committee, Goshen, Ind.

11.3 Cookbook, *With Manna Fed*

Myrtle pulled together many recipes and published a cookbook titled *With Manna Fed* during their second term (1958-1961) and arranged for printing in the U.S. while on furlough, at their personal expense. It is widely used, even today (2006), among Mennonite housewives and beyond. It appeared in five editions. In the introduction Myrtle wrote:

> *The Chaco settlement has only begun. But we experience again and again that God provides us our daily bread. I decided it should be a book "food for body and soul."*

The cookbook was organized by weeks. Each week begins with "Food for the Soul:" a Bible text and reflections on the text, a song and then a prayer.

For the first week in January:

Text

    Deuteronomy 11:12:

        It is a land the LORD your God cares for; the eyes of the LORD your God are continually on it from the beginning of the year to its end.

Reflections

    "Lovingly nestled by mighty forces
    We wait with confidence for that which is to come
    God is present day and night
    And certainly is so during each new day."

    A new year with many days is before us. We read these lines and we ask how do we wait for whatever comes? Do we pray for courage and strength and God's help for every day? His eyes rest on this land from the beginning of the year to its end. What will happen to us is still unknown and we look to the future with confidence. God is with us!

Song

    Begin your days with the Lord

Prayer

    We pray for ourselves that we may devote our lives to the Lord, for our families, that each member remains true to the Lord, and for the church that it act in harmony and peace until He returns.

Anny Thielmann said in a 2006 interview:

We can see the good result of Mrs. Unruh's pioneer work in home-making, is still up to date and valued. But we have almost forgotten who did this important thing.

Edith Siemens Klassen, a pupil in Mrs. Unruh's cooking and household class, said:

Many totally new and different recipes and advice were taught to us, fitting our local situation. There were a few from USA, but with sub- stitute ingredients available here. She tried many different local substitutes and incor- porated these into her recipes. When butter was not on hand we used lard for example. We tried many recipes and after many attempts with substitutes we at last had something tasty. It was important to be thrifty. She was always conscious that substitutes should not cost too

Title page of Myrtle's cookbook.

much. Her goal was to create and prepare tasty foods, which every family could afford. (Interview, May 2006)

Helga Dyck similarly was Myrtle's student who later became an Indian school teacher. She said:

As teachers we taught good nutrition and vegetable growing. Mrs. Unruh gave me guidance and instruction. Nutrition for the Indians was of primary importance. They had to be taught how to grow and cultivate the vegetables first and then instructed how to use vegetables for meals. I tried the recipes at home and then with conviction I could teach the Indians.

Beginning in 1980 I was lead teacher at Cesarea, the central school for the Nivacle Indians where students walked to school from nine villages. We needed to provide the noontime meal otherwise the students could not make it through the day. At home there often was not enough food for the family if the parents were both working or searching for work and away from home. Feeding the children was a means for keeping them in school otherwise they would lose interest and be absent. It was important the food be as healthful and tasty as possible. We cooked with many variations using the same food; beans mixed with noodles, rice and corn. We had a special stew with sweet potatoes, pumpkins and a variety of vegetables, in this way adding diversity. Mr. Unruh would come periodically when parents were invited. He would talk about the importance of growing vegetables and eating vegetables raw, not only cooked. He would also hold a demonstration in the school's large garden, how to cultivate the garden and care for it. Then we would eat a meal prepared mostly by the Indian women. The result was that the school garden got bigger and bigger. One year we had tomatoes in excess. There were so many we sold some. The children had to be taught to eat tomatoes; at first they did not like them. So I tried different recipes and every student was required to eat at least one bite and it went very quickly. Soon the students gained a liking for tomatoes and wanted to take tomatoes home.

To help them become nutrition conscious, after lunch I asked them to write down everything the lunch contained. These meals encouraged the children to attend school regularly and be on time. One time I asked the children, "Who is coming to school next year?"

A student jumps to his feet and says enthusiastically, "I will!"

I ask, "Why?"

And he said, "For the tasty food."

Helga Dyck verifies the lasting effect of Myrtle's nutritional education in the Chaco:

One sees her influence today in many things. Mrs. Unruh in my view laid the foundation for using the restricted variety of food available here. Today's generation likely does not appreciate this. It was her cook book with many recipes that brought about this big change and is today taken for granted. Myrtle created or rearranged the recipes to make locally produced foods useable. (Interview, May 2006) (See 11.3, p. 237)

Preparing a special occasion meal, Yalve Sanga. Photo credit: Mennonite Church USA Historical Committee, Goshen, Ind.

11.4 Working with Indian Missions

In the late 1960s as colony economic development increased, the Unruhs' service expanded to Indian settlement work. Indian settlement later became a massive effort with North American and European support. To stimulate interest in this work, Myrtle was asked to "gather stories and continually report on the work." (*Mennoblatt*, November 1, 1969) She used the *Mennoblatt* as the platform to report on economic, health, cultural and spiritual issues.

The settlement program was patterned after early Mennonite settlements. That is, the Indians were settled in row villages, each family given acreage, a cow, a horse and small tools. The man was to be the breadwinner and the woman was to manage the household. This was a difficult adjustment for the Indians, a seismic cultural shock to their customary communal lifestyle; they had only the Mennonites example to learn from. The Indian husband needed seeds and practical advice only knowing a life of hunting and collecting from the bush having no need for money. The need for sensitive and useful help became an overriding concern. To be settled meant they must plan ahead for the necessities and make purchases in stores. They must plant, cultivate and harvest their food with something left over to sell for money to buy from the store. Moreover, many more children survived their early years; health and educational needs must be met. Myrtle wrote about the many needs for the Indians; economic, health, religious and cultural adjustments. In this *Mennoblatt* issue she wrote with sensitivity about her home economics instruction:

I notice that mission and settlement workers work to help the Indians in all areas. Twenty years ago Lengua women learned to sew dresses and make sewing alterations. Some are elaborate and show talented work. Yet there are too many extremely poor or who have not had the opportunity to learn. We sometimes move to a quick and make wrong conclusions that nothing is being done to help them. Although training courses for teachers, preachers, and farmers are well under way, ladies (Mennonite) and mission workers give instruction to Indian women on child care, health and diet. The Indian women eagerly participate in prayers and telling biblical stories. From her garden each woman brings something and it is prepared for the noon meal. In this way she learns to peel, cut, stir and proper heating. Learning happens in this way because for her it is often entirely new.

In the afternoon they sew, knit or do crafts. One baby was sleeping in its mother's lap while she sewed. Another mother made a swing from her bag for her baby to sleep, rocking the baby to sleep and knitting at the same time. Some children slept on the ground. A crying child was immediately nursed. The sewing hour quickly passed and they proudly showed what they had accomplished.

The women learn eagerly and want to learn more. They want to learn to bake Zwieback. They want to learn to sew men's trousers and how to keep house. However, not all have such desires and not all could master these things. We must support these mission workers in their efforts. The work requires devotion, courage, skill, patience, perseverance and love for the work. There is much to do. And we should prayerfully thank each mission worker for their service. (Mennoblatt, July 16, 1971, p. 6)

These reports went out to MCC and were often published world wide in Mennonite publications. Myrtle wrote about the Indian's need for basic utensils and supplies:

Having adequate supplies on hand is crucial for preparing nutritious meals quickly. Having inventory when unexpected quests arrive also helps one stay calm. A cook learns soon that proper storage is important to prevent spoilage and waste.

To store food is unknown to Indians. Their supplies are few, mainly what grows in their garden and what they carry in their ever-present bag; this bag accompanies them always and contains food,

Myrtle distributing metal buckets, 1967. Photo credit: John Peters.

clothing, shoes and more. It is not the custom for Indians to plan ahead; they live from day to day. Indians do not worry about tomorrow; it is not their culture. We wonder why they do not keep food to eat in the dry season? They were shown that rice, beans, flour and corn could be stored in coffee and milk tin cans with proper lids. Insects can not get to the food and it stays clean. A Chulupi woman said right away, "Yes, cans would be better than bags because the dogs always got into her bag, eating the food and scattering the contents all around." But only a few women would do this, it was easier to depend on the Mennonites to care for them. Several weeks ago I offered an empty Nescafe can to an Indian woman and she refused it saying, "I already have three at home, I do not need more." This year much work has been done but there are so many it will be a long time before we reach them all. (Mennoblatt, June 16, 1972, p. 12) (See 11.4, p. 238)

At other times Myrtle wrote about tensions between the Mennonites and Indians. The Mennonite position was that Indians should emulate the white man's habits and lifestyle. This attitude presupposes the white persons supremacy, thinking the Indian mentally stripped; there is nothing to be learned from the Indian.

Who has not thought the Indians are unobservant and slow to learn? We look for a time and opportunity to teach them. If they are not interested our time and effort is wasted, in vain. But do we ever think we can learn from them?

We came unannounced to a Lengua mission home to show our friends how the resettled Lengua actually lives and keeps house. They were friendly, welcomed us and proudly showed their house, yard and garden. Outside the kitchen pumpkins and a certain weed was growing. Mission workers explained to us the weed was used as medicine but she did not know exactly how. I turned to the Indian woman asking if she used this herb as medicine? She smiled and said it keeps insects out of the beans (while the beans are drying when first harvested). The beans keep until the next harvest us-

ing this herb. I said what a good idea; I would like to try it in our cabinets too! We learned something from the Indians that day, they know the Chaco plants. Another Lengua showed me a plant to make an all purpose glue. Do they not have something to teach us? (*Mennoblatt*, January 16, 1973, pp. 5-6) (See 11.5, p. 238)

Myrtle with Indian family. Photo credit: Mennonite Church USA Historical Committee, Goshen, Ind.

12

Robert Unruh
and the Indian Settlement

Robert Unruh came to the Chaco to manage the Experimental Farm in Fernheim. In unapologetic humility he persevered against harsh realities, leaving a legacy of good will and unanticipated economic progress, the *raison d'être* for this accounting. From the beginning however, the Unruhs were concerned about the indigenous population. This concern shows in activity reports to MCC expressing their concerns and in family letters asking for their prayers. They expressed hope that the economic progress flowing to the Mennonites will visit the Indigenous' welfare too. Bob and Myrtle appeared to fully understand what had been suggested by perceptive observers in the Mennonite migrations' beginning; that the Mennonite adaptation to their Indian neighbors might be the colonists most intimidating sociological issue. The Unruh's vision was fulfilled in part, when European and North American aid was received for Indian settlement. In the beginning however, to actively participate in the Indian settlement program was not anticipated.

In the 1960s Bob's direct participation in the settlement program began. First, some background (See Chapter 12, p. 238).

12.1 A Short Historical Summary
When the Canadian Mennonites came to the Chaco in 1927 there were estimated 500 nomadic Lengua (Enlhet) Indians in Men-

One Indian encampment near Filadelfia, 1955. Photo credit: Phil Roth.

no's settlement area. During the Chaco war the number declined as the Indians moved into deeper bush, away from the war zone. Immediately after the war (1936), "Light to the Indians" was organized by Fernheim for mission work among the Lenguas located at Yalve Sanga. On February 24, 1946, the first six Indigenous men were baptized. These Christian men and their families were issued small parcels of land where they homesteaded. The Yalve Sanga settlement replicated the traditional Chaco Mennonite village. By 1953 the mission settled 50 families in two villages. Each family was granted 1.25 acres of land. This was sufficient to provide for their own subsistence, but was not enough to grow cotton and peanuts needed to provide the income needed for this altered life style.

Soon more Indians, learning about mission amenities began showing up demanding land and settlement privileges. A settlement model was developed where each family received 12.5 acres. A new village was created in each of these years: 1955, 1957, and 1959. The

Indian plowing at Yalva-Sanga, 1964. Photo credit: Nancy Flowers, Standard Oil Co, Mennonite Church USA Historical Committee, Goshen, Ind.

Indian workers pulling peanuts.

first Chulupi (later known as Nivacle) village was created in 1961. (Stahl, 1980, p. 147) Very soon "Light to the Indians" found itself overwhelmed as Indians streaming in from all directions accelerated. The Mennonite Brethren (MB) mission board in Hillsboro, Kans., sustaining Yalve Sanga financially and otherwise, appealed to MCC to share in this mission effort.

Under this increasing pressure, the Chaco Mennonite churches, North American Mennonite Church missions, and MCC organized the Indian Settlement Board (ISB) June 22, 1961. In 1976 the name was changed to the Indian Counsel Bureau, and finally in February 1978, it was restructured and officially registered with the Paraguayan government under law No.37174 as *Asociación de Servicios de Cooperación Indígena-Mennonita* (ASCIM). Statute 37174 granted protection to their indigenous population against all threats, hunger, illness and homelessness. ASCIM's broad purpose was, "To aid the indigenous communities in their socio-economic development."

ISB board members were representatives from the various Indian groups, the three colonies *Oberschulzen,* the missionaries and a MCC representative. MCC did its best to provide an organizational structure for the venture and contributed 75% to the annual budget. A director, medical doctor, educator, agronomist, cooperative advisor (business manager), anthropologist, and women's social worker made up the executive committee. Functional departments were health, education, agriculture and livestock, marketing and money matters, social work and homemaking. (Stahl, 1980, p. 148-49) The director Jakob B. Reimer reported that ASCIM's board had 50 members; 22 Indians and 28 Mennonites. (*Mennoblatt*, October 1, 1980, p. 5)

The settlement project was a complex enterprise in the beginning, chiefly because there was not agreement between MCC and the Mennonites about settlement priorities. (William T. Snyder, Oral History, p.1092) The goal to settle the Indians and aid them to a point of self sufficiency was not achieved for decades. There seemed to be no transitional goals along the way where people could agree that the short term work they set out to do was finished. That said, the Indian settlement program was and still is, unique in the history of the Americas. Throughout the Western Hemisphere, colonizing Europeans had expelled the Indians from the newly occupied regions. In the Chaco the opposite was the case. Indians were welcomed by the Mennonites—to a point. They settled nearby to Mennonite villages and sought Mennonite protection and aid. (C. Redekop, 1980)

Bob and Myrtle Unruh through their MCC connection were instrumental in this important cooperative task between Mennonites and Indians. We looked at Myrtle's contributions in chapter 11. (See 12.1, p. 239)

12.2 Bob's Role Early On

On March 15, 1962 (a few months less than a year after organizing ISB), there was a meeting at *Mennonitenheim* (MCC country office) in Asunción between the Indian Settlement Bureau and William T. Snyder, MCC's Executive Secretary. Present were the three colony leaders (*Oberschulzen*) Jakob Reimer, Menno; Heinrich Duerksen, Fernheim; and Peter Derksen, Neuland; missionary G. B. Giesbrecht, Yalve Sanga; Frank Wiens, MCC Paraguay director; Robert Unruh; Peter Epp, MCC's *Mennonitenheim* manager and missionary J. H. Franz, representing the North American Mennonite Brethren Mission Board. Bill Snyder said, "I'm here to gain insight into the problems associated with the Indian settlement. MCC has received many letters that paint a confused picture."

Snyder wished to engage Jacob Loewen, a Mennonite linguist working for the American Bible Society, to do an anthropological study about the Lengua and Chulupi. The *Oberschulzen* were reluctant. Not recognizing the urgency as did MCC—the Indigenous were by then an important factor to colony economic well being—they did not want to disturb relations with the Indians. They were skeptical and had reservations about the usefulness of Snyder's plan. (See 12.2, p. 242)

At this meeting, Snyder designated Bob as MCC's representative on ISB's board, officially noted in ISB minutes two months later

March 1962 meeting on Indian settlement matters, MCC, Oberschulzen and missionaries. L to R: Robert Unruh, William Snyder, Frank Wiens, Jacob Reimer, G. B. Giesbrecht, Heinrich Duerksen, Peter Derksen, J. H. Franz not shown, 1962. Photo credit: W. T. Snyder, Mennonite Church USA Historical Committee, Goshen, Ind.

in May 1962. The following August, Bob was elected ISB's chairman. This was a critical juncture. Stressful events began to pile up. Heinrich Duerksen served as Fernheim's *Oberschulze* through this critical period and describes one troublesome event: (See 12.2.1, p. 243)

> *The Chulupi Indians were encamped on the Paraguay side of the Pilcomayo river bordering Argentina demanding that we do more to settle them, as we have done for the Lengua at Yalve Sanga. We have already settled Chulupi in villages near Yalve Sanga, Bethanien, Samaria and also Tiberia. We tried to select Indians carefully (for settlement) hoping for stability. The Chulupies were first baptized. But soon unrest among the Chulupies appeared. They wanted more land. This we could not afford financially and administratively. They would not listen to reason.*

In this frame of mind the Chulupi chief, Manuel met with the Chu-lupi at Pilcomayo. They joined forces with more from Argentina and then walked through Neuland to Filadelfia. They said they are settling here in Fernheim, want land and food, this was in September, 1962. The weather was dry and hot and there was no work. But work they did not want any-way. We knew there was no way they could live off the land so the tension grew between the Chulupi Indians and us. There were so many it was im-possible to feed them all. That led to more tension because they said, "You Mennonites have food and we have none."

One day hundreds of Chulupi marched, mostly women, into the street stopping at the Cooperative Building, demanding food and land. They wanted me to speak with them. I came to the window of the Coop-erative Building and said I cannot talk to this many people but I will talk with a few. After a time they disappeared and only the leaders stayed. On the opposite side of the street many citizens (Mennonites) had assembled watching to see how things might turn out. We began to slowly work things out. The Indians were very agitated. I said we wanted to be their friends and to live in harmony together; also that their wish to be settled on their own land was our wish too. Finally I asked what was their immediate need? They said they needed food like sugar, rice, galletas and other things. I said we would deliver some bags to their encampment today. (Duerksen, 1990, pp. 186-187. Also G. B. Giesbrecht, *Mennoblatt*, June 16, 1962, p. 7) (See 12.2.2, p. 243).

Bob recognized the urgency writing to Frank Wiens September 10, 1962, in Asuncion, copied to Bill Snyder, missionary J. H. Franz, and J. Winfield Fretz, in the U.S. He expresses concern that violence might erupt at any moment. This ". . . is a problem that exceeds the colonies means," he writes. Bob says the demands could be met for the present group but more Indians will surely appear wanting the same considerations. He asks, "How does one proceed in this situation?" He asks if MCC has the ability to appeal to international organiza-tions and to the US government, who have before given aid to the

Mennonites. He concludes that intervention is needed to prevent the situation from escalating into an even more serious long term problem using as an example, the African Congo. His proposal is an immediate settlement for a few until more aid is forthcoming. Not only is land for settlement needed but food is the immediate need. But widespread drought prevails across the Chaco, so there is little work or surplus food for the Indians.

Generous international aid did arrive for the longer pull. In the short term however, the ISB had to devise emergency measures. Bob continued efforts to secure international help with ISB board approval and with the *Oberschulzen* working through their governmental channels.

ISB's minutes from September 10, 1962 (same date as Bob's letter), "The priority is for a limited settlement program in cooperation between 'Light for the Indians' and Fernheim Colony." An additional settlement at Yalve Sanga was begun.

12.3 A High Profile Project About to Crash and Burn

But four months later, January 1963, Bob wrote to Bill Snyder, "The project has gotten out of control." Supporting his claim: 1. Too many Indians were promised (or thought they were entitled to) land beyond what was possible. 2. Most Indians are being settled without proper counseling. 3. The project has only one Mennonite manager and he was only half time. 4. There is too little funding to make things happen quickly. And finally 5: If matters are not remedied and the project is not reorganized, the settlement effort will surely fail.

Bob wrote to Wiens on July 27, 1963 (interestingly not copied to others as the usual practice); for the Indian settlement program to succeed, the three colony administrations must honor ISB as exercising centralized control. Bob also wrote there was tension between 'Light to the Indians' at Yalve Sanga and the MB mission board in Hillsboro over land ownership. He sees this more a matter of communication and not threatening the effort but must be resolved before real progress is possible. He asks Wiens, who is himself a MB, to help along an understanding by urging the MB mission board in Hillsboro to decisively deal with the matter. More important, there is serious tension between *Oberschulzen* and ISB, "The *Oberschulzen* want to control the money and ignore the ISB." Bob fears that this settlement effort risks collapse, "Or is it already too late?" At the letter's end, "It is ironic; if this settlement succeeds it will happen despite the Mennonites, not because of them."

This opinion might sound insulting to the Mennonites. But Bob's comment illustrates the high tension at the time. Bob was venting his overwhelming frustration. His tone was, of course, totally out of character. We have no evidence he expressed himself this harshly to committee members.

On August 8, 1963, Bob attempted to resign as chairman. He was committed to the effort but was frustrated because the project was unsupported at the colony level; the three colony administrations were painfully unresponsive. His proposals were not implemented. Bob was elected chairman but his guidance was disregarded. ISB's recording secretary put a good face on the situation by writing, "Robert Unruh would like to step down as chair of the Indian settlement project. The project decentralization has made it difficult for him to advance the project and to find any satisfaction in the work."

What was meant by decentralization? The three Chaco colonies were highly competitive. Each colony wanted its own plan with a separate budget and the ability to make decisions in its own best interest. The settlement program was dysfunctional from MCC's viewpoint because the administrator (Bob) had no oversight or management control over implementation practices. (W.T.S. Oral History, p. 1081)

At the committee's urging, he did continue as chair one more year until his third term ended in August 1964. (See 12.3, p. 244)

12.4 ISB Reorganization

Bob's patience eventually bore fruit but it took many years. While tension between MCC and the *Oberschulzen* remained for some time, the recommendation for central control did happen quickly, at least on paper. Not only did Bob express his own opinion but the interests of MCC as well. Likely the Indian settlement project was debated vigorously, but Bob maintained his clear position; to do what was in the Indian's best interest. "The speedy reorganization of the settlement board is seen as necessary." (ISB minutes, October 29, 1963)

One month later the following reorganization of the Indian settlement board was discussed and recommended:

1. That one administrator will manage the entire settlement area. An immediate search will begin.
2. Accounts of the three colonies be closed and merged into one account.

Oberschulze Heinrich Duerksen, Frank Wiens (behind Duerksen), Robert Unruh (sunglasses), Yalve-Sanga resident with wood working tool, Ann Klassen, Canadian MB mission worker focusing her efforts on empowering Indian women, 1963. Photo credit: Frank Wiens, Mennonite Church USA Historical Committee, Goshen, Ind.

3. Funds from MCC pooled into the same account.
4. Disbursements by the director must first be approved by the executive committee.
5. Director will submit budget and plans to executive committee for approval.
6. Indian settlement leaders accountable to the director.
7. The director's goals are to organize for centralized control and to bring about better cooperation and operational efficiency.

Thus the organizational structure to accommodate MCC was now satisfied. (See 12.4, p. 250)

12.5. Bob's Contribution to Indian Settlement

In a broad manner we might highlight Bob's contribution to the settlement program.

Bob had served for ten years (eight years onsite in the Chaco) when the settlement project was organized. His concern for Indian welfare was well known to the colonists and to MCC. His agricultural proficiency was recognized and sought by the *Oberschulzen* and the missionaries. Because it was a MCC program and Bob was the MCC representative in the Chaco, he needed to articulate MCC's views on the issues. Clearly, MCC's long range view was more global than the Chaco Mennonites. Retrospectively, this is evident from discussions about Indian values and anthropological matters. This variance however, created conflict for all concerned; for the *Oberschulzen,* the missionaries, the Indians and MCC.

This is where Bob's quiet and humble patience must be noted as crucial. Representing MCC he managed to somehow straddle the anthropological issues and stayed clear of arguing the matter. People said he had a 10,000-foot view, he saw things from on high. He did not take sides but remained neutral and objective, with a clear goal in mind. His entire orientation was what was best for the Indians. With this attitude he provided a good example and a lasting contribution. While he gave much good advice, he also led by example.

In August 1964 the Unruhs ended their third term. Bob continued to think about the Indians in the Chaco while working on his masters degree at Texas A&M. He made comparisons and drew parallels. He kept up to date on the Indian settlement work; their poverty pained him. A Newton, Kans., church paper discussing poverty in the world motivated him to write about the Indians in the Chaco. Here are some excerpts:

Humans do not live on bread alone. But the history of mankind is the history of their struggle for daily bread. . . . Famine has killed more humans than war. After World War I twelve million Russians starved. In 1943 famine claimed six million lives in India and China. Hungry people are a social burden. With an empty stomach people cannot work nor study to learn in order to improve their standard of living. They cannot think beyond their present emergency that precludes all else. Starving people have little resistance to disease. In brief, because millions are hungry the economic and social development of a country suffers, indeed the whole world suffers

He then relates this directly to the Indians in the Chaco and the Mennonites' responsibility, as though he was living among them. He fears for the future of the Indians:

The Chaco Indian people are increasing in number; soon they will outnumber the Mennonites. So some Mennonites see only a dark future. They think the only solution is to migrate to Canada. If it were possible for all to emigrate have we fulfilled our obligation before God and our fellow men? I believe not! If the world is threatened by famine as scientists say, then we Mennonites well known as farmers have an even greater task before us. If one believes in self help for the Indians then we must continue to settle them on their own land and give them the equipment and means to succeed. This is the first step and vital. The second step is education where we teach one or more in each village who then teaches his neighbor villag-

Indian school in session, Yalve Sanga, 1968. Photo credit: Robert Unruh.

An Indian farmer on his garden with Robert Unruh.

ers how to farm. Some progress has happened but more needs done. It is hard work without visible results the first years. It might take ten or fifteen years until success is seen. But it is the only solution in my view if we dread famine, communism, etc and want to fulfill our obligation before God and our fellow man. (Mennoblatt, April 16, 1967, pp. 5-6)

Returning to the Chaco in October 1966 (fourth term) Bob continued in a consulting capacity with the ISB. Driving through the Indian villages and visiting the mission stations, to his dismay he discovered no improvement in his two year absence.

Bob working with the Indians. Photo credit: John Peters.

(*Mennoblatt,* April 1 and April 16, 1968) Bob then suggested to ISB that he organize and teach an "Agricultural Course for Indians." The first two classes, one for 36 Lengua and one for 38 Chulupi, began mid-1968. The students were selected with at least one person from each village for broad representation.

The topics were:

Preparing ground for planting

Preserving food

Plant protection against diseases, insects and pesticide use (*Mennoblatt,* August 1, 1968)

Bob also worked with cattle breeding and animal nutrition. (*Mennoblatt,* May 1973, p. 2 and Stahl, 1980, pp. 150-151)

Peter Duerksen from Filadelfia, *Oberschulze* Heinrich Duerksen's son, economic adviser for many years at Yalve-Sanga said,

Mr. Unruh with his specialized knowledge was at that time crucially important. With his kind and interpersonal good nature to the Indians he gained widespread acceptance. He held many meetings with the Indian farmers although already very busy otherwise. Even today it is a mystery how he managed to do it. He did great service by finding seeds for planting. Also with farm animals for the Indians he provided chicks. He motivated the Indians to keep and care for a milk cow to improve family health. In all these matters he was at the forefront. Bob treated Indians as personal friends and they returned the favor, addressing him as 'Bob.' I could tell that Bob was pleased even though the manner of interaction was different from interaction with his Mennonite friends.

Finally Duerksen summarizes the service of the Unruhs saying,

The 1971 ISB executive committee, program supported by three Chaco colonies and churches, MCC and other charities. Far left Robert Unruh, director 1962-1964, Hans Epp medical doctor, Abram Boschmann executive director, Jakob Klassen education, Werner Janz finance & cooperatives.

Plain and simple, Bob Unruh was a man of action. He was there when needed. Not only in the struggle to exist economically, he participated in Indian church building. We failed to recognize and appreciate many things he and Myrtle were doing for the Indians. The progress and development for Indian settlement that happened would be difficult to imagine without the Unruh's participation. (Interview, May 2006) (See 12.5, p. 250)

13

Robert Unruh as Agricultural Advisor to the Three Colonies

13.1 Organizing *Servicio Agropecuario* (SAP)

Bob was the Experimental Farm director in Fernheim. The farm was a joint effort supported by Fernheim and MCC on a roughly equal basis. It was however, MCC's intent that Bob's contribution should accrue to all three colonies. Bob emphasized that his serving Menno and Neuland would in the end serve Fernheim's best interest by advancing agriculture for the region. That concept was a difficult sell, reluctantly tolerated by Fernheim. No serious difficulties arose, though there were occasional objections. For example, Neuland and Menno farmers were invited to a cattle auction in 1967 and this caused some concern among Fernheim's leaders, feeling that good breeding stock might be lost to Fernheim. (See 13.1, p. 252)

Before leaving on furlough following his fourth term in 1969, Bob wrote a letter to the (three) *Oberschulzen* looking forward: "We thought about our work for the next term of service and make the following suggestion: . . ." He then talks about the desirability of cooperation among the colonies in matters of agriculture and cattle ranching. "We must find a way for all three colonies too cooperate in this work." He proposed a centrally located office from which would flow information to all three colony farmers.

With regard to the advisory council for the Indian settlement issues, he stated that he was willing to continue, "as long as it is advisory to agricultural settlement issues." But, ". . . the daily issues about

Robert Unruh, far left foreground, evaluating beef livestock. Photo credit: Robert Unruh, Mennonite Heritage Centre Archives (Winnipeg).

Field Day at the Experimental Farm, 1967. Photo credit: John Peters.

financial matters at individual settlements . . ." he preferred to leave to the committee. Then an unexpected comment; "Somehow it seems to be understood that I have the final word on settlement issues, but such responsibility I cannot and prefer not to take on." Thorough, systematic planning is needed for the future of agriculture for the Mennonites and Indians alike, Bob said. "We cannot leave this to chance." (Unruh, October 13, 1969)

During the succeeding years, comprehensive studies were conducted to learn how a joint advisory council, to incorporate all colonies, might be organized. Using the Experimental Farms 25th anniversary as the reason, an analysis was conducted by Dr. Harold Kaufmann and Professor Leonard Siemens in cooperation with Bob. The task was two fold; to look back and to make recommendations going forward. Looking back the report acknowledged the trials at the Farm were unfortunately not valued or recognized by many colony farmers as vital. And that the farmers were not implementing recommendations on a broad enough scale to be beneficial. The report recommended a stronger "technical advisory service," for the farmers and stronger interaction with them (know as "extension"). This was possible through the creation of a "central office" with staff, experts, and technicians. The recommended site was Loma Plata (Menno) because this new agricultural service for established farmers would dovetail with the agricultural school (later vocational school) planned for Loma Plata (the school became a reality in 1981). (See 13.1.1, p. 253)

After a difficult development period in 1973, *Servicio Agropecuario* was operational in 1974, and located in Loma Plata, Menno Colony. The goal was to "gather agricultural information and through its laboratory and an experimental farm to circulate this material for the improvement and development of agriculture in the central Chaco."

Two departments were organized, one for agronomy and one for cattle. Each department served Menno, Fernheim, Neuland, and the Indian settlements. Service delivery was accomplished through visits, farm field days, and radio programs. The office was supported financially by Menno with 50%, Fernheim 35%, and Neuland 15%. The oversight board was the three *Oberschulzen*. Robert Unruh was the director for farmer's services and Dr. Rudolf Kaethler, DVM, was the director for Animal Care. (Rudolf Kaethler, *Mennoblatt*, March 16, 1974)

Demand for services from cattle breeding increased and that department grew rapidly. By 1981, SAP employed 22 persons:

Office personnel	4
Agronomists	5
Veterinarians	5
Para-technicians	4
Other	4

Two years later, records show 29 persons employed. Giant strides occurred in these years; mechanization increased, cattle improved through genetics and better care with milk production soaring upward. Bob's influence was seen coming to fruition. (*Mennoblatt*, November 1, 1967, pp. 6-7)

SAP as an inter-colony institution ended in 1992 when the demand for specialists' time and for specialists with differing disciplines in each colony, suggested the single service center concept was no longer an efficient method for delivering services.

Beginning in the 1970s Central Chaco agricultural development took off like a rocket. The Chaco had become productive on a scale not imaginable in 1951. Exodus from the Chaco was near zero by the late 1970s. Following are examples showing Robert Unruh's economic contributions to the Chaco Mennonites.

The Chaco was changing even though the weather, soil conditions, and nature remained the same. Mennonites adapted to the climate for agriculture and cattle farming. Following are work highlights with the Mennonite settlements.

13.2 Increased Cattle Ranching and Milk Production

Improvement in ranching and milk production began in the 1950s with Buffelgrass' introduction and better ground preparation methods. Beginning in 1957 bush was cleared to plant Buffelgrass, and genetic improvements were undertaken. In 1961 pure bred cattle such as Holstein, Jersey, and Brown Swiss were flown from the US. In succeeding years Holstein bull calves were brought in from East Paraguay. With the genetic improvements and greater attention to feeding, came increased milk production. Using funds from the USAID credit line, more pure bred animals for breeding were imported from the US. Also imported from Argentina and Uruguay were Holstein heifers. For this the Chaco colonies became Paraguay's leader in milk production.

Jakob F. Hiebert, Hochfeld, Menno Colony was a good example. He agreed to launch a "milk production project" in collaboration with SAP. He reports:

In October 1974 a veterinarian from our advisory office came to my farm and asked if I was willing to start a dairy operation as a demonstrated project. They were looking for a young couple willing to try something new. We were told that it would not be easy because it was an experiment. The entire project was to be documented to study its efficiency. Technical assistance was to come from Robert Unruh, who was to help me in all aspects of the work such as data entry and analysis. The purpose was to learn whether there was a future for milk production in our colony.

Hiebert comments on the reasons he decided to sign on:

One reason we decided to go with the project was my wife's sensitive skin. She had difficulty working outside in the sun. We decided that milk production would solve this issue. One must remember that in those days every person needed to work outside if the field work was to get done on time. It would be difficult for me to do this work alone. We decided to go with this experimental project, making less field work.

Jakob remembers that Bob supported him in every way:

Bob Unruh came to us and we planned the next steps. During our talks and our planning we considered basic and practical questions. Mr. Unruh stressed this constantly. I did not always understand everything but today after 30 years—I am still in the dairy business and think about the hints and advice he taught me. Sometimes he would say: 'One should not just be interested in the money, but the business itself.' He also said: 'It does not matter what work one does, but what is important is that one is interested in the business, that one works and acts responsibly, and that the operation is run orderly.' I took this advice seriously and have tried to stick to it in my business. These principles still apply today.

He also remembered that Bob helped him to finance the buildings, purchase 25 good milk cows and a pure bred bull, and advice on care and feeding and building the silo. Then he said:

. . . There were situations when we were at wits end. Mr. Unruh always came and usually had a solution. And that was the unusual thing about this man; he did not seek personal profit or honor. His priority always was to help each individual and thereby help the community.

Our project was concerned about creating something others could use as model and start their own dairy business. He always appeared sincere, dedicated and persistent, which earned him respect and recognition in our entire community. He also contributed enormously to the construction and development of "Lácteos Trébol."

Hiebert thought the family farm was important for milk production in the Chaco and in conclusion said:

Administrators told me years later during a time when the colony had some financial difficulties: "If you and Mr. Unruh had given up, the entire colony milk production, including the plant, would not have been built.

Jakob also described his personal relationship with Unruh:

> *Bob and Myrtle were not just our teachers and advisors, they were*
> *our friends. . . . Contacts with people in the colonies and the church family*
> *were important to him. We both enjoyed choral music. He loved singing in*
> *the choir of the Mennonite Church in Filadelfia, and we sang in our choir.*
> *His letters always asked: "Do you still sing? Keep it up! We don't just need*
> *to improve our economy, but we also need spiritual development and the*
> *fellowship with other Christians in the church." For me and for our entire*
> *community in the colony he was a helper and a friend. We want to honor*
> *his legacy.*

It took five or six years to bring a steer to a thousand pounds in 1951, but today it can be done in just two years. During the 1950s a cow delivered half a gallon of milk per day but today it is four to five gallons. The birth rate for cows was 60%, today it is 90%. How did these monumental improvements happen? Bob used his successful teaching strategy—demonstration or quotations from other experts—over and over to urge farmers toward improved practices, in this case how best to genetically improve the herd:

> *There is a proverb that says "The bull is half the herd." This is true,*
> *but sometimes people think about saving money and buying a cheaper*
> *bull. Dr. Steward Fowler, director of "Cattle Research at Texas A&M," in*
> *Texas, USA, says: "A good bull does not cost you anything." What does he*
> *mean? A good bull is a great start, but a poor bull can destroy everything.*
> *A bull leaves his imprint on the herd for many years. One mediocre cow*
> *in the herd is tolerable since she delivers but one calf a year, but a medio-*
> *cre bull cannot be tolerated since he produces 30 or more calves a year.*
> *Any bull can produce calves but that is just cattle reproduction, not live*
> *stock breeding. We must produce the best quality cattle, cattle with accel-*
> *erated growth, a well formed quickly maturing body to yield a reasonable*
> *margin of income. . . .*

I believe Dr. Fowler's words are true: "A good bull does not cost you anything." A mediocre bull is expensive, even if he is donated. (*Mennoblatt*, November 16, 1975, pp. 6, 7) (See 13.2, p. 253)

13.3 Importing Breeding Cattle into the Chaco

Bob was not a trained veterinarian, he was an agronomist. Even so, he had an impressive record in cattle breeding in the Chaco. For instance, soon after arriving in 1951, he sent a request for a refrigerator to MCC. The reason was that his plan to introduce artificial insemination for herd improvement and refrigeration was needed. Bob's bold effort to import breeding stock from the U.S. can be pieced together from correspondence and records.

The first breeding stock imported into the Chaco occurred in May 1961, before the Trans Chaco Road was finished. Peter P. Klassen, *Mennoblatt's* editor wrote: "It was a sensational event on May 7 when a huge U.S. transport airplane landed at the Filadelfia airport coming directly from the United States." (*Mennoblatt*, 1961, #10, p. 7)

Large crowd gathered to watch the unloading, first livestock airlift from Miami to Filadelfia, May 1961. Photo credit: Irvin Weaver.

L to R: Four man flight crew, Irvin Weaver, three colony officials. Man with briefcase was Paraguayan customs inspector. Shenk not shown. Photo credit: Irvin Weaver.

The flight departed Miami on May 5, with stops in Panama and Chile, and then landed in Filadelfia at 4 pm on Sunday. The Paraguayan military authorized landing in Filadelfia without a problem. According to Klassen, 1,000 persons were at the airport to witness this groundbreaking occasion.

The large transport airplane brought 18 young pure-bred bulls, 15 Holstein, 2 Jersey, and one Swiss Brown, all had been donated by Mennonite farmers in Pennsylvania for the Mennonites in the Chaco. Thirty pure-bred hogs also came with the same transport. Two Mennonite donors accompanied the transport: Henry E. Shenk and Ervin D. Weaver. They remained in the Chaco for some time to observe and to oversee the animal's acclimatization to their new environment. The flight itself was underwritten by the U.S. Government. MCC arranged for this contribution through its continued good rapport with USAID development program. Earlier relationships included cooperation with STICA, construction of the Trans Chaco road, and the million dollar credit (Smathers loan) for the five colonies. (See 13.3, p. 254)

Third livestock air shipment at Wichita, Kans., before departure, 1968. L to R: Dwight Wiebe, MB Mission Board; Frank Wiens, Paraguay MCC director on furlough in the states; Army Major General Henry Weber; Air Force Brig. General Doyle Hastie; Philip Waltner, Moundridge, KS; LaVerne Graber and Otto Preheim, Freeman, SD who accompanied flight for animal care and Robert Schrag, Mennonite Weekly Review. (LaVerne's second visit to Chaco having helped build the Trans-Chaco Highway a few years earlier when a PAX man). Photo credit: Robert Schrag, Mennonite Church USA Historical Committee, Goshen, Ind.

The second airlift from the U.S. took place in February 1966. There were 36 young pure-bred bulls (one died soon after arriving) and three young pure-bred stallions. As with the first airlift, the orchestration was begun by Bob and carried out on arrival by others in Bob's absence. Arriving in Asuncion, this second flight was met by John Peters, Experimental Farm director and Frank Wiens, MCC country director in Asunción. This shipment, as the first, was a contribution from Mennonites in the U.S. however documents in Paraguay cannot confirm this. John Peters points out that the ground transportation to Miami was funded by Myrtle's home congregation, the Eden Mennonite Church in Kansas. The flight from Miami to Asunción was again

A U.S. Air Force transport plane in Asunción with cattle for the Chaco colonies, September 16, 1968. Robert Unruh arranged the donation from Mennonite farmers in North America. Photo credit: Mennonite Church USA Historical Committee, Goshen, Ind.

Robert Unruh, U.S. Ambassador Hernandez, and Helmuth Siemens observe the unloading, September 1968. Photo credit: Mennonite Church USA Historical Committee, Goshen, Ind.

funded by the U.S. government. Transport expenses within Paraguay were covered by the colonies. From this airlift three bulls went to Friesland, two to Volendam, with the remainder to the Chaco.

The third breeding stock airlift, planned and executed by Bob and John Peters, took place in September 1968. It contained 28 cattle, 15 hogs, and 4 sheep. The 28 cattle cost the colonies (U.S.) $6,031. In October 1974 Bob writes that these 28 cattle brought into the world 1,387 calves. He termed this a "total success."

Jacob T. Fehr and Rudolf Dürksen accompanied another transport in September 1977. Fehr writes:

After repeated recommendations from Robert Unruh and Rudolf Käthler, the Oberschulzen advisory group gave the go ahead to import young bulls to improve cattle genetics. After the cost estimate and other details were studied (from what country to purchase) *it became clear that the U.S. offered the best arrangement. Because Bob wanted to visit several technical organizations and universities, his furlough was extended to four months. He was authorized by SAP to purchase young bulls and three stallions. But a full airplane required 85 animals so Wolfgang Weber's ranch, Remonia, joined with SAP for this shipment. Rudolf Dürksen was Remonia's ranch manager, making the financial arrangements and helped with animal care.*

During August and September 1977 (in the states), *Bob with considerable effort and much devotion arranged to buy 50 young bulls: 22 Herefords, 22 Santa Gertrudis and 6 Brahman, Holstein, Brown Swiss. Also three young stallions. On September 3, I flew to Newton, Kansas, to help Bob during the quarantine time, the documents preparation and to escort the flight to Asunción.*

Bob assembled the cattle on Ted and Edith Krehbiel's farm, Myrtle's relatives in Kansas. This was a small farm where we fed the cattle, ran the needed tests, gave shots, and prepared them for the transport. By September 22 all documents were in hand and we were able to truck them to Houston, Texas. We arrived in Houston after 14 hours with our double-decker truck.

After an eight-hour quarantine, we loaded the 85 animals into an old four engine turbo-prop Lockheed Electra belonging to Aerolineas Argentinas. When finished Rudolf and I boarded, and the airplanes loading door was closed. We made one stop in Panama and arrived in Asunción on September 24, 1977.

In Asunción Dr. Käthler took charge and the animals were brought for quarantine to the experimental station of MAG at Km 315 along the Trans Chaco Road, where they were cared for by SAP until they were cleared for transport. On November 3 and 11 the animals were raffled off to the ranchers who had ordered them. The importation of cattle was and remains an important factor in cattle breeding, which was started by Bob and supported by SAP.

In December 1979, an importation of 82 heifers, 63 bulls, and 5 young horses took place but no details about the origin or how they were distributed were found.

13.4 Artificial Insemination

The introduction of artificial insemination (AI) took place step by step and appears in the *Oberschulzen* meeting minutes on September 25, 1968 showing that semen and instruments came with the third flight earlier that month. John Peters says in a 2003 interview:

In the third shipment of livestock in 1968, Bob arranged with Roy Snyder from Ontario to donate a thermos of semen from high quality dairy and beef bulls. The livestock shipment was to leave from Midwestern U.S. but the thermos started in Ontario, was sent to Mt. Lake, Minnesota, where more semen was added then to Kansas where more was added. So we had a variety of semen with which to respond to the various interests of Chaco ranchers and dairymen. Rudolf Kaethler (veterinarian in training) was not yet in the colonies and we didn't have liquid nitrogen in the colonies to keep the thermos supplied so we would send the thermos to Asuncion for periodic recharging to keep the semen frozen. So Bob and I had to figure out how to learn about artificial insemination. Bob said, well, let's go to the abattoir and examine the female organs after the cow is killed but not yet gutted, then at least we will know what we are feeling for. That's how we trained ourselves in AI. This illustrates the necessity of being resourceful when you are out there by yourself and need to get things done, you figure out how to do it otherwise you face the consequences of failure.

In 1968 however, Fernheim Colony minutes show AI was considered in 1955. Ingrid Epp in 1986 compiled Robert Unruh's 'career highlights' and reviewed her list with Bob, writing that in 1958, instruments for AI were ordered and in 1961 the first calf by AI was born at the Experimental Farm. In 1960-61 Werner Siemens learned the technique for AI with STICA in East Paraguay. Dr. Rudolf Kaethler told about the 1968 semen thermos bottles and liquid nitrogen:

Fresh sperm, with a shelf life of five days, was sent by STICA via airplane and placed in a refrigerator to be used as needed. During his furlough trips to the U.S. Bob took animal care refresher courses at Texas A&M. During my visit to the University he showed me the various departments, the fundamentals of genetic improvement, and he introduced me to various people with whom he had studied. As I understood it, at one point he spent an entire semester where he learned the theory and practice of artificial insemination.

13.5 Radio Programs

An important SAP advisory medium, aside from regular bulletins and farm days, were regular 15-minute radio programs. During these broadcasts, which reached even the most distant homes in the Chaco, Bob gave concrete advice on agriculture and cattle ranching. Topics discussed were fruit trees, vegetables, insect and disease control, news from the Experimental Farm, care of machinery, reforestation, working the bush ground, and many more topics.

Many of these programs, perhaps most of them, were conducted by Bob himself. The written record of each of these broadcasts was perhaps three pages long and generally started with: "Good evening radio friends. This SAP program is conducted by Robert Unruh." Then he stated the theme for that evening. Usually Bob gave concise examples easily understood, with guidance on implementing the practice. A twice weekly broadcast adds up to 100 radio spots each year. (See 13.5, p. 255)

13.6 Pesticides: Use and Application

In the early years, ants, grasshoppers, locust, and aphids were the serious insect pests. Later, diseases and various other pests arrived. First was the problem of finding the best pesticide, and second was finding a supplier, and third was learning how to safely and efficiently use the chemical. During the first decades control measures were not available and later when chemical were available, farmers did not know how to use them. Pesticides were generally unavailable in Paraguay. Bob found it necessary first to determine what control pesticide would work, then experiment on the farm before making recommendations. Colony administrations bought the pesticide and then Bob instructed farmers on proper usage. He also was in frequent contact with STICA and Ministry of Agriculture in Asunción. His ability to find answers to sticky problems was impressive. In 1979 Bob writes:

The use of poisons, especially insecticides, must be used much more intensely this year than was the case in the last 4-5 years. It is extremely important to use the right amount and timing the application. The method and timing of applications will greatly influence the results. For the best results it is necessary to understand how to set and maintain the sprayer. I get many questions about spraying, some I will detail here and try to answer. (*Mennoblatt*, January 16, p. 10)

He then followed with detailed instructions; how much chemical to each gallon of water, the pressure, height of the sprayer nozzles, how to mix these poisons and what are the best times of day to spray. To conclude the article, he called attention to the importance of spraying at the right time and under favorable conditions:

> *It is impossible to spray preventively against insects since one can never tell when the infestation will occur. It is best to wait until the insect population builds up a little because the poison has a short life after spraying on the plant. Where only a few insects come, often natural predators will control the damaging insects. On the other hand do not wait too long or the insects will cause much crop damage; each day delayed is a day of losses. For example in an experiment by the Ministry of Agriculture last year, spraying peanuts two days after worms appeared the yield was lower by 290 lbs. in one field and 420 lbs. in another compared with immediate spraying. A delay of six days reduced the yield in one field by 670 lbs and in another by 1220 lbs, compared with immediate spraying.* (Mennoblatt, January 16, 1979, p. 11) (See 13.6, p. 255)

13.7 Citrus Tree Diseases

Citrus trees grew easily in the Chaco. The fruits were good quality and the tree free from disease. Bob promoted citrus growing for these and health reasons. In 1979 citrus necrosis appeared. It was a devastating development for every person in the Chaco. Bob surmised the disease spread from East Paraguay and recommended drastic measures be taken everywhere in the Chaco:

> *In the last days the feared citrus "necrosis" disease has shown up in several places. We thought it was not present in this Chaco region. . . . The disease can only be eradicated by removing and burning the diseased trees. There is so far no successful chemical control. We will do a survey of locations where trees were recently imported into the Chaco to assess how widespread the problem. The following recommendations come from other countries:*
> 1. *All trees with the disease must be completely destroyed by burning, included the smallest twigs. After the trees are burned the*

> *ground must be fumigated. Also the worker's shoe should be disinfected before they go into another garden.*
>
> 2. *Wait 8 months before replanting citrus trees in the same soil or location.*
> 3. *Fruit from stricken gardens should not be sold to prevent the spreading the disease.*
> 4. *Young trees and fruit must not be brought from East Paraguay into the disease free zone.*

Some people will throw up their hands and say it is impossible to control citrus necrosis! But that is not true. If we begin immediately to keep the disease from spreading we can get citrus necrosis under control and preserve our beautiful grapefruit trees as well as other fruit trees. But there must be energetic and forever watchful attention by all colony people to get successful control. (Mennoblatt, March 1, 1979, p. 10)

In a wide-ranging report on June 15, 1982, Bob wrote about controlling citrus necrosis. In 1979 there were 714 trees diagnosed with necrosis in all three Chaco colonies. In June 1982 only 21 trees are known diseased and marked for removal. He confidently closes the report:

> *We have confidence that within 2-3 years the disease will be wiped out if we are careful not to re-introduce it from diseased trees or fruit coming from East Paraguay.* (See 13.7, p. 255)

13.8 The Ranchers Association, "*Rodeo Trébol*"

Rodeo Trébol was an association involving the three Chaco colonies focused on cattle and horse breeding. It had no direct organizational link to SAP but worked closely with SAP.

Rodeo Trébol was organized in 1972 with 23 charter members. Membership rapidly increased. Article II stated the association's purpose as "Promoting the interest in horse breeding and care, also the promotion of cattle breeding and to provide a forum for the exchange of experience in the form of exhibitions and showing of horses."

An area near Loma Plata on the way to Filadelfia was acquired to set up facilities. Over the years buildings to house and show livestock were built with corrals, grandstands and other amenities for spectators. August 15th was a national holiday that is a traditional folk festival attended by thousands from far and near. The best horses and cattle compete for prizes. In this manner the association contributed to the Chaco colonies economic development. (*Mennoblatt,* September 16, 1980, pp. 10-11)

Bob participated from the outset in *Rodeo Trebol.* In minutes from the first meeting April 28, 1973, "By the influence of Mr. Robert Unruh the association was given from the Showalter foundation (USA) $ 3,000 for the development of exhibition sites." Bob serving as judge for cattle awards and continued his membership until leaving the Chaco in 1983. He periodically reported information about the association during his radio broadcasts on ZP-30.

When the Unruh's left the Chaco in November1983, the association noted the following November 26, 1983:

> *We honor today our very valuable coworker in the cattlemen's association, Mr. Robert Unruh. We want to show our appreciation for his many achievements with*
> > *a. A thank you letter*
> > *b. A plaque and inscription*
> > *c. A photo album from the last exhibition*
> *The president of Paraguay, Alfredo Stroessner and his entourage of 200 persons, was also present at the last exhibition.* (*Mennoblatt,* September 16, 1983, p. 10)

13.9 Unruh Fish; A Mennonite Legend?

What is a legend? An exaggeration? A legend is a morally instructive narrative; a short and often humorous story. Its intention is to portray an important truth in a concrete manner. A legend does so with a story that fits the context of a person or a happening. World and church histories use legends to illustrate morally instructive values to transmit these from generation to generation.

There are at least two Unruh fish legends. One was told by Edgar Stoesz in his book on the Chaco Mennonites, *Garden in the Wilderness*, page 94 and paraphrased below:

Two Mennonite farmers notice Bob with his pick-up truck next to a pond. They wonder what it is he might be doing. They commiserate together that many of Bob's experiments fail or yield questionably valued results at best.

The next morning one farmer overcome with curiosity goes to the pond to see what it was Bob was doing. He finds dead fish floating belly up in the water. He thinks to himself in Low German: "Well, that I could have spared him."

Some months later Bob and Myrtle return from furlough in the US. Myrtle asks Bob to go to the Co-op market and buy meat for the noon meal. Bob asks: "What kind of fish are those in the refrigerated display?"

"These? I don't know, we just call them Unruh fish." Not knowing to whom she was talking, she added, "They are now growing them in local ponds."

No person in the Chaco today has any factual evidence about "Unruh fish." It is thought that Bob possibly experimented with fish in water lagoons since he did hundreds, if not thousands of experiments—no one knows for sure. In spite of many experimental disappointments and the prevailing skepticism about value, Bob's actions were crowned with success, and eventually Mennonites in the Chaco recognized and showed their appreciation. (See 13.9, p. 256)

14

Paraguay Appreciation and the Last Years

Work in Paraguay ended suddenly when Myrtle's health worsened in 1983. Asuncion medical advice supported the idea that Myrtle might be better served by returning to the U.S. They had lived half their adult lives in Paraguay. Bob wrote an open departure letter published in the *Mennoblatt*:

We are soon departing for the U.S.A. As many of you already know our plans are indefinite. When we might return depends on circumstances over which we have no control. God alone knows and we trust him to do what is best. We are happy to have served so long in the Chaco. The first ten years were the most difficult because much of what we take for granted today, did not exist then. What has been accomplished cannot be attributed to us. Many of you encouraged us and faced the difficulties with courage in those very uncertain times. MCC sent workers and gave financial support to promote the work. Other organizations likewise gave substantial contributions. I want to thank the many coworkers from the colonies. And last we must say that God gave us the ability and courage to do this work, it is in the Lord's honor! (*Mennoblatt*, December 16, 1983, pp. 4-5)

Heinrich Dyck, Fernheim *Oberschulze* at the time and chairman of the three-colony *Oberschulzen* committee wrote these parting words of appreciation:

1. They contributed much to the "Servicio Agropecuario" development and helped the institution become accepted throughout the colonies.

2. The introduction of Buffelgrass from North America fundamentally changed our agriculture so that today the cattle industry is the most important industry.

3. The newsletters and radio programs were of important educational value. The information and references guided us in our farm and cattle practices. And the consultations and advice was always given in good time to be of practical value. We know the information was gladly received and employed over a large area.

4. Your personal advisory and farm visits were of great value to those visited. When called upon, no farm too distant or travel too difficult. To Mrs. Unruh we acknowledge your great contribution with a cookbook, your cooking and household instruction to small groups and in our secondary level schools and in different ways to our community. (Mennoblatt, January 1, 1984, p. 7)

Departure celebration for Robert & Myrtle Unruh, November 1983.

Frieda Kaethler wrote an article entitled, "Humans we should not forget:"

No, we will not forget Robert and Myrtle Unruh's service in the German Chaco settlements. They actually belong to us." (Mennoblatt, May 1, 1984, p. 5)

The Unruhs frequently exchanged letters with friends and co-workers. This mutual respect and appreciation became evident when the three *Oberschulzen* invited and paid expenses for the Unruhs to visit the Chaco in the spring of 1986 for several weeks. They toured all three colonies. Bob was invited to SAP meetings and in one meeting his participation was programmed into the meeting agenda. At the last meeting before departure on November 15, 1986, Bob gave these impromptu remarks:

We see how Chaco agriculture expands. We see how you have brought order to the land. If it seems difficult sometimes, remember all problems can be overcome with God's help. When we are given material goods, we must help those less fortunate. But when people are hungry and homeless it is impossible for them to believe the gospel. Bill Snyder, for many years Executive Secretary of MCC once said: "The Chaco might become the bread basket of South America." That was twenty years ago. Today we see it is a possibility. Evaluating the Chaco colonies today we see a large move toward that objective. In past years the concern was to simply exist. Today one is concerned for the advancement of the entire zone. God intends something good with the Mennonites in Paraguay. As God assisted you in the past, so he intends it so in the future." (Mennoblatt, December 1, 1986, p. 5)

Myrtle Unruh died September 23, 1996. To friends in the Chaco Bob wrote on October 28, 1996:

Six months ago Myrtle was diagnosed with colon cancer. She had surgery in August. The surgeon said after the operation that the liver was also cancerous but nothing he could do about that. In November they tried chemotherapy but it was unsuccessful. From that time on she lost the desire to eat and became even weaker. The physicians said there was nothing more they could do so I took care of her in our home until the end.

Radio Station ZP -30 in Filadelfia broadcast a memorial service on September 26, at the same time funeral services were held at Eden Mennonite Church in Moundridge, Kansas, Myrtle's lifelong church congregation.

Edwin Neufeld, Filadelfia, Fernheim colony writes:

A life lived in service to her fellowmen has come to an end. For all those who remember Myrtle, her life was an example to us all.

To confirm this statement so we shall never forget, on May 27, 1997, a monument to Myrtle's memory was erected near the entrance to *Colegio Filadelfia*. It has three bronze plaques, the same text in German, Spanish and English.

Robert Unruh and daughter Elizabeth (Betty) participated in the tree planting ceremony, traveling from Kansas. They stayed six weeks in Fernheim at the colonies invitation.

During this visit many meetings were held to reunite old friends and co-workers. On May 7, Fernheim's colony administration organized a colony wide meeting for those 65 years or older for a reunion at the Experimental Farm. Bob and others reminisced about old times. He closed with the following, speaking for Myrtle too, "We had good memories of the work here. I am pleased that we could be here." It seemed that all who were physically able attended the reunion and were grateful for the opportunity to meet once again. (*Mennoblatt*, May 16, 1997, p. 11) (See Chapter 14, p. 256)

In his quiet, modest way, Robert Unruh plants a Palo Blanco tree to honor Myrtle Unruh, his wife, 1997.

This tree and monument in her memory are on the schoolyard of Colegio, Filadelfia. Myrtle taught home economics here from 1958 to 1977, 1997.

Meetings with SAP staff, farmers and others felt similarly about their last meeting with Bob Unruh. Robert Unruh died Thursday, March 5, 1998, at Betty's home in North Newton, Kansas.

Klaus Kroeker, a co-worker wrote:

Bob Unruh loved the Chaco. He worked tirelessly for improvement and development. He believed he could not do too much. Robert and Myrtle showed in their actions their love for God and their fellowmen by the service they gave to us. (*Mennoblatt*, April 1, 1998, p. 10)

15

Remembrances 2006—
A Lasting Impact

In May 2006, Edwin Neufeld carried out interviews with many who knew or worked with Bob and Myrtle Unruh in Paraguay. These are interesting accounts. The remembrances confirm and extend the Unruh legacy. There are duplications but to paraphrase Philippians 3:1, repetition will give the communication clarity.

15.1 Heinrich A. Wiens, Filadelfia, Fernheim Colony

Heinrich was already working at the Experimental Farm before Robert Unruh came to the Chaco and was an early associate:

We became acquainted easily and closely. Mr. Unruh was serious but polite and tolerant. He taught me how to drive a tractor, a car and how to work in the fields with different experiments and test plots, which was my main work.

We soon noticed Mr. Unruh had American speed. That was not a good idea in the Chaco's heat. That lasted about six months until we came to an agreement. Mr. Unruh had much energy and new ideas. Most were strange to us and we had our doubts. And some things did not work. But he respected our experience and would try again, differently. He expressed clearly that his wish was to create for Chaco people a better life wherever he could. First was a better and reliable food supply—milk, improved pasture with different kinds of grasses, improved cattle breeds; these were the early priorities.

The most important project, Wiens says, was the Buffelgrass. It was the economic development that benefited the entire Chaco. Also other important projects were vegetable, citrus fruit, watermelons. Mrs. Unruh was an important contributor for improving the diet and a teacher for better housekeeping.

15.2 Jakob Rahn, Filadelfia, Fernheim Colony

As a young man from Filadelfia, Jakob worked for many years at the Experimental Farm:

Mr. Unruh was a friend to every person who worked at the station. More than just a boss he put himself on the same level as everybody. There were of course differences of opinion but these were solved in a friendly manner. He never scolded; on the contrary he commended us and encouraged us to take more responsibility.

He assigned me for a time to the tree nursery. He had many experiments. Many small trees were budded to different varieties. Citrus trees from many countries of many kinds from Japan, India, U.S.A. and other countries were flown here. Or people traveling would bring him plants to try in the Chaco. I was amazed by all the connections he had around the world, he most have been well known. We received rose cuttings, vegetable seeds and ornamental shrubs to grow at the Experimental Farm.

He had to accept many failures, like it was with palm dates. Mr. Unruh tried hard and had much time invested trying to dry the dates or otherwise prepare them. He pleaded with farmers to help. But nothing came of it as he expected it would. That was very disappointing for Mr. Unruh.

And still another memory, also disappointing where the pasture experiments. Mr. Unruh brought a great many grass varieties to try out here. At first we planted small plots to be sure the plants would grow here. Some grew but most did not grow at all or very poorly. When people came to the Farm and saw the terrible condition of some plots they would ask,

"What is this?" Some plots did look pitiful.

We said, "Those are experiments with different grasses."

They said, "Why do you waste time and money?" or "This is unneces-sary, we have Buffelgrass!"

Such expressions were painful for Mr. Unruh. He was already warn-ing against trusting only Buffelgrass, "Some disease or problem might strike and ruin the crop so it will no longer be useful," he said. That actually happened later exactly as he said it might.

15.3 Kornelius Kroeker, Neuland Colony

From Sandhorst, Neuland, Kornelius was for many years a farm-er and cattleman. He founded a family company, 'Cabaña Kroeker.' About his introduction to Robert Unruh:

When we settled in Neuland, we knew little about farming. Menno and Fernheim had made some progress. But Neulanders were having a difficult time with farming and cattle breeding. So Mr. Unruh came on many occasions to advise us about crops and cattle. "It is unfortunate that the book I have in English is not also printed in German. It is a big help because I didn't study medicine," he said. The point is, he was eager to help and tried hard in all things even if he was not an expert in a particular area.

I remember well a medicine that he provided, 'Terramycin' that helped much. I thanked him and complimented him for his good work. I was pleased that my words did not go to his head. On the contrary he was always humble and modest; he did not introduce himself by saying, "I am Mr. Unruh." No question asked was silly or unimportant, he always an-swered straightforwardly and essentially. He never changed in all the years I knew him.

Mr. Unruh was always ready to help even if the call came from far away. For example, I scouted my fields regularly. One summer with cotton we knew we had a problem, something was not quite right but I could not find what was causing the problem. I telephoned Mr. Unruh. He came and said there is a worm inside the growing bud. He made a recommendation what must be done. My field had no outward sign of distress although I knew something was not quite right and the damage might have been significant. The recommendation did help and probably saved the crop.

Our neighbor, a widow, came to me often for advice. So it was this time she asks, "Why do you spray when you see nothing?" I told her what Mr. Unruh said and she said, "Come and look at my cotton." Her plants were younger so doing the spraying as Unruh said, her cotton was much helped. The woman got an unusually good harvest. So in this way the assistance Mr. Unruh gives to one farmer helps the whole colony.

What I learned from Mr. Unruh not only benefited me but my several children, so his advice is many times multiplied throughout the colony. How often do we hear someone ask, "Why must I do this?" Answer: "Because Bob Unruh said to do it . . ." And he didn't simply tell us what to do, he showed us how to do it. A good example was a problem with mastitis (a cow's udder inflammation/infection). Unruh would show me then say, "Maybe next time you can try it yourself." In this way he was one of us. His work here was of immense help. We want to keep his memory in high honor.

Susan (Penner) Kroeker, Menno Colony

Mrs. Kroeker says the same thing, telling that Bob Unruh helped her father improve his cattle by making it possible for her father to purchase three purebred bulls from U.S.A. In addition he advised and helped establish planting different grasses and storing feed for off season feeding:

By Mr. Unruh's advice, my father also started working with purebred hogs, the large white ones.

15.4 Klaus Kroeker, Fernheim Colony

Was for some years the manager at the Experimental Farm. Klaus was first an Unruh student in the *Zentralschule* and worked his summers at the Farm. Later he became a full time employee at the Farm. He reports that Bob required exactness:

Working with cotton he marked a certain area. Then the plants were counted. Later the caps were counted. When harvested the crop was weighed. Mr. Unruh was exact in this work in the field and in calculating and evaluating the data. I found the summer work interesting, learning beforehand what might be taught in the next central school year. I traveled with him to villages. Working cooperatively I learned a great deal about advisory activities and strategies for service.

Mr. Unruh was in some ways a slave driver. When something needed to be done, he would not slow up. The work continued through siesta time and sometimes into the evening hours. He demanded this of himself and also the workers. Sometimes he got into trouble by pushing too hard. But otherwise Mr. Unruh was more a leader than a boss. He kept a friendly relationship with us. When tensions rose up it was clear there was no ill will toward us, it was merely the situation. It was not beneath him to apologize to the worker or admit he made an error; honesty and exactness where his highest priorities. But whoever did not meet his standards in their work could expect to hear from Mr. Unruh. But when conflicts arose, Mr. Unruh went out of his way to solve problems with calmness and impartiality.

He never seemed to give up. For example, he was called to look at sick cattle. He studied his literature, sent telegrams to experts for advice. He looked 'under every rock' to catch up and train himself to deal with the emergency. Then he said, "I do not know for sure but we will do this . . . and see if it helps."

In another case not an emergency but a cattle illness no person had seen before, he watched the cattle's behavior, studied technical literature, maintained intensive correspondence with experts in USA and other countries. He decided the illness was caused by ticks, a disease to that time unknown in the Chaco. Only by intense, hard work did Mr. Unruh solve this problem.

15.5 Wilhelm Giesbrecht, Agronomist, Menno Colony

Wilhelm was one of the first trained agronomists from the colonies. Bob encouraged and arranged financing for his first year studying

in Asuncion (grant from the Schowalter Foundation). When agronomists were first hired by SAP Bob was their advisor:

> *I always had great admiration and respect for Mr. Unruh. In the
> beginning he had extensive experience and I was the young beginner. He
> helped me much and contributed to my education. Coming from U.S.A.
> he had broad practical knowledge. Coming from school I had theoretical
> knowledge and knew if I needed practical help, Mr. Unruh could be count-
> ed on for backup. He supplied me with information that I needed for my
> work. He corrected me if in my eagerness as a young agronomist I went off
> the track but diplomatically, never in a negative or degrading manner. He
> was this way with every person—particularly young people. In this regard,
> I don't think there is anyone who can be compared with Mr. Unruh. He
> was always dedicated to help young people, to promote them, making sure
> they were not pushed to the side and always provided new chances. In this
> area he was a constant example the entire time I related to him.*

From the many achievements, Wilhelm sees dairy development
and mechanization as his important contributions. He says agriculture
in the Chaco is today what it is because of Robert Unruh's influence.
With regard to character:

> *What I appreciated most about Bob was his uprightness; even in dis-
> agreements, Bob was straightforwardly honest. He was a sincere Christian
> who didn't need to talk; it was plain to see in his actions.*
>
> *I would honor Mr. Unruh with the honorary title; "Agronomist Rob-
> ert Unruh is the father of agricultural development in the Central Chaco
> of Paraguay.*

15.6 Jacob N. Giesbrecht, Menno Colony

Ex-*Oberschulze* (died August 1, 2006, shortly after this interview)

Oberschulze Giesbrecht says he can not find enough words to
show his appreciation for Robert Unruh. But he stresses that Unruh

surrendered his own convenience to help us in the Chaco. And that his self sacrifice was extended to the Indians also:

> *Robert and Myrtle Unruh were human in every way; conspicuously Christian in their life. They tried their best to be useful to others. Sometimes we made excessive demands of them. This was true not only about the Mennonite Colonies but for the Indian settlements and beyond into the Chaco also. He was a pioneer in the economic expansion for the Chaco region. He motivated young people, providing training and arranging financing. That we now have specialists from the colonies happened mostly from his efforts. His proficiency and accomplishments for his fellowmen have borne much good fruit.*

15.7 Widow Katharina (Boschmann) Neufeld, Fernheim Colony

Now living in the assisted living unit in Filadelfia, Katharina was widowed December 4, 1947. Her four children at the time were aged 7 to 1 ½. Then in Hohenau, Fernheim, she continued to farm until 1965. She tells about the support and help from the Unruhs:

> *Economically it was difficult for me as a widow and particularly difficult for the children. When the million dollar credit program began, I needed a third person to co-sign for credit certification. It did not seem possible for me to qualify in this case for several reasons. In this emergency situation I sought guidance and was told, "Ask Robert Unruh!" Mr. Unruh arranged interest free financing making it possible for me to clear ten acres, plant pasture grass for the cows. That was 1961 and for myself and my children I will forever thank Robert Unruh and never forget.*

15.8 Jacob T. Fehr, Menno Colony

Director for many years with SAP, Loma Plata. In this position he developed a close relationship with Robert Unruh. Their association began while organizing the 1977 importation of 85 cattle and 3 young Quarter Horse stallions by airplane from the USA. (see chapter 13):

Robert Unruh was man of practical experience, rather than a theoretician. He did not give up trying to find answers until solving the problem. Often drastic measures were needed for example, the citrus tree necrosis. Some citizens were angry with Unruh and the bad feeling was painful for him.

With his many skills and demands for his attention, his priority was the Experimental Farm. But if some person called and wanted help, no matter how far or how big or small the problem, Mr. Unruh would attend to it. He exerted himself to answer the request; one interesting case I remember well. A farmer in Menno lost 22 cows in a very short time. The sickness puzzled everybody and resisted treatment. Mr. Unruh worked day and night analyzing grass and feed samples, looking through literature, talking with universities and research institutes. He did not give up until finding the answer—poisoning by seed husks from the Palo Santo tree. In such cases Bob Unruh had no equal.

Fehr says in appreciation to Robert Unruh's lasting service in Paraguay:

Robert Unruh will never be forgotten by any person who knew him. Beginning with the first years, he served everyone while kneeling. Whatever the field was, he constantly educated himself and thus converted himself into an authority not stuck in old ruts. On his post-retirement visits to Paraguay the young specialists—as all persons did—gave him abiding respect for his accomplishments. The same holds for Mrs. Unruh. Their work here will be evident and felt for a long time. I welcome every effort to keep alive the memory of these noble people.

15.9 Walter Thielmann, Fernheim Colony

Neither a farmer nor cattleman but serving many years as a minister, church leader, teacher and choir director:

The Unruhs lived in Filadelfia one block from our house. As children we often went into the Unruh yard to play and thereby learned to know them. In Zentralschule *we soon had a new teacher who spoke a strange mixture of Low German, High German and English; somehow we managed. Despite these difficulties a new world was explained to us. Things we thought we knew were presented from a totally new viewpoint.*

Bob Unruh was the right person for the right time. The history of Mennonites in the Chaco would have happened differently had not the Unruhs been there. More people would have exited from here.

The Unruhs shared their faith with us. They were devout Mennonites and were enthusiastic that Mennonite ideals reach out to every person. An early thing they did when coming here was looked for a way to participate in church life. They participated broadly; Robert loved music and singing. He soon emerged as one of the most faithful choir members I had in my 25 years as choir director. Robert held dear his principles of faith and testified in different ways, sometimes with short sermons as introduction to communion. He took part in Bible study where theological books and writings were studied. He lived his convictions in everyday life. His religious orientation and inspiration enabled him to meet the everyday set backs and disappointments. He was a unified person, body and soul in harmony, daily realized. We hold the Unruhs with high esteem as brother and sister in the church community.

15.10 Johann Friesen, Fernheim Colony, Retired Farmer

Mr. Unruh helped where and whenever we needed assistance. At the Experimental Farm he conducted many trials, not many had good results. Some 'new ones' we partly accepted but not immediately. But he held on and after a time we realized his proposals were good ideas.

With cattle, particularly newborn calves, we continuously had grub problems. There were many losses because the remedy available was not effective and caused injury to the applied area. Robert Unruh introduced a new medicine, a bad smelling gel. We called it 'grub grease.' Because the odor was so offensive most cattlemen wanted nothing to do with it. But it worked if the wound was covered; the grub didn't stand a chance.

15.11 Franz Ens, Fernheim Colony

In 1955 Franz was a student studying agronomy with Robert Unruh in the *Zentralschule*. Later a special association developed between them:

Mr. Unruh's classes were interesting, for example how milk is manufactured in the cow's body. We knew a cow gives milk, but how? We had no clue. He explained that the cow's brain controls the hormonal sequences in the cow's bloodstream where it travels to the udder where a chemical process takes place that produces milk. And more, how the cow processes her feed and what might be done in this process to promote greater milk production. This was all very interesting to me.

On economic matters Franz points to Buffelgrass as significance for the dairy industry in the Chaco. And then to his personal relationship with the Unruhs:

The Unruh's were in a friendly circle that included our family. Mr. Unruh was knowledgeable about farming and took a practical approach. We could discuss topics of faith and religion with him. He was not a person of many words but his participation in church was appreciated by all. They were confident people and for our generation a very good example.

15.12 Rudolf Kaethler, a Veterinarian Working With Robert Unruh and Later Fernheim's *Oberschulze*

We lived a short distance from the MCC house in Filadelfia. All persons sent by MCC to the Chaco became our neighbors. We were acquainted with all those who came on their first day in the Chaco. After they were here for a time our family developed a special relationship with the Unruhs. Although I was at that time still a youngster I took a liking to Mr. Unruh. For example, in my ninth year during summer vacation, he was working on the dirty engine of his Jeep that he had taken apart. He allowed me to help clean the parts before putting the engine back together. At that age the experience was extremely interesting.

Bob arranged for Rudolf to study veterinary medicine in Asuncion:

One evening in September, 1959 Mr. Unruh invited my father and me to his home. Also invited were Abram Esau and his son Heinz from Schönbrunn (village No.8). Mr. Unruh made us an offer; allow the sons to study agronomy and veterinary medicine. He said there was available financing through a foundation (Showalter Foundation, Kansas) and MCC in U.S.A. for the next ten years. This is how I studied and became a veterinarian. It is known that Bob Unruh again and again motivated young people to take university study.

Unruh was concerned that the agriculture economy be diversified. He encouraged vegetable growing, fruit trees cultivation, ornamental gardens and small animal production—chickens, ducks, geese—also beef cattle, dairy and hogs. At the same time he looked for other production possibilities for the Chaco. I was surprised how wide ranging his interests were and how intensely he struck out in so many directions at the same time. When his experiments showed good results he was eager to pass on the information to producers and would continue working to improve production.

Kaethler continues by discussing SAP and Unruh's farsighted planning:

In the late 1960s and early 1970s, Bob was much disheartened and frustrated because the colonies were focused elsewhere and unresponsive, neglecting advisory (extension) activities. So he asked MCC to underwrite a study, compile the needs and give recommendations to develop a new program. MCC enlisted two high powered specialists, Drs. Siemens and Kaufman, to spend some time in Paraguay and the Chaco. It turned out unambiguously that centralized experimentation and advisory services was the method for the future. MCC asked if the colonies were ready to work cooperatively to implement the recommendations. If so MCC would find available specialists and money for the reorganization. In this way Robert Unruh was the initiator for a more purposeful and better organized extension service. It was his vision that bringing colony cooperation and advisory activities together would improve progress for the Chaco.

After twenty years in the Chaco Bob was working shoulder to shoulder on an equal level with former students. Kaethler said:

I noticed from time to time young specialists would ask Bob for help and he would help them perform effectively. My first patient after graduating and returning to the Chaco was a horse with colic. Bob and I drove together since at that time I had no vehicle and frankly was feeling a little uncertain about the situation. On the ride I expressed my uneasiness. Bob gave me a few practical tips not taught in medical school. They were correctly practical things I have applied over and over. His counsel and advice helped me get started in practice as well as in later practice in different ways. He was generous in sharing with colleagues all things he found important and good. I was not an exception, his generosity extended to all.

About Unruh's lasting effect, Kaethler says:

There were important developments with lasting effect and some that later disappeared. For example, poultry production; at its peak, going strong, it happened because Bob designed the correct feed and urged us to use it properly. For ten years poultry was 35% our farm economy. Without the big push into chickens our economy would have suffered through that decade and so Bob was responsible for those good results. That was the 'golden sixties.' But one sees nothing more of the poultry industry. The profitable chicken industry in the 1960's generated capital for expansion into other productive areas and became the foundation for milk and meat production that are today the dominant agricultural industries.

At the same time Bob was devoting much effort to improving milk production by improving genetics. The acquisition of foundation stock was a great concern for him for dairy and beef. Today people take silage for granted. We forget it was Bob Unruh who encouraged this feed resource for high milk production. It was Bob who searched for and found the best plants and seeds to grow better silage.

About interpersonal matters:

Because I grew up and worked so closely with Bob I looked carefully and tried to learn and model myself after his example. But in human terms something about Bob seems almost beyond accounting for. He was at times frustrated and hurt by situations that he believed avoidable, poorly executed and appeared to me as intentionally spiteful. I was then surprised, overwhelmed even, when he met those same people calmly and politely and even tempered as usual, offering continued help. Continually focused on his task, even as more barriers were put forward against his projects, he remained sincere and accommodating to those who obstructed his purpose. (Editorial comment: Biblically, turning the other cheek)

Dr. Kaethler suggests perseverance and service continuity as two factors contributing to Bob's legacy:

The advisors MCC considered urgent and sent to the Chaco colonies never stayed very long. Sometimes not long enough to recognize important inherent characteristics and make contributions before their term expired. They were often replaced with yet another short term advisor. In contrast Robert and Myrtle volunteered to continue for another term. Aside from his expertise, hard work and intuitive nature that led to his inspired opportunities for Chaco agriculture, his work continuity made possible the technological progress and higher standard of living that followed in the

1980's. Bob Unruh's continuity is in my view the most relevant factor that made the expression of his talent possible in the Chaco. . . . It was an enormous achievement; Mr. Unruh in agronomics and cattle ranching and Mrs. Unruh in home economics. (See Chapter 15, p. 256)

Conclusions:

Conducting these interviews, there were many tributes from co-workers and friends expressing appreciation for the Unruhs' service in the Central Chaco. Following are some reoccurring threads in these tributes.

The Unruhs did not come into the Chaco as adventurers, to work a few years gaining interesting experiences to return again to their safe homeland. The Unruhs came into the Chaco to serve their disadvantaged brothers and sisters to help them find a better future. The key words are helping to help others.

The Unruhs faced the hostile and bad-tempered Chaco environment like it was. They didn't attempt to duck the discomfort by withdrawing into comfortable quarters. They adapted better than some colonists did.

Robert Unruh worked tirelessly to elevate the economic situation for Mennonites in the Paraguayan Chaco. He never pretended to know all the answers. Nor did he deem it necessary to dominate others to achieve his goals. Together with the Mennonites in the Chaco he persevered. He somehow knew where to look or who to ask. His soft spoken, patient, generous and determined demeanor was his gift to all.

The Unruhs identified with the Mennonites in the Chaco and took to themselves the colonist's burdens. They took part in colony social, cultural and church life. By these actions they gained respect, affection and trust that led Chaco agriculture and homemaking in new directions.

The results of the Unruh's thirty-two year service are significant, particularly visible and noteworthy in the agricultural economic sector. But their service extensions to the indigenous population and to the religious development for the youth were additionally important contributions.

The Unruhs were sincere Christians who lived and acted their convictions as the testimonials make clear. Edgar Stoesz wrote in 1998,

"Bob and Myrtle Unruh were in the best sense Christ-like (Acts 11:26c) earning the name Christians. With their humble and self-less spirit of service they exemplified what it means to be a follower of Christ.

Addendum

Philip Roth, 2008

Preface

This addendum is intended to share impressions from North American contemporaries of Robert and Myrtle Unruh about their Paraguayan Chaco experience and to describe through the eyes of those who served with MCC in that place and time, the lives and conditions of the Mennonite colonists and this singular place.

The second purpose is to add information and insight into MCC's role in the development of the German Mennonite ethnicity in Paraguay. The addendum is linked to Gerhard Ratzlaff's translated German book by chapter headings and has continuity when read in that context.

Prologue

When Bob and Myrtle returned to North America in 1983 they retired to North Newton, Kansas. Participating in a senior citizens group at Bethel College known as "Life Enrichment," Bob prepared a talk in 1994 about their work in Paraguay. Here are extracts. The original is filed with Robert G. Unruh papers in Mennonite Church USA Historical Committee, North Newton, Kansas.

It was on August 23, 1951, when Myrtle and I boarded the S.S. Brazil in New York Harbor and began the long journey to Paraguay for a five year assignment with MCC. My task was to manage a small experiment station that MCC had begun in 1946 in an effort to help the

Mennonite colonies in the Chaco improve their standard of living. Myrtle's assignment was, in the words of a former MCC worker in the Chaco, "To give a feminine touch to agriculture in the Chaco." We had very little idea what we were getting into but it didn't take long to find out after we arrived there!

The colonies Menno, Fernheim and Neuland were located about 250 miles northwest from Asuncion, the capital city. I think our most indelible impressions arriving in the Chaco was the extreme isolation. The regular route for freight and people was to go by riverboat for 3 or 4 days, a narrow gauge railroad for 90 miles that took 10-12 hours and the last 60 miles by wagon or buggy on a trail through the bush.

There were no graded roads. The only motorized vehicles were a Jeep owned by MCC, a Jeep owned by Fernheim colony and a couple of trucks that had been put together with parts from several different makes of trucks salvaged from the battlefields of the Chaco War. A landing strip for small airplanes was built a few years before but only North American visitors or government officials could afford that method of travel.

Settling of the Chaco was really an agricultural experiment. The only things known were that 90% of the land was covered by dense and very thorny scrub forest and that a few small nomadic Indian tribes lived there. Nothing was known about the soil and only after Menno colony was established was it discovered much of the underground water was salty, some water so bad the livestock refused to drink it. The climate was the exact opposite from the settlers experience. Their move from the temperate climates of Canada and Russia to the sub-tropics, where the temperatures range from 100-115 in the shade for months of the year to light frosts in the dry winter months. Rainfall in the Chaco was very sporadic, sometimes 6-8 months of very little or no rain and strong, hot North winds that cause dust storms that penetrate the houses and cut into to one's skin.

When we arrived, the standard of living was at a subsistence level. Farms were small, 10-30 acres in size and farmers depended on animal traction; oxen or horses. This meant a big share of available cropland had to be planted to feed these animals. There were no planted pastures of *significance. Cattle roamed at will and the cropland was fenced to keep animals <u>out</u>. The only marketable farm product was cotton. Peanuts were grown but only enough to supply cooking oil. Watermelons, melons, squash, sweet potatoes, mandioka and black-eyed peas were grown during the summer months. For other vegetables there was no reliable source for seed and besides, the chickens having free range would eat any seeds they found.*

Refrigerators and freezers were nonexistent. There were very few canning jars so food was consumed as grown in season. Everybody had a few head of cattle that lived off whatever they could find in the bush. When cows calved the calf was tied up at the house to keep the cow coming home. In this way the family got a quart of two of milk every day and the calf got only enough to stay alive. But the cow usually quit giving milk after about four months. A cow produced about 140 quarts per lactation. In the dry season there was no milk for the children.

Food products available in the Co-op store were sugar, flour, rice, beans, and a coffee substitute made from kafir. For the first several years flour was scarce and rationed at two lbs per person per month. Rice, beans and flour were often infested with bugs. Meat was available two, some weeks three times per week when one or two animals were slaughtered. There was no electricity, no powered washing machines, so the housewife had a hard lot. Preparing three meals a day was a real challenge.

After Myrtle found different ways of using the little that was available she began to share these recipes with the housewives. She was also asked to teach teen age girls to cook and bake. Until a building was erected at the secondary school that included a room for teaching Home Economics, she did this in our little 8 by 10 kitchen with the few utensils we had. Out of this came a cookbook, which Chaco housewives still use and cherish.

Farming was very difficult and uncertain. Most field work including planting, weed control and harvesting had to be done by hand. The only equipment owned was one or two walking plows, a one row cultivator, hoes, axes and shovels. Plowing could only be done right after a rain of two inches or more if the weather was not too hot for the animals, up to two acres could be plowed in a long day. But planting had to be done within two days after the rain or the topsoil would dry out so much the seed would not germinate. The warm climate produces insects of all description that attack crops and at that time no insecticides were available. Locusts came in great swarms out of Argentina for a number of years, completely destroying crops. Some fields could not be farmed because of leaf cutting ants that stripped the plants bare. They could clean off an acre in one night. The nests were very deep in the ground so they were very difficult to control.

Many people were very discouraged and wanted to leave the Chaco. Even some North American visitors declared that settling people in the Chaco was a great mistake and that the best thing would be to move them out en masse to Canada or some other country. In those first years we often wondered what our role should be in this situation. We resolved to help wherever we could and that resulted in doing things not directly related to agriculture or home economics, like ambulance work with the Jeep, providing transportation for ministers and visitors and just visiting people to get to know them and their problems.

The experiment farm that MCC started was trying to operate on a budget of $500 a year. Because there were no seeds or supplies available in Paraguay, everything was imported so there was never enough money for very many experiments. Most people were skeptical about the Experimental farm helping them. After all, they had lived there for 20 years! One man said if we couldn't produce rain, we couldn't help them as they already knew all there was to know about farming in the Chaco!

Land covered by the dense and thorny bush was considered waste land and useless. The only method for clearing the bush was with an axe and spade; a slow and tedious process. Even if one got it cleared above the ground it was still useless with all the roots underground. So the biggest barrier to development was the general attitude of the people. To many it seemed like a prison from which they would never escape.

Diversification of crops, better land management, insect control and pastures for livestock were the most pressing needs. To get advice, seeds and plant material I wrote many letters to experiment stations and to agricultural schools in the U.S. and other countries such as Australia, Africa, In-

dia, Taiwan, etc. It took much time to get a reply, sometimes 6 to 8 months, because mail service into the Chaco was extremely slow. The information asked for covered a wide range of agriculture; from growing vegetables, identifying insects and diseases, livestock management and diseases, soil management and farm machinery.

One thing introduced in our first term was Buffelgrass, native to southwest Africa. It proved to be well adapted to Chaco conditions. I came upon it by accident. Abe Peters from Corn, Oklahoma was my predecessor at the Experimental Farm. He left leaving old issues of the Oklahoma Stockman magazine in the MCC house. Since we had no mail for the first month, Myrtle and I read the discarded magazines word by word, cover to cover. One carried an article about Buffelgrass recently introduced into Texas. I thought it worth trying in the Chaco and wrote for information and ordered seed.

It took a couple of years to recognize its potential and to gather enough seed to plant on a larger scale. But after people saw the rapid growth, the drought resistance and the high yield on cleared bush land, they became enthusiastic about it. I consider Buffelgrass the most important thing the Experimental Farm did because it changed the whole attitude of the colonists toward bush land and the Chaco in general. We tried many other grasses and some have proven useful in specific areas where Buffelgrass doesn't do well. But it is still the most widely planted grass in the area and its use has spread to Argentina and Bolivia.

Over the years the farm was instrumental in introducing improved varieties of cotton, peanuts and sorghum that improved yields significantly and introduced new crops such as castor beans, safflower and sesame. Significant also was getting improved citrus varieties, areola cherries and other fruits, ornamental shrubs and shade trees—and that is another story we don't have time for today.

Changes in the Chaco came as a result of many people working together. Farmers became more and more interested in what the farm was doing. Gratefully some were willing to try new methods of soil management and new crops. When mechanization came in the late 1960s, we started *a more intensive extension program. By then farmers had questions about livestock diseases, feeding, pasture management and machinery mainte-nance.*

The Indians working for Mennonite farmers played an important part in Chaco development by cleaning up cleared land, building fences, working in the fields, weeding and helping with crop harvesting. From this grew the Indian settlement program that today has settled over 8,000 Indians.

Other things that played an important role, to mention a few:

1952 – U.S. AID loaning a peanut threshing machine that helped start mechanization

1953 – Private loans from individuals in US and Canada to setup a peanut oil refinery so that oil could be marketed outside the colonies

1954-1956 – Road building by Vern Buller and land clearing with a bulldozer. Regular air service between Asuncion and Filadelfia

1958 – Schowalter grants for the Experimental Farm, a tremendous boost. And funds to educate young persons in agriculture

1960 – First livestock air shipments donated by Pennsylvania Men-nonites. Later shipments from Kansas and Texas followed

Late 1960s and 1970s – Major increase in mechanization, changes in farming technology, Cattle ranching on a bigger scale   Transchaco Road-way opened

ZP-30 radio in Filadelfia, a tremendous help in extension work

1980s – Beef and dairy development through loans from IMF, U.S. and European banks

A few statistics to show the changes:

	1950	*1993*
Cropland	*20,000*	*75,000*
Pasture	*practically none*	*600,000*
Catle	*16,791*	*325,884*
Cattle sold	*practically none*	*100,000*
Milk	*not available*	*15,604,695 gallons*
Tractors	*3*	*1,938*

In 1993 Menno Colony alone:
  31 bulldozers
  34 peanut combines
  25 cotton pickers
  508 milking machines with bulk holding tanks in each village
  103 trucks
  902 pick-up trucks
  952 cars
  2,024 motorcycles
  2456 bicycles
  3627 home refrigerators and freezers

Fernheim and Neuland now have electricity in all villages with correspondingly the same general statistics as Menno. Development continues at a rapid pace. Current plans call for a three-colony slaughter house at Mariscal Estigarribia near the large airport, with the intention to export meat by air. The cost is estimated at $12,000,000.

Note:

The airport was built by Paraguayan President Alfredo Stroessner in 1970. Early speculation that it might become an international hub for commercial air traffic gave rise to the plans for a meat packing facility and drove colony land prices sharply higher. But that did not happen. Later speculation in 2005-2006 that the US might lease it as a military base did not happen either. Thirty-eight years later in 2008 the concrete airport runway, better than 2 miles long sits unused in the middle of nowhere without buildings or improvements.(http://en.wikipedia.org/wiki/Mariscal_Estigarribia)

Introduction

Bob spent much time in the early years on his knees, examining plant disease or insect injury, grafting citrus rootstock and examining sick or injured livestock. Thus the "kneeling" reference.

"Kneeling" to examine crop plants, in this picture grafting citrus trees.

Chapter 1: Childhood and Youth

1.1 The early years in Montana were promising economically until broad weather patterns shifted. From 1919 into the 1930s, the Missouri River basin was tenaciously gripped in a severe drought; pioneering the expansive Montana prairie reversed into a risky venture. Faced with declining grain prices and a nationwide economic crisis after World War I many farmers declared bankruptcy.

In what would prove a cruel trick of nature, a period of above average rainfall produced deceptively good crops. Local ranchers gave glowing testimonials that appeared in promotional literature, contributing to the rapid influx . . . after 1900. New communities sprang up. . . . The end of WWI [1919] brought crop failures and a drop in agricultural prices that hit hard. Montana's post WWI depression extended through the 1920's and right into the Great Depression of the 1930's, ruining many farmers. The overly optimistic promotion of agricultural potential was only part of a larger problem. The end of higher-than-average rainfall exposed a basic truth; 320 acres (1/2 section) proved inadequate to make a living in dry land eastern Montana and most were forced to abandon their dreams of farming in the area. (Montana Mainstreets, published by the Montana Historical Society).

1.1.1 Giant stride as described by Verney Unruh.

A pole with 8 chains spaced around the top hanging down with handles. Children grab the chains and start running around the pole. When they get up enough speed their feet leave the ground and they take 'giant strides' as centrifugal force moves them outward and their feet inches off the ground.

1.3 The new mother was Frieda Schmidt, who left the security and comfort of relatives to marry a man 13 years her senior and become a stepmother to five children. Frieda and Anna were second cousins. In later life Frieda confided to her stepchildren that the decision to marry a widower, many years her senior, with five children was especially difficult because she had an aunt who took a similar route with unhappy consequences. Luckily, Frieda did not share that unhappiness with a marriage that continued until death.

1.6 After an August harvest, Bob and Gordon Sawatsky, a Bethlehem Mennonite student transferring from Grace Bible to Bethel, began their journey to North Newton in a 1936 Willys (nicknamed 'Little Willy') Bob had purchased earlier that summer. Planning to drive straight through the night, Bob dozed off in the wee hours outside Hebron, Nebraska and ran 'Little Willy' into the ditch breaking a front wheel spindle attachment. Fortunately, neither was hurt beyond bruises (despite lacking seat belts and air bags in mid 20th century automobiles). The next morning they arranged to have the car repaired and caught a bus for North Newton, Kansas.

1.6.1 Myrtle was a senior at Bethel and four years older than Bob, her student status a bit unusual. She had been a freshman in 1935, returned to help out at home after her sophomore year, then worked in Wichita as a secretary in 1945-46. Myrtle returned to Bethel in 1946 to finish a B.S. in Economics and Business Administration. After she graduated (1948) Myrtle worked in Bethel's administrative office until Bob graduated in 1950.

1.7 Bill Snyder knew Willard and Verney from serving together in CPS during World War II.

CPS; **C**ivilian **P**ublic **S**ervice during World War II was one alternative service option for conscientious objectors in lieu of military service, performing 'work of national importance.' CPS men served without wages supported by families and church congregations. MCC, American Friends Service Committee and Brethren Service Committee administered most CPS camps. CPS'ers were not released until 19 months after the war ended serving as forest fire control parachuting, erosion and flood control, human medical experimentation subjects (a few died from live virus trials. Others were given starvation diets to study the effects) and mental health hospital orderlies. CPS men were in some cases responsible for institutional reforms in state hospitals and the Mennonite Mental Health program grew from this WWII experience. (http://en.wikipedia.org/wiki/Civilian_Public_Service)

1.7.1 To be sure, Bob's letter to Bill Snyder, December 16, 1950 projects a good sense of his disciplined and scrupulously methodical side—rarely if ever impulsive, hasty, or rushing headlong into something. It might be the only time Bob ever drove himself into a ditch doing something rash was driving into the early morning hours on the way to Bethel College!

Archival correspondence does not reveal the sequence but we might speculate that Abe Peters, director of Fernheim's experimental farm (a joint project with MCC), not wishing to extend his service to a second term, expressed his desire to Miller that December 1950. After hearing back from Orie Miller, Bill Snyder on January 26, 1951, wrote again to Bob and Myrtle that MCC needed a director for the experimental farm in Fernheim Colony, Paraguay. With penetrating insight Bill Snyder observes in this letter that service among the Unruhs' far distant relatives in Paraguay presented a ". . . near perfect situation for all concerned." Later events will show this to be a most prescient assertion.

The Unruh's January 21 letter with a completed application form and Snyder's letter of January 26 letter crossed in the mail. After more letters are exchanged, the Unruhs agreed to a five-year first term in Paraguay. Snyder says MCC will have Voluntary Service young men already in Paraguay keep an eye on things until the Unruhs arrive in Paraguay later in the year.

1.8 Regarding Bob's personality: He was the personification of humility. He never appeared to take himself too seriously. He didn't waste emotional energy on trivia and was ethically beyond reproach; there was no sense of a hidden agenda. He was not prone to deep philosophical reflection about existential matters or broad strategic issues. Bob and Myrtle were serious persons engaged in important and moral business with a job to do and they somehow did it without being noticeably assertive.

Bob was not gifted with a commanding presence. That is, others were not automatically deferential by reason of a dominant personality or striking physical appearance. Bob was not the "take charge" executive type. He was not a "salesman," given to hyperbole or profound synoptic utterances or inclined to articulate a majestic vision to others. An added difficulty, Bob's conversational German never quite met muster. He was focused on and devoted to his clear-cut task as he understood it to be. Not inclined to make waves or stir up the water, he appeared to go out of his way to avoid conflict (not aggressive), being at ease with himself and self-assured.

Bob did however project the aura of a man on a mission; focused and disciplined. He was remembered as a good listener, approachable. He always took time to respond to others often with nothing more than a smile of reciprocal recognition. He was without pretense or self importance, never projecting self-absorption or the slightest arrogance. He was perceived by co-workers as steady, reliable, predictable, the same today as yesterday with no reason to expect a different response tomorrow.

And most important to their contributions in Paraguay, Bob and Myrtle showed repeatedly that they were thoughtful, considerate and accommodating "can do" persons. One North American co-worker, John Peters, sums up Bob's approach as, "You know, this is a good thing to do and we need to find a way to do it, never mind the difficulties."

1.8.1 Bethlehem Pastor John Franz's Attempted Lynching
A near miscarriage of vigilante justice

In the spring of 1918 with World War I not yet ended, intense history unfolded in eastern Montana that in a back-handed way strengthened the Bethlehem Mennonite community.

Anti-German sentiment was running high against German ethnic groups who continued German language instruction. This sentiment impacted many Mennonite congregations, particularly those west of the Appalachians, who continued German in spoken word and in singing. Montana passed the Montana Sedition Act of 1918 that authorized 'Council of Defense' committees throughout the state to roundup suspected subversive persons and to enforce regulations by destroying or at minimum, removing from circulation German books and literature wherever found.

April 25, 1918, the *Yellowstone Monitor* Glendive's only newspaper, a weekly, included the following on a page with legal notices:

GERMAN BANNED IN SCHOOLS OF MONTANA
Helena, April 23.— The state council of defense today ordered that use of the German language in public and private schools cease in the state, and in the pulpit. Preachers using German must hereafter use English or remain silent. German books and histories must be thrown out of public and private school libraries. John G. Brown, a Helena attorney, was hired as special prosecutor for the council to see that these orders are obeyed. The council also ordered that every able-bodied man in the state go to work at some useful task at least five days a week, whatever his financial condition be. A long list of books, German and in other tongues that are under

the ban will be issued and their disuse enforced. Librarians, school officials, ministers, etc., who disobey the order are warned that punishment will be severe.

On Saturday, April 6, 1918, the Dawson County sheriff, county district attorney in two cars along with a posse, drove unto the Independent School house yard, where Rev. John Franz, his wife and several other couples were attending a meeting to deal with school business matters. School age children accompanying their parents were playing in the school yard. One man entered the school building and motioned for Rev. Franz, seated in the assembly, to step outside. He did so.

It is not known whether Rev. Franz and Sheriff Twible were acquaintances. But Rev. Franz recognized Twible and Dawson County's district attorney in the group. Outside, Franz was forcibly hustled into one car. No explanation for this seizure was given except the off hand comment, "You are the man making all this trouble." And something in the vein, "We're taking you for a ride."

With the commotion outside, the school meeting halted and Mrs. Franz coming outside rushed to her husband. In the third trimester of pregnancy, clinging to the car, she was roughly pushed and fell to the ground in a brief scuffle. This swift and unanticipated event must have come as a great surprise to everybody, not the least to Franz. We might assume it was known county wide that Franz had earlier gone to Helena (state capital) to arrange non-combatant status for Mennonites (perhaps more than once). Moreover, he was receiving newspapers and church material printed in German; one was his hometown newspaper from Mt. Lake, Minnesota with a section written in German. These details combined to support and embellish public perception of Mennonites as German sympathizers and Rev. Franz as their leader.

The two cars departed with Rev. Franz. A few miles out-side Glendive along a tributary to the Yellowstone River the cars stopped. Now, trees are a rarity on the highland plateaus in Eastern Montana but here stood a high and sturdy tree on the river bank. Imagine Franz's sense of foreboding as men swing a heavy rope over a sturdy lower, horizontal limb. This tree might have served frontier vigilantes administering frontier justice to bank robbers, cattle rustlers and sundry outlaws, some years earlier. (Montana was second only to Texas in vigilante lynch-ing.) There must have been some uncertainty and not 100% agreement about doing this deed, because the sheriff or the county attorney stopped the lynching at the last minute when Franz appealed, especially to the sheriff, reminding him that he had taken an oath to uphold the law and administer justice. Franz related that his grandfather and father were naturalized citizens, that he was a natural born citizen of United States; did they want this breach of justice part on the county's record and their names attached to his unlawful death?

News of Franz's abduction rapidly spread through the Mennonite community. The Bethlehem Church board quickly met and decided five men would accompany Regina and her two school age sons to Glendive in one member's automobile (auto's were rare, horses and buggies still the dominant means for transport). Arriving in Glendale around 4 p.m. and going to the jail, Sheriff Twible was not inclined to allow Mrs. Franz admittance to see her husband. Twible finally relented when she persisted. Once inside the jail she then refused to leave. Af-ter considerable argument and her pregnancy in consideration along with Rev. Franz's pleas, Twible instructed his deputy to clear out a closet area to accommodate Regina and her two sons.

A public hearing in Glendive's city hall was held Mon-day evening, about 7:00 p.m. Around 200 persons attended.

Searching Dawson County Court records for that period comes up empty for documentation on a hearing. Legend has it Regina and her two sons waited outside; we're not certain whether by her choice or by officiating mandate.

It didn't take long. Franz later said many people fired rapid questions. One question was, "Why do Mennonites refuse to buy war bonds?" His answer corresponded to "Because we see little difference between financing a war and directly killing another human being. Rather than buying war bonds we have contributed more money to war relief (Red Cross) than any other community of our size in all of Montana."

The hearing's outcome: Bethlehem church services in the German language prohibited. That Franz report to the district court quarterly accounting for his activities, until the war declared over and third, a $3,000 bond was required for his release and for the duration until the case closed. The church board met the next morning and individually pledged their real estate as security for the bond. The Franz family was home together once again by evening, Wednesday, April 10.

At the district court's next meeting within a month, the bond was cancelled and Rev. Franz received a letter stating his case was dismissed and closed.

The *Yellowstone Monitor,* Thursday, April 11, 1918, ran on page four a one paragraph note, mixed with other social news.

Rev. M.(sic) Franz of Retah was arrested the latter part of last week by Sheriff Twible on sedition charges. Rev. Franz is pastor of a German Mennonite colony and was charged with having spread German propaganda and having opposed the draft. Wednesday he was interviewed by the authorities and denied being disloyal. The evidence not being strong enough to warrant conviction, he was cautioned regarding his future actions and given his liberty.

Rufus Franz, Rev. John Franz's oldest son states that the treason charges against the Bethlehem Mennonites were brought by several non-Mennonite neighbors who were later discredited and fled from Dawson County fearing reprisal from non Mennonite citizens who regarded their Mennonite neighbors with respect. Rufus also mentions that a few years afterward, one member of the lynching party drove to Rev Franz's homestead and asked for Franz's forgiveness - instantly granted. That man later became a district judge. This appalling event shook the community deeply.

Mullet, Cindy *Glendive Ranger Review*, November 22, 2001, "Glendive pastor nearly lynched"

Franz, Rufus M. *Mennonite Life*, October 1952, pp181-184, Rev. John Franz's oldest son, an eye witness

75th Anniversary Bethlehem Mennonite Church, 1987,

Dick, La Verne J., *The Mennonite*, April 2, 1964,

Bauman, E. H., *Coals of Fire*

――――――――――

Verney says:

"This incident is part of our family history as dad and mother (Anthony Unruh and Anna Albrecht) *planned to be married the next day on Sunday afternoon, April 7th. Of course with the pastor in jail it appeared that the wedding would have to be postponed."*

Leslie fills in the details:

"Dad and a friend who had a car drove to Lambert, about 20 miles, to talk with the Congregational minister to ask him to come to Bethlehem Mennonite church to perform the wedding. The harness maker in Lambert was a friend of Anthony's and agreed to bring the minister that afternoon, so the wedding was held at 3:00 p.m. on April 7, 1918 after all."

Verney adds:

"Of course the wedding was to be a happy day, but there was a cloud over the wedding because Rev. Franz was away, his fate uncertain. On Sunday, nobody in the community knew for certain what might happen next.

Chapter 2: Mennonite Colonies, 1927 to 1945

2.2 From Robert Snyder, one MCC voluntary service young man in Paraguay in a 2003 interview:

Darrell Albright and I were the first VS'ers assigned to Paraguay, arriving August 1949. Bill Snyder requested we look after the Chaco Experimental Farm when Abe Peters left in April 1951, until Bob Unruh would arrive later in the year. We had some really memorable experiences on the Experimental Farm. Did you ever see grasshoppers being hatched? Grasshoppers would drill about a ¼" hole about 3" deep to lay eggs. Right beside the field where we had peanuts growing, there was a little sandy area with a barbed wire fence. We had an infestation of grasshoppers there all around the edge of that peanut field. The holes were visible if you knew what to look for. One time we came upon the grasshoppers starting to hatch. Little tiny grasshoppers, ¼" long were coming up out of these holes, I mean just boiling up out of the ground, hundreds of them from one hole. They just covered the ground then. We ran to the barn and got some grasshopper poison we had there, sawdust with poison on it. We went out and made a line by scattering this stuff along the fence. Some of them had already come together and started moving in one direction together. Because they completely covered the ground, a layer deep, standing there watching it was just like the earth was moving. They came to this poison stuff and started eating on it. Pretty soon they started dropping. Well then, more grasshoppers would walk over the dead grasshoppers, so we'd make another line. We kept doing this to stop them because if they got to the peanut field, they'd have the field stripped even though they weren't flying or fully grown. By that time some may have grown to maybe 1/2 to ¾ inch or more in a day's time, they grew fast. They'd come to the fence and start climbing up the post and we would stand there and watch as they climb up the post then no place to go they would jump off. So, there was a fountain of grass hoppers, just like a water fountain! I mean that sounds unreal but that's the way it was. By standing there and watching them move we were able to scatter the poison just ahead of them, to stop them. Some of them got by but we saved the peanut crop. They all seemed to hatch at the same time. We monitored for a couple of days until we saw they were pretty well under control.

2.4 Gerhard Ratzlaff reports that G. G. Hiebert was a Russian Mennonite fruit grower from California. In 1921 (following World War One, shortly after MCC was organized for relief activity) Hiebert served with MCC in Russian on a relief project. In April 1930 for one year he served MCC in Paraguay to help with Fernheim settlement.

2.5 MCC purchased *Corporacion Paraguaya* in the "crisis year" 1937. It is not clear exactly what assets MCC received in exchange for a $57,500 payment for corporate stock. It appears to be a transaction intended to break the connection and ease the tensions between the colonies and the inept management of *Corporacion Paraguaya*. In 1952 *Corporacion Paraguaya* was cleared from MCC's books in a "liquidation;" again it was not clearly recorded what assets or to whom transferred. The "liquidation" might have been little more than an offsetting accounting entry against equity on MCC's balance sheet. (Willard H. Smith, *Corporacion Paraguaya*, from *The Mennonite Encyclopedia*, 1955, IX-3-3 MCC Paraguayan Immigration, 1920-33, Mennonite Church USA Historical Committee, Goshen, Ind.)

There possibly were sound reasons to close Palo Santo. As highminded as Casado's experimental station endeavor appeared to Mennonites, Palo Santo was simple arithmetic and good business for the Casado enterprise. With two Mennonite migrations in three years and anticipating further development into their extensive Chaco land holdings (stemming from an early miscommunication during Menno's migration, Paraguayan officials were expecting a 20,000 Mennonite migration altogether. (J W Fretz, *Pilgrims in Paraguay,* Herald Press, Scottdale, Pa. 1953, p.15) For the minimal cost of housing and food, Casado Corporation received valuable data for planning their own corporate expansion into the Chaco. (Palo Santo was near Casado's operational western edge in the Paraguayan Chaco.)

But after five years, the great distance from villages with too little systematic interaction for colonists to comprehend what was happening at Palo Santa (editor Siemens certainly gave his best effort), likely cooled Mennonite patron farmer support. Second, the disruptive Chaco War (1932-1935). Third and most important, the Casado Corporation likely saw no potential return on their investment with no migrations since Fernheim five years before. These three contributing factors likely compounded into a clear and easy decision for the Casado principals to cut their costs and close down *Palo Santo*. (Author's reasoning, no supporting documentation)

2.6 Without the means to finance Esau's training, Fernheim's *Oberschulze* Jakob Siemens appealed to MCC representative Harold S. Bender during Bender's visit to the colonies in 1938. (It appears Bender was highly regarded by Fernheimers having helped them through Germany in 1929.) Bender on the spot pledged $90 a month for one year to support Esau's education and to expand the gardening project. In his report to MCC's executive committee months later Bender cited his commitment and recommended viewing favorably any future Fernheim request for increased funding for agricultural development writing, ". . . it will be money well spent." (MCC files, Paraguay, Mennonite Church USA Historical Committee, Goshen, Ind.)

2.7 An excellent book with interesting detail on this disquieting interlude; John D. Thiesen, *Mennonite and Nazi?: Attitudes Among Mennonite Colonists in Latin America, 1933-1945,* Herald Press, Scottdale, Pa., 1998. A worthy read.

Observation on the struggle for survival: leaders who suffer the consequences of their decisions generally make better decisions than leaders in a position of privilege who do not directly suffer the consequences of their decisions. Such was the case colonizing the Chaco; <u>every</u> person suffered the consequences of every decision.

Chapter 3: Experimental Farm, 1946 to 1951

3.1 B. H. Unruh advocated Fernheim's loyalty to National Socialist Germany [the *Third Reich* or Nazi Germany]. MCC broke off their working relationship with Unruh when his views and letter writing to Fernheim leaders became offensive to MCC. (MCC files, Paraguay, Mennonite Church USA Historical Committee, Goshen, Indiana) North American Mennonite missionaries in Argentina made a failed attempt to "pour oil on troubled waters" in Fernheim; on balance the effort might have created more resentment toward North Americans in Fernheim. (Richer descriptive details in Thiesen's 1998 book)

3.1.1 "*Big brother in the north helping little brother in the south*" was an expression attributed to O.O. Miller at some point in the 1930s speaking to an administrative assembly in Fernheim, according to legend. At times in later years Orie Miller used variations of the expression and in 1955 in his brief public tribute at Fernheim's 25th anniversary celebration. (MCC files, Paraguay, Mennonite Church USA Historical Committee, Goshen, Ind.) No written documentation was found to support the assertion that Miller was the author, although plausible.

3.2 MCC's country office: The shift from dispensing transitory emergency aid through gifts (1920s) to resettlement and helping aid recipients become self-supporting, meant MCC navigating uncharted territory. Bill Snyder's tenure first as MCC Associate Executive Secretary, then as Executive Secretary in 1958, gave expression to this self sufficiency concept as "development," the trademark of his twenty-four year administration. (W.T. Snyder Oral History, 1982, throughout text)

The first Paraguay country director was Willard H. Smith, a history and political science professor from Goshen College (1929-72) in Goshen, Indiana. One of several recommendations from Smith to

MCC's executive committee in 1945 was to expand the Chaco's agricultural output.

Goshen College faculty and staff played a prominent role in Fernheim's early development. In addition to Smith, Harold S. Bender, Goshen's professor in church history, Bible, sociology and dean, also on MCC's executive committee, helped Fernheimers through Germany 1929-30 and traveled to Paraguay representing MCC after 1930.

Sanford C. Yoder, recently retired Goshen College President (1923-1940) and Secretary for the Mennonite Board of Missions (1921-1944) took an active interest in Paraguay colonization visiting the Chaco in August 1940 and authored a book about his trip, *Down South American Way* (Herald Press, Scottdale, PA, 1943). His visit came after the Argentinean Mennonite missionaries failed attempt at intra-colony reconciliation and following an unyielding letter from MCC to Fernheim's *Oberschulze,* making clear MCC's position against the apparent weakening of Mennonite principles and cautioning that Fernheim ran the risk of losing privileged status and their nearly complete independence from Paraguayan government oversight. Yoder mentions the colonist's courageous physical struggle, expressive emotional discouragement, observations about Fernheim's prevailing religious and educational commitment and obliquely the burdening and stressful ideological conflict over German political allegiance using the words "important" and "startling." (S.C. Yoder, *Down South American Way,* pp. 131, 134) He also arrived with a $50 contribution from MCC for Fernheims secondary school (*Zentralschule*) "but refused to hand the money over because of the school's political atmosphere." Yoder is remembered; "a shrewd man who could be firm and yet reconciling." (*Mennonite and Nazi?* pp. 138-140)

Christian L. Graber, Goshen College business manager (1924-1949) who served as MCC South American director 1954-56 to organize the Trans Chaco Roadway and again in 1963 when commissioned by MCC to evaluate and make recommendations on Chaco Indian Settlement after the settlement program hit a bump in the road following a Chulupi Indian uprising (chapter 12).

3.2.1 STICA: Bill Snyder's liaison and rapport with influential US Foreign Service bureaucrats, and his shrewd comprehension about the way things work politically in government power circles were decisive factors in successfully getting US government aid to the Mennonite colonies several times. For instance, urging MCC personnel to develop good working relationships with STICA operatives—both U.S. and Paraguayan—in Paraguay is an early example. MCC personnel performed well and ethically in these ground level positions and built favor and confidence among US bureaucrats that Snyder then leveraged to build his case for the next aid block to the Mennonite colonies. As the Unruh story unfolds we will notice this important Bill Snyder thumbprint again and again. Of course, as Paraguayan Mennonite development progressed, he discreetly played down his ability to lean on big government, something not widely endorsed by North American Mennonite constituencies in mid-20th century. (Arguable intuition, no supporting documentation)

3.3 Menno Klassen (1917-2000) was born in Laird, Saskatchewan. From 1922 until young adulthood he lived in Neuanlage, near Altona, Manitoba. He completed a four-year agriculture degree at the University of Manitoba. After graduation he worked for the Rhineland Agricultural Society based in Altona, promoting 4-H, animal health, and special crop production programs. He also shared in the leadership of the Altoona Youth Forum. Later he worked in Paraguay with the resettlement of Mennonites refugees from Russia and Europe. . . . He remained an advocate for various peace and justice causes and volunteered in many church committees such as Moose Lake Camp, long after his retirement in 1982. He was married to Agatha Enns (1918-) and together they had five children. (www.mennonitechurch.ca/programs/archives/holdings/papers/Klassen,%20Menno%20fonds.htm)

3.4 A later agreement in a few years; MCC agreed to split annual farm operating expenses 50/50, to pay 100% for machinery and equipment and to pay the full salary, benefits and travel expenses for a North American director. In Abe Peters and Robert Unruh's case, salary and benefits exceeded many times over the annual farm operating budget split 50/50. For Bob's first years the annual funding was $500 or $250 each from MCC and Fernheim. There was some miscommunication or at least unclear agreement on the 50-50 split. It was Fernheims position that the experimental farm should be self supporting, generating enough revenue from farm products sold to support the non-productive experimental projects. At years end when accounts were squared, Fernheim administrators would request MCC make up (offset) farm operating deficits, if any. It appears off the record, the Experimental Farm cost Fernheim very little out-of-pocket.

3.4.1 In a 2003 interview about work at the experimental farm in 1951, Robert Snyder, said,

Near the farm was where the first Moro Indian fatality happened. We went out to the abandoned house, did a little hunting. I think Abe Peters was with us when we went out to look at the place. By the time we got there the house was abandoned for some time. They were vulnerable because the house was remote, not in a village.

After that, a year or so before I got there, there was another attack. A

young couple was sitting down to lunch, again in a remote location north from Menno Colony. The Indians came out of the bush and got into the house. The wife hid in a corner and one Indian came down on her with a knife-like weapon but couldn't get a good swing. She turned away and the knife caught her on the face. Apparently he thought he had done his damage. The husband was on the floor unconscious and they

Mr. & Mrs. Bernard Plett, 1951. Photo credit: Robert Snyder.

rammed a spear through his leg into the floor. Then suddenly they were gone. That's the story as I heard it. I can't remember the names. (Mr. & Mrs. Bernard Plett, both survived)

The experimental farm would have been a good place to hit; it was isolated and first in line from the bush in the north to Filadelfia. We had a spot in the bush a little distance (from the buildings) *where we got our wa-*

Abandoned Stahl Homestead, 1951. Photo credit: Robert Snyder.

ter at a well. We'd take a barrel on a wagon out there (to dip water with a bucket from the well and transport to the house) *with horses and we'd keep an eye out, especially at high noon or near evening; we were careful and alert.*

(Later Moro attacks also happened in the heat of mid day to late afternoon.)

C. J. Dyck, interview 2003:

I remember that Abe Peters had a constant concern that he might get killed by Indians on the farm. One of the precautions Abe took was to plant tall crops far away from the buildings and beans and low grow-ing crops close by so that they could not hide close in and sneak up on his house.

Abe Peters is remembered by Fernheim farmers who knew him as something of a loner and Mennonite maverick but friendly and easy-going. It was said he carried a revolver and on occasion demonstrated that he was a competent marksman. (In conversation with a Fernheim Farmer in 2002 and Maurice Kauffman, 2003)

Chapter 4: Journey to Paraguay

On the second stop in Uruguay, Bob visited a Uruguayan show-place farm. He was impressed with the outstanding program development and made connections that might come in useful later on. (Family letters)

4.1 Robert Snyder recalls his stay at Hotel Casado:

On our first trip to the Chaco, up the river to Puerto Casado, we arrived at night and went to the hotel. We had four choices:

1. Just an empty, open room, no doors

2. A room and one blanket

3. A room, blanket and bed

4. A room, blanket, bed and mattress

We were forewarned to take mosquito nets and sleeping bags, so we took number 4. During the night we could hear the mosquitoes trying to get to us through the nets. By morning it was chilly and we shivered even though we were fully dressed but still cold.

—Myrtle writes October 14, 1951 in a family circle letter:

We left Asuncion on a Saturday evening and traveled [upriver] *by riverboat until midnight Tuesday. Through some misunderstanding we did not have any cabin for the trip but on Sunday morning we got one because someone cancelled. When you travel without a cabin you sleep on a filthy mattress on the dining room floor with whoever else happens to be as unfortunate as you. . . . The food was what we classed as terrible and the drinking water was just taken up out of the river. So we just did not drink any water. But 3 ½ days is a long time to do without water when it's so hot. We managed by drinking bottled orange drink that may have had as many germs, but at least it was a commercially sold product.*

We got to Puerto Casada at midnight, only 14 hours late. We went to the hotel [only one hotel in Puerto Casada with open windows and* shutters, no glass or screens and only a few interior doors] *where we tried to sleep and in the morning took the Auto via to End Station.*

At End Station [end of the railroad 90 miles into the Chaco interior from the river, the only access to the colonies with 62 miles more to Filadelfia] *we got on a colony truck which was loaded with freight. The passengers were all piled on top and enjoyed a rather rough trip which included ducking under low overhanging branches and three 'mate' stops. . . . The first 25 miles of the road was terrible. In all of Montana you couldn't even find a badlands road like it. But we finally are here. Bob Snyder was here at the MCC house and had a kerosene lamp burning, the electricity is out of order for another week* [usually 2 ½ hours every evening]. *We set our things into the house then went over to the neighbors to eat. We can get tomatoes and cabbage at the farm, flour and sugar at the cooperative but right now there isn't much else to eat but noodles and meat. Most of the gardening is done in the winter here, planted at the same time you do. We still want to try* [vegetable] *planting now, as soon as it rains, to get something to eat. Otherwise cooking here will prove quite interesting. I plan to can tomatoes sometime this week. A few cans of imported fruit* [from Argentina or Chile] *are for sale. They tell us oranges, lemons and grapefruit will be ripe in another month. Everyone is wishing for rain since it hasn't rained much since May. They had a shower the day before we arrived or we wouldn't have any water at our house.*

The houses here are fair and some really quite nice, only one is very modern with an indoor bathroom. Our MCC house needs a few gallons of paint, a few leaks in the roof fixed and the floor smoothed out." [A one room addition to the house had a badly deteriorating concrete floor and an unusual piece of furniture for the Chaco, an upright piano, one of only a few pianos in the three colonies.]

It was terribly hot in church this morning. I resolved to take a towel to church from now on. . . . The sermons [usually more than one] *alone lasted 1 hour and 10 minutes and of course, Sunday school is only for children at 7:00 a.m.*

Yerba Mate tea: "*Mate*" derives from an Indian word "*mati*" meaning gourd. *Mate* or correctly *Yerba Mate* (sometimes referred to as *Tetera* in Paraguay) is a water tea beverage brewed from dried leaves and stems from the Yerba tree (*Ilex-Paranguariensis*, similar to laurel or holly) growing in subtropical regions of South American and consumed originally from a gourd (*guampa*)—later a cow horn and today any suitable container—through a hollow metal or wooden tube with a filter on the lower end, "*bombilla*" (little pump). It is equivalent to a group coffee break except that every person in the group drinks from the same container and uses the same *bombilla* and might last longer than any reasonable North American employer would tolerate. Dr. John Schmidt termed this practice "community immunization." *Mate* had high caffeine content and helped the colonists physically cope with the harsh environment. Second to the physical stimulation was the social aspect. (*Garden in the Wilderness*, p. 183)

Auto Via. A Ford Model A (vintage 1928-31) retrofitted with steel wheels that ran on the narrow gauge railroad between Puerto Casado and End Station (Km.145). It sometimes pulled a small, open railroad car with wooden benches for seats, much like an open trolley car. The Auto Via might run the 145 kilometer trip (90 miles) in about 3 – 3.5 hours (if it didn't break down or run into conflict with the train traveling the single track) compared with 10 or more hours by train, because it traveled faster and didn't stop for all passengers along the tracks wanting to board, as did the train. It did not run on a schedule rather as prearranged charter and was considered 'luxury' transportation costing more than train fare.

"Roads" were paths of least resistance through the bush and impassable after heavy rain. By 1951 the trails were straightened somewhat to accommodate an occasional truck, mostly 1940's surplus cobbled-together military trucks. A loaded truck one-way took 12 hours, 7 hours under perfect conditions. Trucks traveled two or more together in case one broke down. Horse and wagon caravans planned one round trip per week. There was no mechanized method to level and maintain

Train between Puerto Casado & End Station, 1955. Photo credit: Phil Roth.

Chaco road after a rain on the way to Bolivia, 1956. Photo credit: Phil Roth.

Freight caravan to End Station, 1955. Photo credit: Phil Roth.

these trails, the first bulldozer arrived in 1953; a gift from Northern District. When a mud hole got too deep or impassable, a convenient detour around the spot simply became the new trail.

Leroy Unruh, MCC VS worker assigned to STICA, working for a few months at the Experimental Farm, in a 1954 activity report, "The Chaco has the worst roads I have seen. . . . some roads have a third detour around the mud holes. They just cut a new trail through the bush."

Chapter 5: First Term

5.1 Telephone: used equipment donated by Canadian Brethren, installed in 1948 by Orval Myers, a Columbus, Ohio Mennonite civil engineer. The Unruhs had one of a few phones in Filadelfia and a phone at the farm. Inter colony connections only, no connection to the outside world. That is, a person in Neuland might phone anyone with a phone in Menno or Fernheim. The system was useable only during daylight hours because an operator must make the connection

Typical Chaco truck at End Station. One headlight, cobbled-together grille, no windshield, wooden cab and roof, 1955. Photo credit: Phil Roth.

by physically moving pin connectors and sending out the correct ring signal (multiple phones on the same line required a differentiating ring for each phone). (Stoesz & Stackley, *Garden in the Wilderness*, CMBC Publications, Winnipeg, Manitoba, 1999, p.141)

Maurice Kaufmann, Ph. D. (Plant Pathology) was the first North American serving in Menno colony, 1960 to 1963. He worked closely with Bob in MCC's effort to broaden Experimental Farm representation throughout the colonies. In a 2003 interview he said:

One time I had a Menno farmer on the line, he was speaking Low German and we didn't understand each other too good. Of course the central operator could listen in on calls if they wanted to. Suddenly a male voice interrupts with "Mr. Kaufmann can I help you out?" in a heavy accent. So the operator translated for us. Occasionally I would visit him, his office above Oberschulze Reimer's office. He was an interesting fellow who knew just about everything going on in Menno and then some beyond Menno.

5.2 Ants: 3 ½ years later, February 1955 in letter to Bill Snyder in support for a North American funding drive to buy and ship insecticides for controlling ants, Bob wrote:

One cannot imagine what damage these ants can do until one sees it. They are leaf cutting ants that cut the leaves from the plant and carry them into the nest using the fungus growing on the leaves for food. They might clear an acre or two in one night . . . Many farmers have not been able to raise a crop for five or six years because of ants. Now that we have an effective poison (methyl bromide) *we can do more good with something like this than a clothing shipment or even direct contributions since this an opportunity to help colonists help themselves.*

For a few months every year, it was necessary to pull one's bed away from the wall and be certain the bed sheets did not touch the floor. Setting the bed posts in open tin cans filled with a little water – checking every few days the bed had not shifted touching the can's side or move against the wall and adding water to offset evaporation—were prerequisites for a peaceful night's sleep.

5.2.0 MCC responded with 144 jars for the farm (12 dozen one shipping unit) as a trial shipment. This was not an original idea to pack the jars. MCC knew from experience that filled rather than empty jars when mishandled broke easily. Whether filled or not is unknown. Also illustrating conditions: the Unruhs were without butter for their first 6 weeks in the Chaco. None was available in the Cooperative store; similarly no vegetables, only tomatoes. Myrtle was without refrigeration until July, 1952, nine months after arrival when a kerosene powered refrigerator shipped from the US arrived. She also waited **twenty** months for a gasoline powered Maytag tub and wringer washing machine—a Chaco first. Bob engineered a small cooler to cool fresh warm milk, butter and eggs (extends shelf life for a few more hours). He took an open wooden box, knocked two opposite sides out replacing the sides with screen, partially filled the box with charcoal, laid a burlap bag over the box with a leaking bucket of water on top. The slow dripping water cooled by evaporation. And in a letter home January 10, 1952 Myrtle made her first request from her family; please send baking yeast. She tried yeast available in Fernheim but found it erratic and undependable.

5.2.0.1 In January 1952 Myrtle was asked to teach conversational English to twelve teenage young women. The class met three evenings every week. Bob reported a gas shortage prevailed. If not sick he would have been traveling with horses.

The pressure cooker was found at the farm. Using a pressure cooker over a wood fire was tricky business. The cooker had a safety release for excessively high pressure to avoid an explosion but needed uninterrupted temperature monitoring to control the pressure. Knowing when the cooking was finished was an art not convertible to scientific measurement.

5.2.1 Cattle were taken for granted; to provide scarce resources and to spend time for livestock care was considered unwise to colonists. Bob reflected that genetics, scarce quantities of low quality feed and inadequate attention, were the three reasons for the scrawny condition and low productivity. Bob's preference to import higher quality bulls from North America as permanent colony assets was put aside because funds to buy and for shipping were not available.

So in February 1952 Bob and Myrtle made their first trip outside the Chaco, flying to Asuncion for a meeting with STICA principals. It was the beginning of a herd improvement program. He arranged for shipping four Holstein bulls to the Chaco on loan from STICA. STICA required the cows serviced be certified tuberculoses and brucellosis free to prevent the transmission of the diseases when the bulls were returned to East Paraguay. From February 1952 activity report:

We came back to the Chaco feeling that there is no place like home, even if it is the Chaco with all its inconveniences, heat and insects. Our house was well taken care of in our absence by the spiders and termites. Every room was full of cobwebs and the termites had built their runways over the side of the kitchen stove as well as about a foot above it straight into the air! Where did that many come from in a week's time? It certainly doesn't take them long to take over a place."

5.2.1.1 Most Chaco households had a family cow and chickens, even in Filadelfia. Lacking refrigeration, milk and eggs required near immediate consumption.

Robert Snyder mentioned this "small experiment" in his 2003 interview:

> *I remember Bob's method of getting a point across. Early on most farmers eyed him with suspicion. But not long after he got there, Bob bought a milk cow and put her in his back yard in Filadelfia. He dug a pit about 3 feet wide and deep and 8-10 feet long in his Filadelfia yard and got kafir to make silage. He fed the little cow silage and other good feed and she became sleek and healthy looking. It wasn't long until he was carrying milk to the house by the bucketful. The street by Unruh's corner lot was well traveled and people saw what was going on. Shortly a farmer from village # 9 dug a silage pit. It was interesting to see how people took a liking to Bob and Myrtle, how both of them fit into the community.*

Imagine the quiet in 1952 in the Chaco without machines and electricity to introduce noise into the environment. No cars or trucks running on hard surfaced roadways, no tractors, lawn mowers, sirens, loud speakers or radios, airconditioning fans, trains and only a once-a-week airplane. When the rig was started up in downtown Filadelfia the loud and unfamiliar noise was heard from one end of town to the other.

Menno Klassen and Abe Peters seperately had tried kaffir silage a few years earlier and their trials failed; the silage spoiled. Bob reflected on possible reasons for this failure; either cut at the wrong stage of plant development, cut too coarsely, insufficiently packed or improperly sealed. But he decided silage was an important component to improved animal productivity. It was a good omen when *Oberschulze* Duerksen's family dug their first trench silo. Two years later Fernheim bought a used silage cutter from STICA. A MCC volunteer, Leroy Unruh on loan from STICA working in East Paraguay, filled 15 silos the following year in 1955.

5.2.1.2 April 1952 Activity report:

To keep life from getting too dull, the Moro Indians made another raid mid March (the fourth recorded attack, second with fatalies). *This time they choose the Lengua Indian worker's camp outside Wustenfelde. The attack came at about four o'clock. . . . Three died and one was severely wounded.*" (Wustenfelde about 9 miles northwest from Filadelfia).

5.2.1.3 Robert Snyder and Darrell Albright were assigned to clear a roadway adjacent the telephone line in 1951. Snyder said:

When we arrived in the Chaco before Abe Peters' departure, Darrell and I were given our first assignment to cut a road following this straight telephone line because this cut off a lot of distance from the roundabout original access. We used Indian labor for a long time. The road was cut through the bush with axe and machete all the way. We used the Jeep to push and pull some of the larger logs.

5.2.2 The school year began in March. Bob taught a class in general agriculture. Myrtle helped the art teacher with textile painting in addition to a conversational English group. Ending the report:

As we go along from day to day, we seem to find more things to do all the time. Sometimes we are almost frightened when we think of the immense assignment that is ours. We keep hoping and praying that we shall be able to carry out a small part of it.

5.2.3 The Unruh's MCC activity reports were usually one type-written page and on rare occasion written by Myrtle. As the first year ended, Bill Snyder adds this next to last sentence to one letter. "We certainly enjoy your activity reports and do not find them at all too long." Bob didn't take the hint; his later reports rarely more than one page. Three years later in August, 1955 Snyder tried again, more forcibly this time:

> *I notice you always manage to get your report on one page and that is a virtue because brevity helps in getting your points across. However if you get a literary urge we would also be glad to see your report a bit longer just in case you might be leaving something out that doesn't fit on one page. You are our only direct connection to what is happening in the colonies.*

Only three months after answering Kliewer's request, Bob writes in a letter to family February 8, 1953:

> *I have in mind to bring in a bull from the States. A half Holstein-Red Sindi from the University of Louisiana. Red Sindi is a milking strain of Zebu that was developed by Sam Higginbottom in India (Allahabad Agricultural Institute). They found a cross between Red Sindi and Holstein or Jersey can stand the heat and produce a lot of milk. Bringing in a bull like that will do as much for the colonies as any one thing we could do to grade up their cows. I realize half or more of milk production is proper care but maybe by the time we get some good cattle in here they will see the need for good care too.*

5.2.4 Applied agricultural experimentation in any environment is a slow, tedious and worrisome process with wrong turns and dead ends at best. Operated with limited money resources, lacking tools, equipment and located near earth's end where it took two months to get an order filled—sometimes longer—all compounded by anxious patrons (Fernheim farmers) and underwriters with other pressing priorities (MCC), Bob's task was daunting, not for those lacking the will to endure.

During Abe Peters' tenure as farm director (1949-1951) his home congregation in Corn, Oklahoma sent a used 5-foot Allis Chalmers pull-type combine. Bob needed to borrow Fernheims Farmall M tractor to pull the combine. In an interview with Ray Funk in 2003 (MCC financial administrator in Asuncion 1950-52):

Abe had more of a problem being accepted (by the Chaco Mennonites) than Bob did because he tried to do things in a big way, to mechanize cotton and wheat farming with expensive equipment and that didn't go over too well. He may have had the right idea but the timing wasn't quite right. . . . Bob took his time developing different projects in cattle and crops, he didn't rush into anything. He took a lifetime to do what he did in the Chaco and that I think was really his strong point.

5.2.4.1 Moro Indian sightings became a constant concern throughout the northern villages and the northerly-located Experimental Farm. Cotton harvest at the farm came to a standstill when the Lengua workers refused to go to the farm after footprints, clubs and Moro possessions were discovered about 150 yards from the buildings, Bob wrote in his March 1953 Activity Report.

Peters and Schmidt incident: The Mennonites at first rejected help in the search from their Lengua Indian workers but after three days searching without success, agreed. They were found shortly afterward with Indian help. (Christian L. Graber, *Coming of the Moros,* 1964, p. 52)

5.2.4.2 Bob finished his April 1953 report: "This week we finished screening in our house porch so we will have more room to store things we didn't dare leave on the porch for fear the Indians would walk off with them." Abstractions as in titled property had no history in Indian experience.

5.2.5 Correspondence shows that in the beginning Bob had difficulty getting responsive action from MCC for repair parts and supplies. It didn't help that MCC and church agencies needed to wait until their annual meeting to get approval for gifts or for distribution of funds. If ocean freight was involved it seemed to take another four to six months for paperwork, customs, crating and shipping. So he began bypassing MCC, going directly to suppliers, friends and relatives in North America. But MCC needed to arrange shipping for lower ocean freight rates and at other times partially contributed to purchases. This circumvention caused record keeping confusion and some grief for MCC, for which Bob was called to account (gently) by W. T. Snyder. Some MCC departments underwent reorganization in 1957 and that helped somewhat. (MCC files, Paraguay, Mennonite Church USA Historical Committee, Goshen, Ind.)

Bill Snyder is remembered by MCC workers as a person who could, "Call one to account and make you feel good about having been disciplined." (Wm T. Snyder Oral History)

There is mystery surrounding this tractor. On February 24, 1953 Bob wrote to Menno Diener, MCC purchasing director, investigating the possibility of a farm tractor but did not press the matter with follow-up correspondence. And no correspondence was found showing who was involved or what happened between February and April, only that Frank Wiens, MCC's Country Director, counseled Bob late April 1953 to write to Bill Snyder and lay out the reasons for his claim that an Experimental Farm tractor was important, which Bob did on May 2, copied to Wiens. On May 9, 1953—seven days later, before his May 2 letter could have arrived in Akron – Bob writes again to Snyder, "This is to inform you that I have heard from my friends in the states concerning funds for the purchase of the Farmall 'M' tractor. This will be a loan of $ 2,300 for five years @ 4% interest. I am signing a note to cover this loan. This leaves you free to accept contributions to cover payment of the note, if you wish to do so."

This became the third farm tractor in the colonies—all three in Fernheim. MCC paid and arranged ocean freight. The Farmall M arrived June, 1953, less than two months after the hurried letter exchange when ocean freight alone took thirty days minimum, New York to Asuncion. Clearly, Bob was working privately on this deal for many months, although nothing turns up in family correspondence. Who the "friends" were and whether MCC covered the note repayment remains a mystery.

5.2.5.1 Bob had been reporting to Akron more or less every other activity report through 1952 on the interest in both Menno and Fernheim colonies about moving to southern Bolivia. These archived reports show margin check marks and annotations indicating Akron's deep concern and attention to this matter. His March, 1953 report states:

Among the colonists there is still a good deal of unrest and talk of leaving. There are many showing interest in Brazil and Argentina and some will likely move if conditions here do not improve soon. . . .

Those with family connections and the means were leaving for Canada or other parts of South America from 1947, jeopardizing those that remained by increasing the burden to support the infrastructure. In 1951 for example, 120 persons departed the Chaco for Canada.

Bob reported that a large cotton company located near Santa Cruz, Bolivia was selling land and financing machinery on ten year notes, taking payment in cotton delivered to their textile factory. The main crops planned were cotton, sugar cane, peanuts, kafir and wheat. In a two-page letter dealing solely with migration intentions to Bolivia, written to Orie Miller on September 4, 1953 and copied to Frank Wiens:

On the last tour of investigation they brought back soil samples and I did several tests for them. It is considerably better soil then found here in the Chaco.

Colony statistics show for a five year period, 1951 through 1956:

	Menno	Fernheim	Neuland
Net population leaving	96	332	980
Total population change	+23%	+5%	-10%
Ratio births over deaths	10:1	10:1	8:1

Neuland Colony took the biggest hit in this period moving to Canada and Germany; almost all Neulanders having German citizenship. Fernheim Colony only held its own by reason of ten births for every death but from an economic viewpoint the statistics suggest a decline in short-term productive capacity due to out-migration.

In a family letter dated November 8, 1953, Bob wrote about the Experimental Farm work. "We feel that we are coming closer to accomplishing what we came down here for." He mentions making progress toward his strategy of employing younger men at the farm who are first generation Chaco-born, more inclined to put down roots in the Chaco and who are more open to learning new farming methods than their fathers. He hopes to multiply his effectiveness in this way. Moreover, he wants to put the Experimental Station farm workers on a voluntary service (VS) basis, but that idea is a hard sell. Bob thinks the reason is twofold. First, the VS concept is foreign to colonists. Second is impoverishment; every working age person needs earned income to simply exist. The concept of a young person taking time out to volunteer is a North American innovation perceived in the Chaco as irrational.

He ends by describing an activity:

We (the farms nursery technician Hans Unruh and Bob) did go to a village about 20 miles south. Left early in the morning and got back about 8:00 p.m. It was a hot, windy day so we were plenty tired by the time we got home. This was a younger village, about seven or eight years old and the people are very poor yet. Most have a small two room house and a roof on four posts they call a barn and that's all for buildings. They are young farmers that grew up in the Chaco and none have ideas about leaving, so a person is encouraged to see what they are doing with so little. They really appreciate the help they do get.

5.2.5.2 In anticipation for Orie Miller's visit in June and in July for Fernheim's 25th anniversary celebration, Bob wrote to Miller on March 12, 1955, suggesting MCC fund *Oberschulze* Duerksen's son Harold in an agricultural curriculum in Asuncion as a potential replacement for himself,

I think we should do everything possible to help a thing of this kind get started. . . . and if we can get the young people here started in getting their education without leaving the continent, we will have accomplished a great deal toward helping the people help themselves.

5.2.6 The heavy meal at noon with a one hour siesta following. Every place of business is closed and the streets deserted during siesta time. Absolutely all activity ceased during this mid-day siesta.

5.2.6.1 In periods of drought, the Unruh's small cistern to contain rain water from the house roof would go dry. So Bob put a 55 gallon barrel in his Jeep, drove to the nearest community well and transferred one bucket at a time to the barrel. He could only fill the barrel to

Drawing water from a cistern with rope and bucket, Filadelfia. Neta Klassen, Fernheim Cooperative employee, 1955. Photo credit: Phil Roth.

a level where the water didn't splash out on the drive home. Then from the Jeep he dipped the water to a second barrel on the back porch. Anticipating cistern construction and a two room addition with outside open porch, Bob writes in December 1953, "It will seem wonderful not to carry water for half a block every day." The cistern was finally constructed January, 1954.

Roof spouting empties into an above ground opening. The tank is underground to reduce heating and evaporation. A very few cisterns were equipped with a hand pump to pump water into a small overhead holding tank (20 – 30 gallon). From this tank, water flowed by gravity to one spigot in the kitchen. Inside bathrooms of course, were not possible without electricity, water pressure systems or a septic system.

Maurice Kaufmann in 2003:

When we got to Menno we didn't have a source of water for the house. I was told there was a well at some distance, about 200 yards behind the house. I had a fifty-five gal drum on a sled to pull behind the jeep. When I got to the well I looked down and saw frogs in the water. So I thought there's something wrong here. So I went to see Oberschulze Reimer and he was in a meeting in his office, really bad timing on my part. He invited me into his office and asks what I wanted and I said,

"I must be going to the wrong place for water because I looked into the well and there are frogs in the well."

He replied, "Well, if there aren't frogs in it, don't drink it!"

I imagine the farmers in his office were thinking, "What a brainless American!" If the well water was salty and unusable, the frogs wouldn't live there. I hope, all things considered, we made a contribution but we were pretty naïve when we arrived there.

. . . Bob was deeply respected on just about any ag related topic. He had a way of listening with no air of superiority and treated everybody with respect. I never heard any depreciating comment from him about anyone. I had the feeling there was mutual respect between Bob and the colonists.

5.3 MCC planned that Vern Buller and the five PAX boys, would show good faith and serious intent with Menno, Fernheim and Neuland in an effort to build a Trans Chaco Roadway from Asuncion to the Colonies. Only a few colonists believed such a fantasy project—first seriously proposed by J. Winfield Fretz in 1951—stood a chance of becoming a reality. (Gerhard Ratzlaff, *The Trans-Chaco Highway, How it Came To Be,* p. 244). On balance, some in the Chaco were not overjoyed about the prospect of a Trans Chaco Road (at first) believing easy access and increased commerce would risk losing social control. There was speculation in 1955 that the roadway might at some future time connect with the Pan American Highway (it happened); the sociological impact might then be enormous. They came to Paraguay believing religion central above all else and to escape worldly secular pressures doing violence to their education and culture. Easy access would almost certainly reverse this social segregation. C. L. Graber, MCC Paraguay director on special assignment June 1954 to organize MCC's road construction effort in Paraguay, once mentioned in 1955 to the PAX men that getting support from Paraguayan ranchers and from the Paraguayan government was easy. That however, "Not every person in the colonies thinks the Trans Chaco Roadway is a good idea."

5.6 Younger brother Verney said in 2003 that the presumed reason for Bob's sterility was a punishing bout with measles in his early teens.

Betty, Bob and Myrtle, Filadelfia house yard late afternoon, 1956. Photo credit: Phil Roth.

In 1956 the Unruhs learned about a baby boy available for adoption in East Paraguay. Without telling Betty their intention to adopt a baby brother, they were about to surprise her when the little boy's father suddenly decided not to sign off on an adoption. Disappointed, Bob writes that on the other hand, they were relieved they had not mentioned the matter to Betty who might not understand the disappointment.

Chapter 6: Buffelgrass

The Buffelgrass myth a possible adaptation from real life. John Peters says:

> *Bob did a lot of connecting and importing of seed. I found in an ag journal a new variety of Bermuda grass but there wasn't seed available. I wrote to the Professor at Gainesville, Fla. (articles author) asking if there was a way to introduce the grass into the Chaco. In about two weeks an envelope arrived. That was high speed in those days. In the envelope was a plastic pouch with a rhizome of the new Bermuda grass. That was all. Because a couple of drops of water had been placed in the pouch the rhizome was already sprouting when it arrived. We planted the rhizome under the lattice shade Bob already had constructed and within a month we had a patch of Bermuda grass growing. It was just unreal, it doesn't always work that well. . . . that strain of Bermuda never came to much. . . .*

Buffelgrass was the catalyst setting in motion a chain reaction, the springboard to an economic expansion no person saw coming or might have associated with so ordinary a thing as pasture grass.

First, Buffelgrass' introduction made possible in the Chaco colonies a dairy and beef industry.

From that foundation, the dairy and beef industry made possible the $1,000,000 US Government AID Smather's Loan in 1958. How so? The Smathers loan was not a grant; it was a loan that needed to be repaid. Using loan capital to purchase productive assets that generate revenue over and above the cost to service and repay the debt leads to capital appreciation and economic expansion.

Buffelgrass through this sequence made the Smathers loan "credit worthy." That is to say, the five Paraguayan German ethnic colonies, as viewed with a banker's detached, cold and calculating eye, were seen as a good risk from an earnings standpoint (Smathers loans were not collateralized). Without Buffelgrass' timely introduction, the Chaco colonies might have missed the Smathers Loan opportunity.

And third, the Smathers loan was the point where the colonies began planning their own affairs; the point where the 'failure syndrome' was overcome and began to lose its psychological grip on colonists. The Smathers experience gave colony leaders the confidence to pick up the ball and run with it. As a strategic step in helping the colonies toward self sufficiency, the loan repayments were structured to move from the colony Cooperatives directly to the US Government. MCC purposely avoided becoming brokers or middlemen, after helping to plan and set up the loan with USAID. (William T. Snyder, Oral History from 1943 to 1982, p.596, 1474, 1623 and throughout the transcript)

In Snyder's transcript (p. 20) is the implication that the Smathers loan planning process was the first time the colonies were required to work closely together on "macro" economic matters. The planning process developed a little friction and heat, but it brought the colonies closer together toward inter-colony cooperation on Chaco development matters.

*The **United States Agency for International Development** (or **USAID**) is the United States federal government organization responsible for most non-military foreign aid. An independent federal agency, it receives overall foreign policy guidance from the United States Secretary of State and seeks to "extend a helping hand to those people overseas struggling to make a better life, recover from a disaster or striving to live free and democratically.* (http://en.wikipedia.org/wiki/United_States_Agency_ for_International_Development)

Smathers Loan*: In 1956 Senator Smathers from Florida succeeded in adding a special provision to the foreign aid bill for economic development and social reform in Latin America that became known as the "Smathers Amendment."* (Robert Harrison Wagner, *United States Policy Toward Latin American,* Stanford University Press, 1970, p. 101)

There are two other factors to consider. MCC modified their standard three-year term to five years for the Unruhs first term to offset the high first-term transportation and setup costs in Paraguay. A three-year first term might not have given Bob enough time to follow through with his Buffelgrass experimentation to a successful conclusion. And, had the Unruh's not returned to the Chaco after their first term, the Buffelgrass story might not be worth telling. For example, Bob worked through many stubborn agricultural problems for the dairy and cattle industries for 25 years. And for 32 years he encouraged, financially through MCC and the Schowalter Foundation and with personal appeals, Mennonite young people toward advanced training to pick up where he left off; that is, to replace himself.

This is the point in recording the Unruh story; Bob selflessly laid the foundation for a flourishing agricultural industry in the Chaco. Bob and Myrtle were catalysts for change. Not to forget it was the Chaco Mennonites who affected the change with willful, resolute determination.

Chapter 7: Second term

7.1 What is the explanation for a nineteen month long furlough following the first term? In a letter to Orie Miller in January 1956—eight months before their first term ended—Bob listed four conditions for a second term:

1. He wanted to devote his energy 100% to the farm; no longer MCC's representative to the Chaco colonies. Too much time lost from more productive work was his reasoning.

2. A new four-wheeled drive pickup. The Jeep was worn out when he arrived five years before. He kept it running but again at the expense of productive work.

3. A five-year term was too long; a second term must be shorter. He had fallen behind in the rapidly advancing world of scientific agricultural technology due to the Chaco's isolation.

4. There were health concerns stemming from long intervals with a poor diet.

Then Bob tips his hand, "We feel we cannot give a definite answer until we have been home and look things over there." This doesn't sound like much enthusiasm for a second term.

The Unruhs moved into the farmhouse on Bob's 320 acres purchased in Montana in 1943 and re-established themselves as Montana dry land farmers for the 1957 crop year. Younger brother Leslie recalls the 1956-57 and 1957-58 winters were unusually harsh and that the house was in disrepair and not winter-worthy. Betty was 5 years old, soon to start Kindergarten and likely missed her Chaco playmates. And we learned in chapter 1 that 320 acres on the Montana prairie was inadequate to earn a living. There was no archived correspondence found regarding their decision to return to Paraguay or relevant correspondence with MCC about the second term.

7.3 A possible reason silage feeding enthusiasm waned; dairymen were pushing beyond nature's limits. From John Peters:

The practice was to harvest the sorghum seed, then cut the stalk for silage. Feeding that silage in the winter, the milk production would always drop off, better than no silage but not as high as summertime production. The experimental farm depended on money from both seed and milk. I suggested making silage from the whole plant. The Fernheim manager wasn't too happy about losing the seed sale money. I said, 'Well maybe the wintertime increase in milk sales will be more than the money from seed sales; we should try it to find out.' Boy, did the farm's wintertime milk production soar. That became a new recommendation; one of my successes.

7.5 John Peters:

Ivan Glick, a New Holland dealer in eastern Pennsylvania adopted the MCC farm program. He worked closely with MCC and Bob. Ivan arranged the importation of a forage harvester and repair parts, also the first milking machine for the farm, as I recall. I'm not certain Ivan was involved, but I was always impressed by the many small baby chick shipments arranged through Akron. Maybe 300 to 400 chicks at a time would arrive in Chaco, airfreight all the way in 48 hours.

7.6 Schowalter Foundation, Inc. was a Mennonite philanthropic organization, founded in 1954.

Its chairman in 1957 was O. O. Miller. It was organized with six trustees representing the General Conference Mennonites, the Mennonite Church and the Holdeman Mennonite Church conferences. These three groups were named in the will of Jacob A. Schowalter (1879-1953), which bequeathed most of his assets to the Foundation. Foundation income was designated for relief work, training of ministers and missionaries, and for the promotion of peace. The total appraised value of the estate was $1,157,000. Assets grew to $10,298,000 by 2003. Schowalter immigrated to America from Germany in 1883 at age four, eventually settling in Harvey County, Kansas, where he lived the rest of his life (a bachelor). He acquired his wealth through wheat farming, land investments, and oil. (http://www.gameo.org/encyclopedia/contents/S371.html)

October 28, 1960 in a letter to the family, Bob writes:

Our term is up beginning April next year. Akron wants us to come back again. Sometimes I think we have been here long enough but on the other hand the work is really starting to get interesting now that we have a little more money to work with.

By December 1960, a third, three-year assignment was agreed upon. In their agreement letter they informed MCC that they anticipated their third term would be their last service term in the Chaco.

Chapter 8: Third Term

John Peters in a 2003 interview:

"We only had one week overlap for orientation before the Unruh's departure. . . . I was swamped with work immediately and so it was just fly-by-the-seat of my pants."

John Peters:

Here is a good example of the Unruh's generosity. When the Unruh's returned in 1966 we were living in their MCC house in Filadelfia. Looking back, we should have moved elsewhere, it was really their home and they should be living in it. But the Unruhs said, "No, you stay another year until your furlough, we will live in another house temporarily."

Chapter 9: Longing to Grow Wheat

9.3 W. T. Snyder responds to the August 1954 activity report, writing to Bob:

I am sharing your activity report with Marion Kliewer (MCC publicity director) *who will give an account of your wheat harvest* (to North American church papers). *We must be careful not to describe the Chaco as a 'New Ukraine' . . . Your work in agriculture I am sure, gives new hope to many folk in the Chaco. . . .*

However guardedly optimistic this activity report, the 1954 wheat harvest was the exception rather than the rule.

9.5 Tradition (as a cause) had a profound effect on colonist behavior. Bob kept trying to grow wheat because it was his nature to be accommodating to the colonists' needs. It took 21 years before Bob came to terms with the reality that growing wheat in the Chaco was intractable. That certainly qualifies in most minds as persevering or resolute. Another reasonable person in Bob's position might have flatly said after 10 years, "Enough is enough, let's not waste our time and resources, urging on a dead horse."

Chapter 11: Myrtle

11.1 In a 1952 letter home Myrtle wrote, "I was very much surprised at the poor diet served in the hospital. . . . I suppose it gets even worse when there is a dry winter and vegetables don't grow." In a February 8, 1953 letter to family Myrtle mentions managing the hospital kitchen with one helper when Dr. Dollinger and staff go to East Paraguay to participate in the Kilometer 81 leprosy mission dedication.

By January 1952 Myrtle was asked to teach twelve teenagers conversational English. The class met three times each week.

Bob mentions secondarily in a letter to Bill Snyder on other matters May 2, 1953 that, "Myrtle's latest project is a class in homemaking she and Mrs. Dollinger (the German surgeon's wife, Erika, who lived next door) are jointly supervising for some teenage girls. They will be taught a little of everything about housekeeping . . ." It was the informal beginning, taught in the Unruh home, for what later became a formal home economics curriculum in Filadelfia's high school.

In February 1954 the Unruhs wrote a one page letter addressed simply to 'Dear Friends,' thanking them for their support into the first three years of their first term. This letter mentions Myrtle's activities; she is giving English lessons, has four piano students, teaching typing to another group and baking class with teens in her kitchen to a fourth group. Later in their second term all this informal activity, except piano, became structured under the *Zentralschule*.

Myrtle observed that young mothers with small children were excluded from Sunday church services and other functions. So she organized a weekday afternoon (once a week) in their home for socializing, babies welcomed. A Bible reading, prayer and unstructured fellowship follow.

11.3 There was a story circulating; Bob was asked whether Myrtle cooked at home the recipes published in the book? He replied, "Yes indeed, she tried them all on me first!"

Myrtle's surviving siblings say she became an accomplished cook in her high school years—not surprising the second child and oldest daughter in a family with seven children. Number two and oldest daughter in a large family might have had something to do with Myrtle's organizing ability and her skill for "getting the trains to run on time."

MCC agree to do the shipping to Paraguay, holding a few copies (in German) for North American distribution. There was continuous correspondence for almost a year trying to sort things out, mostly because not enough copies were printed.

Nomadic Indians encountered on an overland trip to Boliva, about 70 miles northwest from Filadelfia, 1956. Note three dogs and one kid goat, protected as valuable possessions. Photo credit: Phil Roth.

11.4 Indians were always accompanied by dogs. Living in the open in grass huts and sleeping on the ground, they needed dogs for early warning signs of approaching threats and at night to keep the wild life at bay.

11.5 An extract from a commemorative for Robert Unruh, March 6, 1998 that speaks as much to Myrtle as it does to Bob. By Edgar Stoesz:

> *Bob and Myrtle lived in a plain, adobe house—the kind the pioneers lived in and eventually replaced, but Bob and Myrtle added a few functional features. It was a shelter from the elements, what a house is supposed to be. For the Unruhs this house became a place to recreate, to entertain people from near and far and to experiment and invent. Perhaps too, a flower in a vase and the smell of good cooking. Nothing fancy. But functional, orderly and open to others – always.*

Chapter 12: Indian Settlement

Bob grew up about 160 miles from a Cheyenne reservation in Montana. One reference was found to a Bethlehem Mennonite Church youth group visit and interaction with Cheyenne youth at this reservation (2003 interview with Kenneth Deckert). In addition, Mennonite film maker William Zehr, produced a movie in 1955, *The Call of the Cheyenne*, about Montana Mennonite church mission efforts to Native Americans. So an Indian connection for Bob might have been longstanding. Mennonite Church USA Historical Committee, North Newton, Kansas has viewable videos of this movie, unhappily not available for viewing until after this book's release.

From the Indian settlement beginning in 1936 the conventional Mennonite wisdom declared the Indian farmer needed to be apprenticed to a Mennonite farmer for several years as a training mechanism and to weed out those without the capacity for self-discipline and reliability. Even after apprenticeship he probably needed constant supervision on his own farm for several more years.

12.1 From a review essay by Gerhard Reimer, professor emeritus of German at Goshen College on the German book by Peter P. Klassen, *Die Mennoniten in Paraguay,* volume 2, 1991:

> *Almost from the beginning the Mennonite settlers were concerned about helping the Indians to change from a wandering or nomadic culture to a sedentary one. Walter Quiring warned against the "development of a Chaco proletariat . . . that would simply be there for the purpose of providing ambitious German farmers with cheap labor." He was also aware of the conflict that could arise out of the difference between what the missionaries preached and how the white settlers lived. . . . An eventual encounter between the whites and the Indians seemed unavoidable, however, and at that point the Germans* (Mennonites), *will need to be involved or "they will become guilty of the destruction of their brown neighbors."* (http://www.goshen.edu/mqr/pastissues/oct02reiner.html)

North Americans are inclined to romanticize about Indians. Figuratively speaking, rubbing shoulders with them daily tended to amend fantasy notions.

For instance, in the 1950s, Lengua and Chulupi (Nivaclé) Indians roamed through Filadelfia during the day looking for chore work, chopping wood or cleaning up the yard or digging holes for planting trees or fence posts in exchange for food or clothes or whatever the homeowner wanted to offer in exchange. They were not averse to begging; if shown in advance an item in exchange, they might insist on handling the item and then walk away with the item in hand, without doing the work. An Indian face might appear at the window any time of the day usually at meal time, except siesta time midday when everything was shut down and shutters closed. (Most houses then had no glass or screens, only wooden shutters to close for shielding against mid day heat, high winds and sand storms.) There was little sense of European modesty or privacy; they were

Typical nomadic Indian shelter near Yalva Sanga, now abandoned, 1955. Photo credit by Phil Roth.

uninhibited, more like a child's naivety. They were dressed mostly in tattered clothes given to them by Mennonites, sometimes discarded Paraguayan military attire and generally barefoot. They tended to be hygienically scented. Frequently eye cataracts were observed and dental hygiene was desperately needed.

An explanation for the peaceable Indians withdrawing from the war zone; the Paraguayan military sometimes shot them on sight:

The Chaco Indian tribes isolated by the inhospitable landscape lived without much contact and interference from outsiders until the Mennonites arrived and more particularly the Paraguay-Bolivia War. The Paraguayan military considered all Chaco Indians sub-human.(http://countrystudies. us/paraguay/34.htm).

Another indication: Gerhard Reimer, translating Peter P. Klassen's *Die Mennoniten in Paraguay,* volume 2, 1991:

The following story is told by Frieda Kaethler: Kazike Molino and his wife were working in the fields for the Kaethler's when the Paraguay military moved in during an incident in the war with Bolivia. Because the Indians had betrayed the Paraguayans to the Bolivians, they were now free game for the Paraguayan soldiers. When Frieda's mother saw two soldiers with loaded guns sneaking up on the two unsuspecting field workers, she called to Frieda, her 11-year-old daughter, to run and warn them. The two escaped and the blame for their escape now rested with the Kaethler family. Not wanting to take the young girl who warned the two Indians, the authorities instead took Mr. Kaethler and his son to the military post. Fortunately they were soon released because the Paraguayan officer in charge knew and respected Mr. Kaethler.

Also told by Frieda Kaethler (Die Mennoniten in Paraguay), illustrating Mennonite involvement in this new environment was that her mother had once offered to buy one of the unborn babies of Kazike's wife so that she would not kill it. At that time family planning for these Indians

Two Indian men in their Sunday best, 1955. Photo credit: Phil Roth.

*consisted of suffocating unwanted children immediately after birth by fill-
ing their mouth with sand.*

Having Indian representation on ISB's board was an MCC innovation, regarded at first as absurd by colonists. (Stahl, 1980, pp. 148-
149)

Lem Metzler, MCC worker with ISB & ASCIM from 1973 to
1979 said in 2006:

*In a legalistic sense Indian welfare was really the Paraguayan
government's responsibility, not the Mennonites. By 1975 the known
and registered Indians equaled the Mennonite population. The annual
growth rate was astonishing, particularly when factoring in the Moros.*

In contrast to usual European colonization where the indigenous
were removed to isolated locations, in the Chaco the Indian settlements were at first adjacent to colony lands. In time the Indian settlement lands were surrounded by colony property.

12.2 Snyder's "confused picture" comment was an expression for
MCC's disappointment that Indian settlement was not progressing as
hoped and the reason for Snyder wanting to employ Loewen to better understand the issues and move the settlement program forward.
Snyder said in 1982, ". . . made us feel that here in North America
we had to know more about this problem, that we had to bring more
competency to bear on it than we had (up to this point)." (William T,
Snyder, Oral History, p.1018)

2002 essay review of *Mennonites in Paraguay,* Peter P. Klassen,
1991, by Gerhard Reimer:

*Pressure to settle the Indians increased in the early 1960s. With
the help of MCC, the anthropologist Jacob Loewen was sent to study
the situation. Loewen brought to the discussions an awareness of the
cultural upheaval experienced by the Indians as a result of the settlement*

project. He pointed out that the Indians were a traditionally matrilineal culture. J. Winfield Fretz also brought a sense of cultural awareness to the situation at hand: "During thousands of years he [the Indian] *learned that land is to be owned and used in common and that nobody whosoever has the right to buy or sell it." And now they were proposing to make landowners out of the Indian! In spite of such considerations, as the Indians continued to immigrate into the Chaco the movement to settle them could not be stopped.* (http://www.goshen.edu/mqr/pastissues/oct02reimer.html).

12.2.1 Fernheim *Oberschulze* Duerksen had served as ISB's chairman from ISB's beginning. Bob didn't want ISB chairmanship; being assertive or performing a chairman's role was not his persona; he knew it to be so and so did the *Oberschulzen*. They hoped Bob might be an acquiescent link to MCC on Indian matters. From their position, there was no downside to electing Bob chairman. The *Oberschulzen* could control spending as MCC money was channeled through them, thereby overriding Bob's decisions. (W.T.S. *Oral History*, p. 1081)

12.2.2 About the Chulupi demonstration: ". . . This revolt was a good thing in the long run because it brought the whole Indian issue to the colonies attention." (W.T.S. *Oral History*, p. 1019)

This uproar had intricate contributing factors building up for many years. Competition arose between two Chulupi chiefs that created tensions and conflict within the Chulupi tribe. Neuland paid annual tribute in homegrown produce to Chulupi for colony land the Indians disputed as theirs and promises made and broken by the Paraguayan Bureau of Indian Affairs officials for land to call their own. Indian livestock roamed into Mennonite gardens and cropland. When Mennonites lost their patience and killed several offending animals, the Indians retaliating by killing Mennonite livestock and stealing from the Mennonites. The Mennonites then arrested and held in confinement a Chulupi for stealing. Complicating matters was the Mennonite feeling the Indians were being incited to riotous behavior by an "outside and unknown" source. If that was not enough anxiety, things somehow went wrong with a food distribution under the USAID "Food for Peace" program (arranged by MCC but implemented by colony administrators) to the point where some Chulupi rejected the food and continued to protest. (Mennonite Church USA Historical Committee, Goshen, Ind., IX-12-4 MCC files Paraguay 1962-1969)

12.3 J. M. Klassen (MCC Canada Executive Secretary) brought back from Paraguay (date not stated) that the ISB was perceived by colony leaders as an institution kept alive to please MCC. The *Oberschulzen* did not enthusiastically support ISB. (W. T Snyder *Oral History*, p. 1092) *Oberschulzen* reasoning was not found in archived reports or correspondence. But they clearly had reservations about the programs path or the eventual consequences. Might MCC's initiative been perceived as potentially drying up the labor supply? Possibly the *Oberschulzen* not wanting to be seen by their constituencies as irresponsible if a labor shortage did in fact develop, caused them to be less than forthcoming. (See *W. T. S. History*, 1982, bottom of p. 873)

Matters were complicated by Loewen's report that criticized the Paraguayan Mennonites for rigidly trying to "remake" the Indians into Mennonites for Mennonite benefit rather than adjusting the settlement program to the Indian culture for the Indian's benefit. To make matters worse, MCC mishandled presenting Loewen's report to the colony leaders by giving a rough draft summary to the USAID in Paraguay before Loewen's draft was edited with some of the undiplomatic language toned down. The Mennonites were in the dark and offended when USAID people wanted to discuss the provocative Loewen report (thrust on them by MCC) and they had not yet gotten the report from MCC. "We weathered that storm but it was not easy." (*W. T. S. History*, 1982, p. 869-870)

There appeared to be some indecisiveness on MCC's part, trying to reconcile the anthropological studies they had underwritten to the down-to-earth realities. Balancing personnel and money resources to Loewen's ideal was not easily done. The realization that the settlement difficulties were extremely complex generated a feeling of trespass; if not directly working at cross-purposes, at least there was some measure of mutual incomprehension on Indian matters and MCC might set an already troubled program backwards. Having financed the study and gratified that it shed light on the issues, the report did not clear up practical ambiguities, so it wasn't immediately clear what to do with it. (See *W. T. S. History*, 1982, 871 and top of p. 1168)

A decade later MCC was chagrined when the Loewen report and other anthropological studies were used in the Paraguayan political arena, ostensibly to unseat the Stroessner government (if true, the tactic didn't work). The Chaco Indian settlement later came to the attention of the World Council of Churches, getting world-wide attention. "We have a tarnished image to this day on our handling of the Indians." (*W. T. S. History*, 1982, p. 872, 873, 1436) (As Gerhard mentions, ultimately European and North American governments gave generously, an upside to the bad press.)

"Bob Unruh had to administer this thing while working things out with very strong, aggressive *Oberschulzen.* . . . They reserved too many decisions for themselves. . . . They preferred not to use the board. . . . They wanted to proceed independently." (*W. T. S. History*, 1982, pp.1081, 1092, 1093)

It would have taken Herculean leadership ability to create positive results in this impaired atmosphere. Abundant patience—Bob's signature strength—allowed time to work its magic.

Yet another complicating factor for ISB was MCC's decision in October 1964 to restructure the MCC—Paraguay connection. From 1930 to 1964 MCC worked with the *Oberschulzen* to arrange aid funding offered as subsidies and grants. By 1964 MCC aid had expanded to six standing programs; the Experimental Farm, Km 81 leper hospital, programs for education and social aid, a mental sanatorium, *Christlicher Dienst* (Paraguayan Mennonite voluntary service) and ISB.

*Things were not working out in the Indian Settlement Board and
the colonies were getting on well on their own in their economic development having* (independently from MCC) *negotiated a $700,000
grant from the German Government for 29 different projects in 1964*
[p.1091]. . . . *these* (events) *contributed to our feeling that it was time
to turn over activities to a responsible Paraguay Mennonite organization.*
(*W. T. S. History*, 1982, p. 1093)

As a church relief organization, MCC wanted to work with Mennonites in Paraguay through a single church committee. Snyder was
asking for one, unified five-colony Mennonite Church organization
to work with MCC. However logical from MCC's prospective, this
proposal created a structurally disruptive problem for the Paraguayan Mennonites. Considering a thirty-four year dependence on MCC
support channeled through them, we might appreciate that the *Oberschulzen* felt they were losing control; that their grip on MCC money
was slipping away. (Mennonite Church USA Historical Committee,
Goshen, Ind., IX-12-4 MCC files Paraguay 1962-1969, Oct. 23, 1964
Memorandum)

Indeed, four years later in a MCC annual report dated November 29, 1968, MCC came to terms with the issue:

*The frustration was due, to a large measure, of Akron failing to rec-
ognize the strong authoritarian organizational structure of the Mennonite
colonies where everything culminated in an Oberschulzenrat* (a committee
of five *Oberschulzen* organized in 1957 to work cooperatively on the
Smathers loan allocations). *This august body rules supreme and may not
be bypassed.*

Snyder said in 1982 that, "I had some emotion about drawing
the curtain on MCC's participation in Paraguay. . . . yet it was the only
way to go." And, "There were leadership qualities there in people that
came out only when it was necessary for them to take the lead. . . . it

was amazing how quickly everybody caught on and moved ahead in Latin America when we decided to pull out our director (1969)." (*W. T. S. History*, 1982, pp.1094, 1298)

John Peters said in his 2003 interview:

I remember when Orie Miller, Bill Snyder and J. M. Klassen were in the colonies talking with the three colony leaders; how does MCC transition to less direct involvement by Akron and more responsibility from the Mennonites? We would spend all day meeting with the colony administrators. In the evenings Bill, Orie and J. M. would come to our house for supper and rehash what happened during the day. One evening Orie Miller said, 'You know, the Mennonites are afraid.' And then J. M. quoted the scripture, '. . . **Love casteth out all fears**.*' There was a reflective pause and Orie quietly said, 'We don't love enough . . . we don't love enough.' This was a very impressionable event so we remember it clearly. So there was that struggle and at the same time Bob and I did our thing. . . .The bottom line was that Bob and Myrtle were totally immersed in their work there – they were just totally dedicated to doing what was best for the Mennonites and for the Indians.*

It took into the late 1970s for the dust to settle. In the meantime ISB suffered through two reorganizations to emerge as ASCIM in 1978. MCC had not yet divested all Paraguayan assets (mostly land for Indian settlement) when Bill Snyder retired in 1982. (*W. T. S. History*, 1982, p. 1094)

Moro (Ayoreo) Indians, September 1963. Photo credit: Frank Wiens, Mennonite Church USA Historical Committee, Goshen, Ind.

The Moro Indians: following the Stahl tragedy, there were four more attacks on Mennonites with injuries but no fatalities. Altogether, three incidents between 1947 and 1950, three Lengua fatalities in 1952 (see chapter 5) and two attacks in 1955, the fifth and last assault only a few miles north from Filadelfia.

Bob's first indirect experience with Moros came early March, 1953. In his activity report for that month:

Cotton picking at the farm has been delayed due to a visit by Moro Indians. They were not seen but something scared them and they ran off leaving war clubs and feathers about 150 yards from the house. The Lenguas of course refused to come back to pick cotton. At approximately the same time Moros were seen near a village Northeast of Filadelfia and also near a village to the Northwest, maybe 30 to 40 altogether.

On December 5, 1961 Bob writes to MCC:

. . . As you know the Moro Indians have been a constant menace to the colonies for some years. About a month ago very clear evidence was found they were near the farm. No attack occurred but a week later more fresh tracks were seen. . . . the parents of some workers (Mennonite) became so concerned that we were forced to evacuate a wife and child and have hired a man to do the cooking. Now again within the last ten days more fresh signs, so that we must be constantly on guard.

. . . We have the feeling that the time is not far away when the Moros will come out of the bush and when they do, the problem of knowing what to do with them and how to handle them might be greater than that of making contact with them. We would appreciate your thinking on this problem as to what MCC's attitude on this is. Above all, we think it would be in order to request church wide prayer for the situation here.

In a letter to family dated a month later, January 14, 1962:

Things have settled down a little at the farm. There are no recent signs of Moros, I am beginning to see some hope. Most Mennonites thought we should arm to the teeth and be ready for the worst. One worker did start carrying a revolver and others had rifles. We finally voiced concern about this tactic and a few people started thinking more sensibly.

But in the next month Bob wrote:

Last week we had another Moro scare at the farm. For two nights in a row there was a fire burning at the edge of the bush, about 200 yds from the buildings. They have never done this before near the colonies so maybe they have peaceful intentions, but one can never know for sure. They are never seen during the day. The oil company experience has been that one day they are friendly and the next day ready to kill whoever they see.

Bob's reckoning was not far from the mark, later in 1962 about sixty Moros settled in with a Catholic mission station, forty miles Northwest from Filadelfia. In January, 1963 two Moro men, five women and two children walked from the Catholic mission to Filadelfia. Bob wrote:

You can imagine there was a lot of excitement in town. They were friendly and content to stay in the shed on our old lot. During the day they wandered all over town looking at everything. They wanted in the worst way to trade us some beads for our dog but we didn't let ourselves be talked into that one. . . . the colony decided to take them back to the army post (Estigarribia) about 25 miles away. . . . Plans are being worked on what course to follow when they come again, little doubt a larger group on the next visit.

From that point Moros with friendly intentions where occasionally encountered. John Peters said his pickup truck was occasionally hi-jacked (1966):

A few hundred yards to the side of the road from Filadelfia to the farm was a Moro encampment. Occasionally on my drive back to Filadelfia several Moro women would stand in the roadway with their arms outstretched blocking the roadway so I would need to stop. Then they would pile into the back of the pickup for a ride into town. By 1966 people were becoming more comfortable about the Moros. There was an effort to get them to trade away their spears and weapons. By hindsight that probably wasn't the best idea . . . it only hastened their dependency on the Mennonites although in reality it was going to happen in due course.

We leave the Moro story here only to say the New Tribes Mission (NTM) already working with Ayoreos near the Bolivian border eventually established a Paraguay 'mission control' operational base in Filadelfia with radios and an airplane hangared on Filadelfia's airport to stay in touch with several NTM missions north from the colonies.

12.4 One MCC trouble-shooter for that period was C. L. Graber, who organized the Trans Chaco Highway effort in Paraguay 1954-56. Graber was commissioned by MCC as Special Assistant to Paraguay for Indian Settlement. He appeared in the Chaco in March 1963, staying for six weeks to do a settlement program evaluation and reorganization. It is a reasonable assumption that Bob's letters, September 10, 1962 and January, 1963 helped set this initiative in motion.

ISB's Reorganization in October followed Graber's recommendations presented to MCC one month earlier in September.

12.5 But ISB's struggle to perform continued for another decade and longer. Lem Metzler said in 2006 about his MCC experience as Indian agricultural counselor and educator, 1973 to 1979:

Colony communication (with MCC) was not their strength. The failure to communicate and drag their feet was the colonies method of equalizing or throttling back MCC's exercise of power and control over ISB; it came across as being at times uncooperative. I think Bob tried hard to accommodate the Chaco Mennonites and should never be faulted for the work he did with the Indians. . . . the sticking point was that MCC owned the program and controlled everything. The truck and equipment belonged to MCC. MCC owned the land . . . Poor communication (south to north was the mechanism that) *didn't allow MCC's power to flow. . . .*

Visiting the Chaco in 2007, a Mennonite was heard to say, "We have lived with the Indians for over 75 years and still do not really understand them."

This account illustrates a poetic reckoning. From MCC's beginning in 1920 the guiding principle was to help the aid recipient through a difficult period or in Paraguay's case, into a self sustaining economic position, gradually disengaging and moving on to the next opportunity for service. The irony was that the Paraguayan Mennonite fear of being abandoned as receiver of MCC's support and the love/hate relationship that often accompanies growing independence, was now visited upon them by the Indians. The roles were reversed; in a parallel dynamic as the Mennonites to MCC, the Indians were to the Mennonites. As the Mennonites reacted in fear of being cut loose and adrift, likewise the Indians did not want to break their dependency on their benefactors (the Mennonites), needing the security and comfort from the Mennonites as protectors and employers.

History is replete with abuse and exploitation in such circumstances. The Mennonite Chaco colonization and Indian settlement experience suggests the fabric of religious underpinning avoided such abuse and exploitation.

We only scratched the surface on this absorbing and crucial interval. Given that it might be unfinished business, a fluid history still in progress, the Indians from 1927 to 2000 were vital to Chaco colony survival. Further, the Mennonite Chaco colonization might have progressed at a much slower pace had it not been for the Lengua and Chulupi Indians, the Mennonite Brethren Mission Board and MCC's importunate leadership.

Chapter 13: Agricultural Advisor

13.1 Recall that in agreeing to a third term in 1961, the Unruhs informed MCC that they anticipated the third term as their last in the Chaco. Recall also that from his first term Bob lobbied for a second MCC agricultural worker to share the load. For one or both of those reasons MCC recruited John Peters, an agronomist from Canada, to begin in September 1964 as the Unruhs finished their third term. After graduating from Texas A & M University with a masters degree, the Unruhs did return to Paraguay in October 1966 for a fourth term. In a letter to family, August 1963 one year before their third term expired, Bob said he was busy, expresses optimism for an improved working environment in the Chaco and hoped to continue on in the Chaco. But no correspondence with MCC was found showing an agreement for a fourth term.

The three colonies have to this day carried on a friendly competition with one another. It might be that in the long run, this competition among the colonies stimulated and aided progress when each tried to outdo the other two (an inference, no documentation). However, MCC's position was that inter-colony cooperation would more efficiently advance all three colonies to a higher level than each colony going its separate way, duplicating efforts. Moreover, a rising tide lifts all boats; Fernheim might leverage its front-runner position by sharing its progressive leadership in agricultural development. MCC's philosophy was more than economic conjecture; it included the principle and Mennonite ideal for mutual assistance.

John Peters said in 2003 about the 1967 Experimental Farm cattle auction:

Through the farm's breeding program we had calves for breeding stock that were clearly superior to the average. The invitations were sent out and at the last minute Fernheim Oberschulze Duerksen suggested to me that only Fernheim farmers should be allowed to bid for the calves. His reasoning was that since the Experimental Farm was Fernheim's all the benefits should accrue to its members. I found myself in a pickle. Finally I said, "It is too late to put conditions on the sale having sent the invitations out." I held my breath waiting to see what might happen next. Fortunately they saw the wisdom for a three colony sale and the sale came off well.

Before the sale Bob spoke to the farmers about animal husbandry; caring for the animals, the likely disease problems, good feeding practices and nutrition, how to employ breeding stock and the characteristics to look for in good breeding stock.

13.1.1 MCC unilaterally initiated an Experimental Farm assessment by commissioning Dr. Harold Kauffman, an authority on tropical plant pathology (a former MCC worker) and Professor Leonard Siemens, Professor of Plant Sciences, University of Manitoba, Winnipeg. Another purpose for the study was to work out a cooperative research and extension program for all five colonies, including Friesland and Volendam in East Paraguay.

Among other things, the report suggested a five-colony "Agricultural Advisory Council." That an "overall program director for the five colonies" be named by the Council. That an agricultural extension specialist concentrating on Indian matters be designated (Lem Metzler was the first specialist). And that Bob Unruh as a one person show, was carrying an unrealistic burden of responsibility without a supporting staff. "Such a workload is not a reasonable expectation from one person…" (H. Kauffman & L. Siemens, Report on Agricultural Experimentation and Extension Study in Mennonite Colonies of the Chaco and East Paraguay, Summary Note XI, August 1972, p.20, Mennonite Church USA Historical Committee, Goshen, Ind.)

13.2 Lem Metzler said in 2006:

Before Dr. Rudolf Kaethler, the first colony born veterinarian came on board (1969), *Bob was the colony and Indian vet, by default. In the first week after our arrival, Bob got a call early morning as we were getting up before breakfast* (Lem and Alta stayed with the Unruhs for a week until their house was available), *to please come right away to one of the eastern villages in Fernheim. A cow started calving yesterday and was having difficulty. The calf was dead and sideways and the cow had absorbed the amniotic fluid internally. Between labor contractions Bob would go in and straighten the calf. The farmer and his wife were bringing Bob soap and water to work up lather for lubrication. The calf was finally delivered and the cow saved. The morning air was still cool but Bob worked up a real sweat.*

Bob trained colonists and occasionally Indians at the Experimental Farm. These people were comfortable going back to Bob as a reliable resource person, always ready and able to help them. He was providing a (agricultural) *safety net for the colonists. . . . I never heard a disrespectful remark from colonist or Indian about Bob. . . . Bob never did or said anything without first giving it much thought and consideration.*

13.3 Irvin Weaver said in 2007:

MCC and Eastern Mennonite Conferences gathered 18 dairy bull yearlings and 30 hogs for the Chaco. My brother Levi and I donated one Holstein calf. The U.S. Government under the Marshall plan provided an unpressurized surplus C-46 airplane and pilots to fly the cattle from Miami to Filadelfia. We departed Miami May 6, 1961, stopped overnight in Arica, Chile then early morning flew across the Andes direct to Filadelfia, arriving Sunday afternoon about 3:15 p.m. There were many people on the airport and so close to the runway the pilots at first didn't want to land. Someone said people were leaving church to be at the airport, so the churches stopped services early. A Paraguayan customs official was there to meet us and check the cattle before unloading. We were the first international flight permitted to land at Filadelfia. We spent many days touring the Chaco before flying to Asuncion for the return home. The hospitality was great.

13.5 In response to an inquiry from Edgar Stoesz in 1996, Bob said:

I remember the frustration of trying to reach all 1,250 farmers, scattered over an area of 6000 sq miles, as they began to see the potential of the Chaco, realizing they had much to learn. Our field days at the Experimental Farm and regional meetings in all three colonies (as well as one-to-two day meetings with the Indians) *were successful to a limited degree but the biggest help in reaching even the remotest farmers was the radio station . . . Sometimes Myrtle and I came home after a hot, dusty day to find a big watermelon on our doorstep.* (Stoesz and Stackley, *Garden in the Wilderness*, 1999, p.95)

13.6 The chemical age began in the 1930s, getting into high gear after World War II, so agricultural chemical pesticide technology world-wide was state of the art by 1970.

13.7 Citrus tree necrosis is a generic term for premature tree decline related to vascular cell tissue destruction usually around the bud union near ground level. The first symptom is yellowing leaves followed by stunted growth in later years. The tree becomes incapable in pumping fluids back and forth between its below ground and above ground system. Fruit production declines; the fruit is smaller and ripens prematurely. Growing branch tips die back and the tree dies a slow but certain and early death. Interestingly, the control measures Bob recommended for this and similar virus induced diseases have not changed in fifty years.

John Peters in 2003:

Bob was in some sense a visionary about details. He would come to understand that something specific should be done. My approach was to ask, what are all the problems around this idea, what will make it difficult or impossible, the reasons it should not be done? That wasn't Bob's style, he would say, "This is a good thing to do and we should find a way to do it, never mind the difficulties."

13.9 However fishy the Unruh fish story might be, fish were introduced into the Chaco by someone. It was a good no cost protein source for humans (a logical benefit for the Indians), not needing a manufactured food source. But in years of extreme drought, not many survived. One way or another, a few did survive and occasionally turned up for dinner. John Peters tells another Unruh fish story:

Myrtle goes to the Co-operative store to buy groceries. At the meat counter is a sign, "Fish." Myrtle inquires where the fish came from. The clerk not recognizing Mrs. Unruh says, "Just Unruh puddle fish but they taste good, better than most fish we sell."

In May 1977 while home on furlough following their sixth term, Bob and Myrtle were awarded the Distinguished Alumni Award from Bethel College.

Chapter 14: Appreciation

The tree planting initiative was initiated by Myrtle's cousin, Kenneth C. Kaufman, Ph.D. He recalls a close relationship between his mother Martha Kaufman (Myrtle's aunt) and Myrtle. With frequent letter exchanges and small gifts his mother emotionally supported the Unruhs in Paraguay. His mother was a bit ahead of her time with a master's degree from Witmarsum seminary at Bluffton College, Bluffton, Ohio. She might have encouraged Myrtle's attending and graduating from Bethel College. Dr. Kaufman wrote the plaque's inscription.

Chapter 15: Remembrances

W. T. Snyder, *Oral History*, 1982, page 1472:

We have a beautiful pattern of long-term approach to development in South America with Bob Unruh. . . . He worked slowly year in and year out to develop better pastures, to upgrade the livestock. . . . He did not bring in prize heifers or prize bulls that could not be afforded. Ultimately the things colonists laughed at were accepted (became standard practice) *because Bob was there to work out the problems—and there were problems galore.*

Commemorative Inscription, 2008. Photo credit: Wendy Teichgraf Kehler.

Tree and monument as it appeared in 2008. Photo credit: Wendy Teichgraf Kehler.

Acknowledgements

Arriving under cover of darkness the night before, walking down Filadelfia's main street after 47 years, I discovered the building, formerly Fernheim's administrative office was now a museum, *Museo Jacob Unger*. There was a young man near the doorway. I extended my hand and hopefully asked, "Do you speak English?" "Yes." He then continued in perfectly phrased and spoken English, "My name is Gundolf Niebuhr, curator and historian, please come in." We sat in the morning shade under brilliant and penetrating sunlight—a unique, serene low humidity atmosphere that might only be found in the Paraguayan Chaco—and ran through much Paraguayan Mennonite history in the next hour. During that conversation Gundolf noted that he had a file drawer stuffed with material about Robert Unruh. He pensively hoped some bilingual person, who understood agriculture and could evaluate each paper, would put the clutter into organized form.

A week later in Asuncion I met with Gerhard Ratzlaff author of *The Trans Chaco Highway: How it Came To Be*. After publication of his book in German, Paraguayan Mennonites often remarked, "How could the story of how the road came about be forgotten so quickly?"

Something about these two comments dented a receptive neuron in my brain and fixed an undeletable impression. The Unruh legacy was recognized throughout the Chaco but little known outside the Chaco beyond contemporaneous MCC co-workers. Perhaps the Unruh story should be recorded before it too was forgotten? Why not research MCC's archived papers in North America, drive across the country to Montana and Kansas, do a few interviews and put together a short quasi-biography for the sake of history preserved? Gundolf and Gerhard, many thanks for the inspiration.

Returning stateside I looked up Edgar Stoesz who lives not far away in Pennsylvania. Edgar said he doubted there was much recorded material; he remembered that Bob's filing cabinet was in his head. "Yes, Bob and Myrtle were 'atypical' MCC workers staying in one place for 32 years, but don't make too much of that; they did what every church worker does—goes to work doing the best they can with whatever they have to work with. The Unruhs were indeed humble and resourceful persons, no question. And they would be embarrassed to know you misrepresented or inflated their true selves. Go look and see what you can find."

Next stop Newton, Kansas and a brief visit with Robert Krieder. More good advice. "Write with crisp detail. Allow other people to tell the story. All you can share on their humble, low-key approach is good. . . . Most development literature focuses on the expatriate as the agent of change. We might use more information on the role of the indigenous respondents as agents of change. Keep rolling."

Then pay dirt. The first of two rich veins was Verney Unruh, Bob's younger brother. He provided early life details, a helping hand with research, good follow-up ideas, persons to interview, a flow of additions and corrections to the several rough drafts and strong morale support. Verney was a Bob Unruh carbon copy in good humor, helpfulness and humility, it was an enriching encounter. Daughter Elizabeth (Betty) joined us to share papers and pictures. Together we interviewed two of three talented granddaughters, Tanya and Olivia.

In Montana there was a rewarding meeting with Leslie Unruh, another brother and Les's two sons, Doug and Dan. They said, "It was always exciting and a fun time when Uncle Bob came home on furlough." Then information from Mrs. Toni Marchwicki with the Dawson County Historical Society in Montana. Information and data began to pile up.

On the way home to Pennsylvania, the first of several stops in Goshen, Indiana, to the Mennonite Church USA Historical Committee Archives. Dennis Stoesz, Archivist, and his staff rolled out the red carpet; they looked up obscure documents, patiently responded to questions about confusing details and puzzling connections in the documents, and allowed me to work alone into the night. Rich Preheim, Director of the Historical Committee gave counsel that sent me off in a rewarding direction. Without their help this project might have turned into twaddle.

Robert Snyder, a storyteller par excellence with pictures and a prodigious memory for detail, did some last-minute research in Bethel College's library and archives.

John Peters spent hours with me thumbing through his 2x2 transparencies and recounting detail after detail. He responded to countless emails for more detail and more great stories.

C. J. Dyck told stories that he said I dare not print; pity, but here are accounts retold with permission.

Also interviewed were Frank and Marie Wiens, Ray Funk, Benjamin Swatsky and Kenneth Deckert. I corresponded with Ozzie Goering, John Gaeddert and Peter Voran. I had a memorable meeting in Bluffton, Ohio, with Dr. and Mrs. Maurice Kaufmann, who concealed from me his impending death a few months later, with amusing and high-spirited stories.

Then the vein ran out, into solid granite with an absence of detail about factual events between 1951 and 1983. I contacted Gerhard in Paraguay, hoping to find a way to research material in Paraguay (details in German I could not read); the second rich vein opened up. Gerhard began knocking on a few doors. One of Bob Unruh's mentored students, veterinarian Rudolph Kaethler was at the time Fernheim's *Oberschulze*. He said, "Great idea, but let's do it in German." Dr. Kaethler enlisted another Fernheim kindred spirit and mentored student, Edwin Neufeld, to mine the archives and dig into interviews. Then Dr. Kaethler asked Neuland and Menno administrators to jointly underwrite the project with Fernheim. There was no stopping the ore train on its way to the smelter now. That lump of rough ore had morphed into a bigger-than-expected book. And in the process I turned over enough interesting detail on Indian settlement to do a second book! (If there is someone out there who wants to write that story, I have the research to get you started.)

My greatest admiration and gratitude goes to all those in Paraguay who contributed, big or small, to the end result, with interviews, information, old and new pictures (Wendy Teichgraef) and those who spoke candidly about their Chaco experience. Gerhard Ratzlaff gave tirelessly in countless e-mails with suggestions and modifications for the English version.

At Gerhard's suggestion, Erwin Boschmann came on board to translate the German Unruh book entitled *Robert and Myrtle Unruh Dienst an der Gemeinschaft mit nachhaltiger Wirkung*, 2007. Erwin was born in Fernheim, graduated from Bethel College (Awarded Bethel's Distinguished Alumnus Award in 1998), received his Ph.D. in Inorganic Chemistry from University of Colorado and retired in 2004 from Indiana University at Purdue.

Edwin Neufeld and Gerhard Ratzlaff and Erwin Boschmann did the heavy lifting on this English book. I did my level best to compile and bring some structure to the North American interviews, documents and correspondences. The Addendum details tied to Gerhard's chapter headings are secondarily intended as insight into the connection between MCC and the Mennonite colonies. I hope you find them helpful to your understanding; sometimes poignant and eloquent and at other times straightforward, matter-of-fact commentary.

And chronologically last, Herman Bontrager and Edgar Stoesz graciously offered critical analysis. Coming down the home stretch, my appreciation to editors Laura Sayre and David Rempel Smucker, to MCC librarian Frank Peachy and to Lois Ann Mast with Masthof Press, all who suffered through an inexperienced writer's sophomoric ineptness.

Along this six-year route, unexpected good events happened, such as bits of information, fortuitous personal connections and turns in the right direction that added to the story. As things came together, there was a conscious awareness of extraordinary coincidence.

About the Authors

Gerhard Ratzlaff

Gerhard Ratzlaff was born in the Paraguayan Chaco wilderness in 1941. In 1947 he began primary and secondary schooling in Neuland Colony, later attending Filadelfia's Bible School and continued theological studies in Curitiba, Brazil and Buenos Aires, Argentina.

Following graduation he became a teacher and missionary in Paraguay for four years. He then studied history at California State University where his interest was researching and recording Mennonite history.

He has served as a preacher, a leading minister, a conference leader and a member of various committees and other organizations. For six years he was the South American representative on the Mennonite World Conference Executive Committee. He taught at the Mennonite Bible School (today part of the Evangelical University of Paraguay) in Asunción for thirty years and was the archivist at the historical library.

Mr. Ratzlaff, now retired, is married to Luise Voth. They have three adult children and four grandchildren.

Philip A. Roth

Phil did his two year I-W alternative service with MCC in the first group of ten PAX men to Peru in 1954. After six months in Peru, anticipating the Trans Chaco Roadway, MCC transferred five men to Paraguay to build inter-colony roads in the Chaco. An uncle having volunteered his 8mm movie camera for two years resulted in the only movie about road building and life in the Mennonite colonies for that period. A compact disc copy resides with the Mennonite Church Historical Committee, Goshen, Indiana and the Historical Library in Asuncion, Paraguay.

He is a third generation fruit grower in south central Pennsylvania, growing apples, peaches, and grapes. In youthful exuberance he found applied physics interesting. Regarding airplanes as the ultimate machine led to a pilot's license at age 16. He was an airline pilot for a few years in his twenties and has been flying privately since. A frustrated engineer, he continues to modify farm machinery in his farm shop and uses hobby time making compost and biodiesel as an advocate for sustainable agriculture.

Index